Austin A30, A35, A40 1951-67 Autobook

By Kenneth Ball
Graduate, Institution of Mechanical Engineers
Associate Member, Guild of Motoring Writers
and the Autopress Team of Technical Writers.

Austin A30 1951-56
Austin A35 1956-62
Austin A40 Farina Mk 1, 2 1958-67

Autopress Ltd. Golden Lane Brighton BN1 2QJ England

The AUTOBOOK series of Workshop Manuals is the largest in the world and covers the majority of British and Continental motor cars, as well as all major Japanese and Australian models. For a full list see the back of this manual.

CONTENTS

ISBN 0 85147 152 8

First Edition   1969

Second Edition, fully revised   1969

Third Edition, fully revised   1970

Reprinted   1970

Reprinted   1972

Reprinted   1973

845

Printed and bound in Brighton England for Autopress Ltd by G Beard & Son Ltd   A

ACKNOWLEDGEMENT

My thanks are due to British Motor Corporation Ltd for their unstinted co-operation and also for supplying data and illustrations.

I am also grateful to a considerable number of owners who have discussed their cars at length, and many of whose suggestions have been included in this manual.

Kenneth Ball
Associate Member Guild of Motoring Writers

Ditchling Sussex England.

INTRODUCTION

This do-it-yourself Workshop Manual has been specially written for the owner who wishes to maintain his car in first class condition and to carry out his own servicing and repairs. Considerable savings on garage charges can be made, and one can drive in safety and confidence knowing the work has been done properly.

Comprehensive step-by-step instructions and illustrations are given on all dismantling, overhauling and assembling operations. Certain assemblies require the use of expensive special tools, the purchase of which would be unjustified. In these cases information is included but the reader is recommended to hand the unit to the agent for attention.

Throughout the Manual hints and tips are included which will be found invaluable, and there is an easy to follow fault diagnosis at the end of each chapter.

Whilst every care has been taken to ensure correctness of information it is obviously not possible to guarantee complete freedom from errors or to accept liability arising from such errors or omissions.

Instructions may refer to the righthand or lefthand sides of the vehicle or the components. These are the same as the righthand or lefthand of an observer standing behind the car and looking forward.

CHAPTER 1

THE ENGINE

This manual covers four engine sizes of 800 cc, 848 cc, 948 cc and 1098 cc capacities. Engine design is much the same throughout, so that instructions will apply to any one of the engine sizes, but the particular model will be mentioned if methods of overhaul or tuning vary.

					Capacity (cc)	Bore (mm)	Stroke (mm)	Comp. ratio
A30	..	..	..	..	800	58	76.2	7.2:1
A35	..	..	..	..	848	62.94	68.26	8.1:1
A35	..	..	..	..	948	62.94	76.2	7.2:1 and 8.3:1
A35	..	..	..	..	1098	64.58	83.72	7.5:1 and 8.5:1
A40 Mk I, A40 Mk II (early)			..	..	948	62.94	76.2	7.2:1 and 8.3:1
A40 Mk II (later)..		..	..	..	1098	64.58	83.72	7.5:1 and 8.5:1

1:1 Engine type

This four cylinder in-line engine has pushrod operated overhead valves working vertically in a detachable head of cast iron. These can be seen in **FIG 1:1**, where all the features which are mentioned can be identified. The valves have renewable guides and the stems are fitted with oil seals. The pushrods operate from tappets lifted by a chain-driven camshaft on the lefthand side of the engine. The camshaft has three bearings. On some engines the front one has a steel-backed whitemetalled liner, the other two running direct in the cylinder block. On 1098 cc engines the three bearings have steel-backed whitemetalled liners. The single-roller chain which drives the camshaft is tensioned by two synthetic rubber rings. End thrust on the camshaft is taken by a plate bolted to the front of the cylinder block. An integral skew gear to the

AAB

9

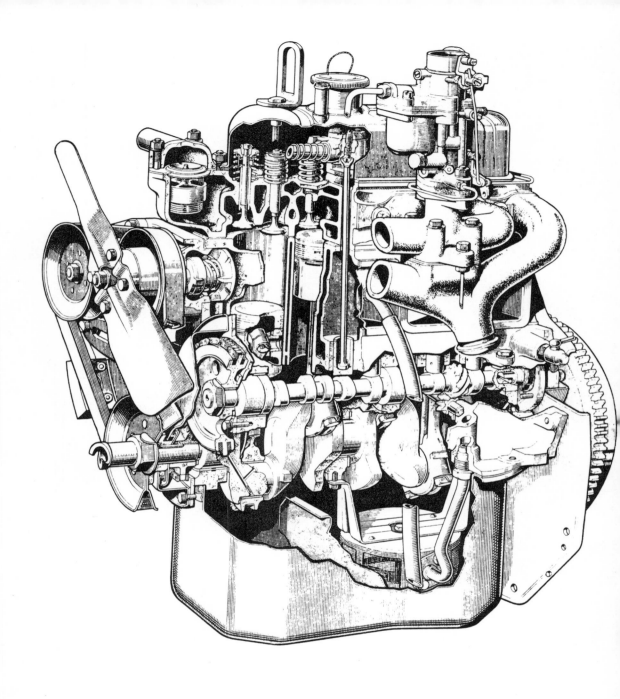

FIG 1:1   Cutaway view of the 948 cc engine. The other engines are basically similar

rear of the camshaft drives a transverse shaft which drives the distributor. There is also an eccentric on the camshaft for operating a mechanical fuel pump.

The crankshaft runs in three bearings. These bearings have renewable shells with surfaces of different alloys, selected to suit the loads imposed by varying power outputs. End float is restricted by thrust washers on each side of the centre main bearing. The connecting rods have big-ends which are split diagonally so that they will pass upwards through the bores. The big-ends have renewable bearing shells, and like the main bearings these have different alloy surfaces.

The earlier cars have split-skirt pistons and gudgeon pins clamped in the small-ends of the connecting rods. Later cars have solid-skirted pistons and fully floating gudgeon pins which are located by circlips. Four piston rings are fitted, the top three for compression sealing and the bottom one for oil control.

The oil pump is bolted to the back of the cylinder block and has a slotted shaft which engages a driving pin in the end of the camshaft. Of the two types which can be dismantled, the Burman has sliding vanes in a slotted rotor, while the Hobourn-Eaton pump has inner and outer rotors with specially shaped lobes. Oil reaches the pump from a strainer in the sump, and then goes under pressure to a relief valve on the righthand side of the engine. This valve restricts oil pressure to a safe maximum when the oil is cold and thick, returning any overflow back to the sump. The oil then proceeds to a gallery along the righthand side of the engine where, at the rear end, will be found an oil gauge union, or an electrical pressure-operated switch connected to a warning light on the dash. Above this fitting is a banjo union with an external pipe leading to a fullflow oil filter just forward of the starter motor. This contains a felt element which cleans the oil and passes it on to the main gallery to supply the bearings. If the element becomes clogged with dirt, a relief valve in the filter opens to allow unfiltered oil to bypass the element and go straight to the bearings. On early engines, the same position is occupied by a throw-away type of bypass filter. This takes a small quantity of oil from the main stream, cleans it thoroughly and passes it back to the sump. Branching off the main oil gallery are passages which take oil to the main, big-end and camshaft bearings. From the front camshaft bearing oil passes at reduced pressure to the overhead rocker gear and the timing chain. Draining down the pushrod tubes it then lubricates the tappets and cams.

1:2 Overhauling

The owner who is competent to do his own car repairs may not have had any training as an engineer. This is no disadvantage if he is prepared to be clean, careful, systematic and observant. We appreciate that working on an elderly vehicle will pose many problems in dismantling, but a little science will often solve such problems without recourse to brute force. For this reason, and also to ensure that each operation is tackled in the right way, we would suggest that a few minutes spent in reading 'Hints on Maintenance and Overhaul' at the end of this manual will be time well spent.

Although the Introduction to this manual has already made the point, we feel that it would be helpful to repeat the information that the righthand and lefthand sides of

a vehicle are those seen from the driver's seat looking forward. It is essential to remember this because there will be innumerable references to location in this way.

Another item of information which will be found particularly useful in this chapter is that No. 1 cylinder is at the front of the engine. The firing order is 1, 3, 4, 2. Further technical information will be found in the Appendix at the back of this manual, and there is a 'Glossary of Terms' to help with descriptions of unfamiliar expressions.

Working on the engine:

The BMC engine is so well known for accessibility that tuning or dismantling is readily carried out, either in or out of the car. Neither is it difficult to remove the engine with adequate lifting tackle, the gearbox either coming out with the engine or staying in the chassis. In the case of the A30 and A35 the engine should be removed from below, for all the other models it should be removed upwards.

1:3 Removing from car

Taking out the engine and gearbox complete:

The following is the general procedure. Where it differs on some models the points will be covered separately.
1 Detach the bonnet from its hinges.
2 Drain the oil and cooling systems.
3 Unclip the radiator and heater hoses (if fitted), and remove the radiator by unscrewing the four fixing bolts from the side flanges.
4 Disconnect the battery positive lead.
5 Remove the sparking plugs, and the distributor cap with leads.
6 Lift off the air cleaner and disconnect all electrical leads, earthing straps, carburetter controls and fuel pipes.
7 Unclamp the exhaust pipe from the manifold and remove the stay to the bell-housing, if a stay is fitted.
8 Remove the hydraulic slave cylinder from the clutch housing and unscrew the speedometer cable from the gearbox.
9 Working inside the car, remove the gearbox cover plate and lift out the gearlever, taking care of the thrust button and spring and the anti-rattle plunger and spring if fitted (see **FIG 6:2**).
10 Disconnect the propeller shaft at the rear axle end and withdraw it backwards from the gearbox.
11 Support the gearbox on a trolley jack and remove the crossmember.
12 Remove the nuts holding the front mounting rubbers to the engine bracket. Lift the engine slightly and remove the mounting brackets from the car frame.
13 The engine and gearbox can now be lifted forward and up.
Variations of the above procedure are as follows:

On the A30 and A35:

1 Release the clutch pedal pull-off spring, and remove the nut, locknut and washers from the front end of the operating rod. Release the pedal shaft support flanges, remove the pin from the spherical bush and slide the shaft free from the gearbox.
2 On A30 cars remove the two setscrews from the clamping plate under the gearbox rear cover. On A35 cars take out the two setscrews passing through the

transmission tunnel from inside the car. From below remove the nuts securing the crossmember.

3 Lower the engine and gearbox on to a trolley after checking that all wires and controls have been detached.

4 Lift the front of the car on blocks until the engine and gearbox can be pulled out forwards.

On the A40:

1 Remove the battery.

2 Remove the crossmember under the gearbox by taking out two setscrews from inside the car and two from below.

3 Arrange slings so that the engine will take up an almost vertical attitude when lifted. It will then clear the front crossmember. Follow the upward and forward motion with a trolley jack under the gearbox.

Leaving the gearbox behind on all models:

1 Do not drain the gearbox.

2 Take the weight of the gearbox on a jack and remove all the setscrews and bolts from the bell-housing flange. Pull the engine horizontally forward until the gearbox first-motion shaft is clear, and then proceed to remove the engine. **Do not let the weight of the engine hang on the shaft or the clutch driven plate hub.**

Separating the engine from the gearbox when out of the car:

Remove all the bolts and setscrews holding the bell-housing to the cylinder block and rear engine mounting plate. With the gearbox fully supported so that it cannot hang on the first-motion shaft, the units are drawn apart.

1:4 Dismantling the engine

It would be useful at this stage to point out that many of the following sequences can be adopted with the engine still in the car. For instance, with the head off and the sump removed the big-ends can be split and the pistons with the connecting rods pushed upwards out of the bores. The tappets can be removed through the engine side covers. With the radiator off, the water pump and the timing gear can receive attention. For the other major operations it is best to work with the engine out of the car. The inlet and exhaust manifolds can be removed as a unit complete with the carburetter if desired. The manifold assembly is attached to the head by six studs, nuts and washers, the four large inner washers bridging both inlet and exhaust flanges. The hot-spot can be separated by unscrewing the four long screws in the middle. Renew the gasket between the joint faces if it is damaged. Leave these screws finger tight until the manifold nuts are tightened fully. If the manifold gasket is replaced with a new one, fit it with the perforated metal face to the manifold.

1:5 The head, valves and rocker gear

FIG 1:2 shows these parts in exploded form. To take off the head, slacken the holding-down nuts a little at a time to avoid distortion. Also slacken top clip 18 on bypass hose 19. **If the engine is in the car, do not attempt to remove the head until the water system has been drained.** There are nine holding-down nuts to be taken off. The small nuts on top of the righthand side of the rocker pedestals do not prevent the head from lifting,

but if the valves are to be removed then the rocker gear can also be released. If the head sticks, do not drive a screwdriver between the joint faces, but tap the sides of the head with light hammer blows on a piece of wood. Alternatively, the sparking plugs can be replaced and the engine turned over by hand, when the head should free itself.

If decarbonizing is necessary, do most of the scraping with the valves still in place so that the seats are not damaged. The valves have 45 deg. faces and a single spring. Inside the spring is a shroud and an oil sealing ring of synthetic rubber. To remove the valves pull off the hairpin circlip round the cotters and compress the spring with a suitable tool. The cotters can then be removed and the spring released. The cap, oil sealing ring and the shroud can be separated from the spring, which should then be checked for length to see if a replacement is needed.

Examine the valve seats and the seatings in the head for wear and deep pitting. The valves can be reground by a garage, and a well-equipped garage can also machine away badly worn seats in the head and fit inserts if necessary. Worn valve guides can be pressed out and then replaced by driving in new ones until $\frac{19}{32}$ inch projects from the machined valve spring face as shown in **FIG 1:3**. The seats must then be recut to ensure that they are concentric with the guide bores. The valves can be ground in with a rubber suction tool. When reassembling springs on earlier engines, fit the oil sealing ring with its chamfered face downwards in the shroud. Later engines have the assembly shown in **FIG 1:4** where a ring of circular section can be seen. This must be pressed over the valve stem until it reaches the bottom of the cotter recess. Both types of ring are easier to fit if they are soaked in clean engine oil for a short time. It is most important to fit new sealing rings at every overhaul or oil sealing may suffer.

To strip the rocker gear, unscrew the locating grub screw from the top of the front pedestal. Note that this pedestal is drilled for lubricating oil which passes into the hollow rocker shaft and thence to the rockers. Remove the splitpin, plain washer and spring washer from the front end of the shaft, when all the rockers, spacing springs and pedestals can be drawn off, taking care to mark them for correct reassembly. All the parts can be seen in **FIG 1:2**, which also shows the locking plate for the locating grub screw. There may be one of these on top of each pedestal on later engines, but it is possible that there may be one only on the front pedestal. The rocker shaft can be cleaned internally by removing the screwed plug from the end. The rockers, which are bushed, may be forgings, or made of steel pressings. These cannot be mixed in one assembly, but a complete set of pressed steel ones can be substituted for forgings and vice versa. In addition, the bushes in the pressed steel rockers cannot be replaced. When reassembling, start with the front pedestal, securing it with the locating grub screw. The rocker shaft should have the screwed plug in the end towards the front of the head. Tightening the pedestal nuts will also clamp the rocker shaft.

Important:

To remove the rocker assembly with the head remaining on the cylinder block it is necessary to drain the radiator and slacken all the cylinder head securing nuts, because

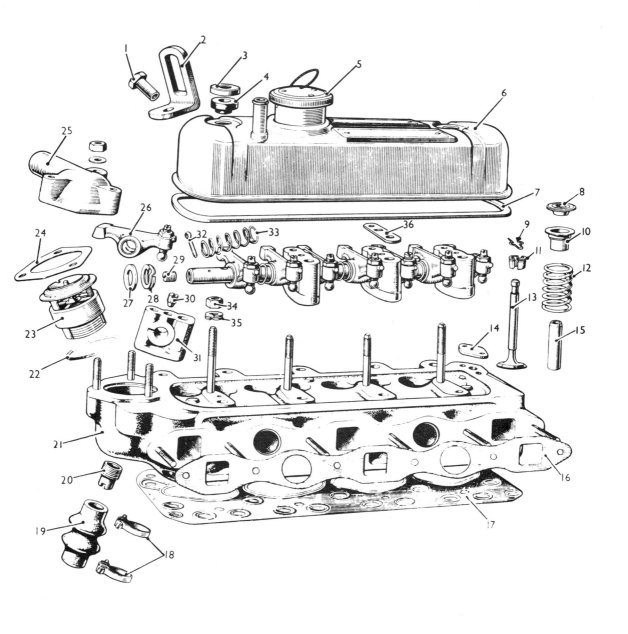

FIG 1 : 2   The cylinder head components

Key to Fig 1 : 2   1 Valve rocker cover cap nut   2 Engine sling bracket   3 Cup washer   4 Rubber bush   5 Oil filler cap
6 Valve rocker cover   7 Rocker cover joint washer   8 Valve spring cap   9 Valve cotter circlip   10 Valve oil seal retainer
11 Valve cotters   12 Valve spring   13 Valve   14 Cover plate   15 Valve guide   16 Joint washer   17 Gasket
18 Hose clips   19 Bypass hose   20 Bypass tube   21 Cylinder head   22 Thermostat joint washer   23 Thermostat
24 Water outlet elbow joint washer   25 Water outlet elbow   26 Rocker   27 Plain washer   28 Spring washer
29 Rocker shaft plug   30 Locating grub screw   31 Rocker shaft pedestal   32 Splitpin   33 Rocker spacing spring
34 Rocker bracket nut   35 Rocker bracket washer   36 Rocker bracket plate

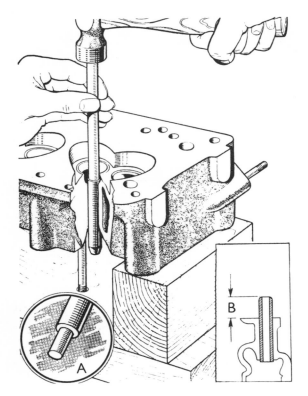

FIG 1:3 Using the stepped drift (A) to remove a valve guide. (B) shows the projection above the top face

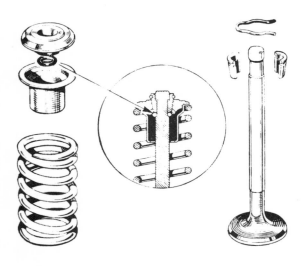

FIG 1:4 Valve assembly showing correct position for oil sealing ring

four of the rocker shaft pedestal nuts also secure the head. **Failure to slacken the five external cylinder head nuts may result in distortion of the head, with subsequent water leakage.**

With the rocker gear out of the way, the pushrods can be lifted out, storing them in the correct order for replacement. Their stems should be straight and the ends examined for wear. At the bottom, the ball-ends locate in barrel tappets. These can be removed by turning the camshaft until each rising tappet can be lifted out, keeping these in the correct order too. They can be seen in **FIG 1:5**, being actually located inside the side covers. New tappets are fitted by selective assembly so that they just fall into their guides under their own weight.

1:6 The valve timing gear

To dismantle the timing chain and chainwheels, and to remove the camshaft, proceed as follows. **FIGS 1:5** and **1:6** will enable the parts to be identified. First slacken the generator bolts and remove the belt. Flatten the locking plate under the starting dog, unscrew the dog and prise off the pulley. The timing cover is secured by four large and six small setscrews, each fitted with a spring and a plain washer. Where the fan pulley boss passes through the cover, there is an oil seal either of felt or of synthetic rubber with lips. If there has been leakage at this point renew the seals. If the timing cover is being replaced after a new seal has been fitted, it is best done, in the case of the rubber seal, by filling the lips with grease. The fan pulley hub should be lubricated and the boss pushed and turned gently until it enters the seal. The timing cover, with the pulley left in place, is then fed on to the crankshaft with the keyway and key in line. After this the cover can be carefully turned until the securing bolt holes are lined up.

With the timing cover off, the next item to be found on the crankshaft is a dished oil-thrower which must always be replaced with the concave side facing forwards. To dismantle the chain-drive unlock and remove the camshaft chainwheel nut and lockwasher. Now ease both chainwheels forward a little at a time with small levers. After removing both wheels and chain make a careful note of the packing washers which are on the crankshaft immediately behind the crankshaft sprocket. If new camshaft or crankshaft components have been fitted, check the alignment of the two chainwheels on reassembly. This is done by placing a straightedge across the sides of the camshaft wheel teeth and measuring the gap between the crankshaft chainwheel and the straightedge with a feeler gauge. This measurement will be the thickness of the packing washers required behind the crankshaft wheel (see **FIG 1:7**). There is a synthetic rubber ring on each side of the camshaft wheel for the purpose of tensioning and silencing the chain. If these are worn or the chain is noisy replace with new rings.

1:7 Removing the camshaft

1 Disconnect the vacuum pipe and low-tension lead from the distributor.
2 Take out the two bolts and flat washers securing the distributor to its housing. **Do not slacken the clamping plate bolt or the ignition timing will be lost.** Now withdraw the distributor.
3 Unscrew the third bolt and remove the distributor housing.

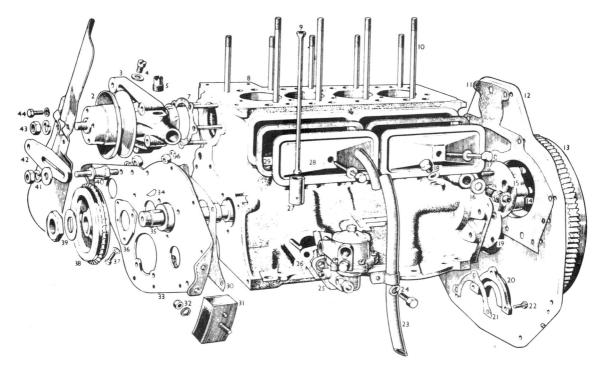

FIG 1:5 An exploded view of the crankcase assembly

Key to Fig 1:5   1 Fan blade   2 Water pump pulley   3 Water pump   4 Water pump screwed plug and washer
5 Water pump bypass tube   6 Nut and washer for water pump stud   7 Water pump joint washer   8 Cylinder block   9 Pushrod
10 Cylinder head studs in block   11 Rear mounting plate joint washer   12 Rear mounting plate   13 Flywheel and starter ring
14 Oil pump   15 Cylinder block drain tap   16 Washer for drain tap   17 Setscrew and washer for side cover
18 Oil priming plug and joint washer   19 Oil pump joint washer   20 Crankcase rear cover   21 Joint washer for rear cover
22 Rear cover setscrew   23 Crankcase vent pipe   24 Setscrew and washer   25 Petrol pump   26 Petrol pump joint washer
27 Tappet   28 Cylinder side cover (front)   29 Joint washer for side cover   30 Front mounting plate joint washer
31 Rubber mounting   32 Nut and washer for rubber mounting   33 Engine front mounting plate   34 Woodruff key
35 Camshaft   36 Camshaft locating plate   37 Setscrew and shakeproof washer   38 Camshaft gear and tensioner rings
39 Nut and lockwasher   40 Pillar for adjusting link   41 Nut and washers for link   42 Dynamo adjusting link
43 Nut and washer for pulley   44 Setscrew and washer for fan blade

4 Screw a tappet cover securing bolt, or any suitable rod with a $\frac{5}{16}$ inch UNF thread, into the end of the distributor drive spindle and withdraw it as shown in **FIG 1:8**. Use a $\frac{5}{16}$ inch BSF bolt on the 800 cc A30.
5 Behind the camshaft chainwheel is a triangular plate secured to the cylinder block by three setscrews and shakeproof washers. By removing this and the mechanical fuel pump if one is fitted, the camshaft can be withdrawn. Invert the engine so that the tappets fall clear.

The triangular plate controls the end float of the camshaft. If this exceeds the figure given in the Technical Data section the locating plate must be replaced with a new one. The plate also has a small lubricating hole drilled in it. This must be replaced with the small hole towards the righthand side of the block.

Check the camshaft bearing journals for wear and scoring, the diameters and clearances being given in the Technical Data section. Examine the bearing liner, or liners, in the cylinder block for signs of scoring or pitting. All the 1098 cc engines have three steel liners with white-metal bearing surfaces. The other engines have only one which is at the front, the two rear camshaft journals running direct in the block. It is a highly-skilled job to replace liners and reamer them in position. The camshaft must also be examined for wear of the cams and the distributor drive gear to see if this is enough to warrant renewal.

When the camshaft is being replaced in the block, remember to align the drive pin in the rear end of the camshaft with the slot in the end of the oil pump driving spindle so that they will engage properly.

1:8 Sump, clutch and flywheel

The sump:

This is secured to the cylinder block by fourteen bolts, shakeproof washers and flat plates. It can be removed either in or out of the car. With the sump drained and removed it will be possible to see the gauze strainer from which a suction pipe runs up to the oil pump. This can be seen in **FIG 1:6**. Detach this oil pipe from the crankcase

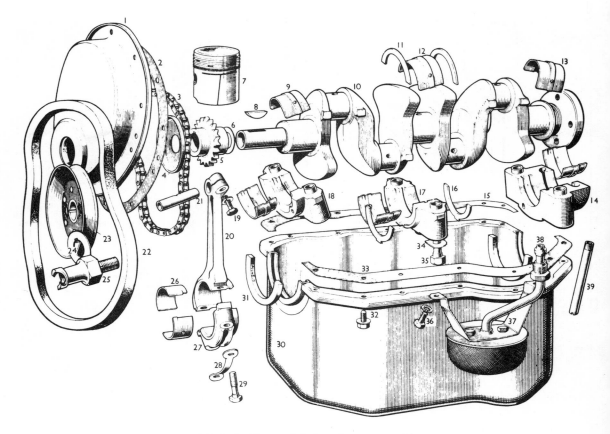

FIG 1:6   The crankshaft and sump assembly

Key to Fig 1:6   1 Engine front cover   2 Joint washer for cover   3 Timing chain   4 Crankshaft oil-thrower   5 Crankshaft gear
6 Packing washers   7 Piston   8 Woodruff key   9 Front main half bearing   10 Crankshaft   11 Thrust washer (upper)
12 Centre main half bearing   13 Rear main half bearing   14 Rear main bearing cap and dowels   15 Oil sump joint washer (right)
16 Thrust washer (lower)   17 Centre main bearing cap and dowels   18 Front main bearing cap and dowels
19 Clamping screw and washer for (20)   20 Connecting rod, less cap   21 Gudgeon pin   22 Vee-belt for fan and pulley
23 Crankshaft pulley   24 Lockwasher   25 Starting nut   26 Connecting rod half bearing   27 Connecting rod cap
28 Lockwasher   29 Setscrew for connecting rod   30 Oil sump   31 Cork sealing washer   32 Setscrew and captive washer
33 Oil sump joint washer (left)   34 Main bearing cap lockwasher   35 Setscrew for main bearing cap   36 Setscrew and
shakeproof washer for strainer bracket   37 Oil strainer   38 Suction pipe   39 Drain pipe for rear main bearing cap

and then unscrew the two bracket bolts from the rear main bearing caps, and the strainer will come away. Never use rag to clean the gauze but scrub it well with a stiff brush in petrol and leave to dry. The sump must also be cleaned in the same way. If leaking or damaged, the joint washers should be renewed, every trace of the old washers and any jointing compound being scraped from the joint faces. Now examine the cork sealing washers to be found in half-circular housings at each end of the sump. These seal on the front and rear main bearing caps and the ends should just stand proud of the sump face. If they leak or are damaged they must be renewed. Grease the new packings and press them fully home in the housings, using a round object the same diameter as the crankshaft main journals. The ends should stand proud of the sump by approximately $\frac{3}{32}$ inch. The four ends of the joint washers will overlap these raised portions, so that when the sump is replaced the cork is compressed and a perfect oil seal made.

Removing the clutch and flywheel:

With the gearbox parted from the engine, the clutch and flywheel can be taken off. Slacken the screws holding the clutch cover flange to the flywheel, doing this a turn at a time and crossing from side to side until the spring pressure is relieved. Do not dismantle the clutch, but refer to **Chapter 5.** The four bolts holding the flywheel to the crankshaft are locked by tabs on two locking plates.

With the bolts removed the flywheel and starter ring will pull off the crankshaft register without trouble. The ring is a shrink fit on the flywheel and can be replaced with a new one if worn. Cut partly through the ring with a hacksaw

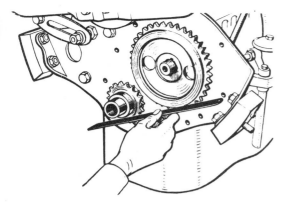

FIG 1:7 Lining up crankshaft and camshaft gear teeth

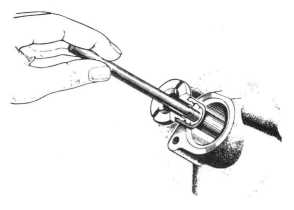

FIG 1:8 Using threaded rod to remove the distributor spindle

and then split the cut open with a cold chisel, taking care not to damage the register on which the starter ring fits. Now heat the new ring all round to an even light blue surface colour, the equivalent to a temperature of 300°C to 400°C (575°F to 752°F). **Do not overheat or the hardness of the teeth will be impaired.** The heated ring is placed on the flywheel with the cutaway on the gear teeth facing the flywheel register, when it can be tapped lightly into place. Allowed to cool naturally, the ring will be a permanent shrink-fit and immovable.

1:9 Connecting rods and pistons

The connecting rods:

The big-ends are fitted with renewable steel-backed bearing shells and are split diagonally. The caps have machined lugs mating with the rods to ensure accurate alignment, the bolts being locked by a plate. The small-ends are split and clamped on the gudgeon pin in the 800 cc, 848 cc and 948 cc engines (see **FIG 1:9**). The 1098 cc engines have rods with bushed small-ends for the fully floating gudgeon pins shown in **FIG 1:10**. There is a jet on the righthand side of each rod which lubricates the cylinder wall, the bearing shells being drilled to pass the oil from the big-end supply.

Before splitting the big-ends make certain that each rod and cap is marked with the number of the bore to which it belongs, starting with number 1 at the front. Unlock the bolts and unscrew them about a quarter of an inch. Now tap the bolt heads lightly, when the cap will separate from the rod. Remove any carbon from the top of the cylinder bores and push the pistons and rods upwards and out. The caps and their bolts should now be replaced on the rods in the correct order and the right way round. The bearing shells are steel-backed, the bearing surfaces being in different alloys to suit the power output of the engine. Reference should be made to the Technical Data section at the back of this book for details of the correct type to use. **Never mix different bearing alloys in one engine.** The bearing surfaces are precision machined and do not require bedding in. Note also that there is a tab on each shell which mates with a notch in the rod or cap. If the shells are scored, pitted or breaking up they must be

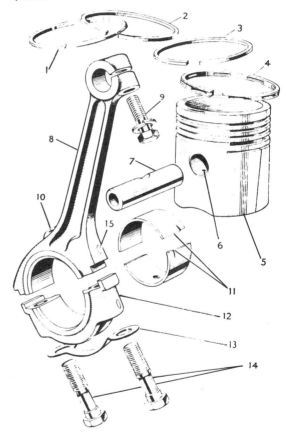

FIG 1:9 Connecting rod and piston assembly for 800 cc, 848 cc and 948 cc engines

Key to Fig 1:9   1 Piston ring, parallel   2 Piston ring, taper
3 Piston ring, taper   4 Piston ring, scraper   5 Piston
6 Gudgeon pin lubricating hole   7 Gudgeon pin
8 Connecting rod, less cap   9 Clamping screw and washer
10 Cylinder wall lubricating jet   11 Connecting rod bearings
12 Connecting rod cap   13 Lockwasher   14 Setscrews
15 Mark on rod and cap

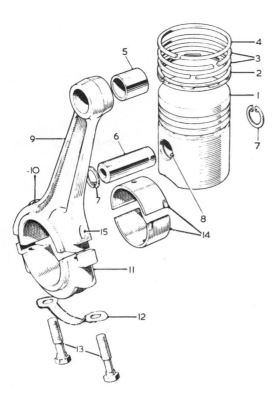

FIG 1:10 Connecting rod and piston assembly for 1098 cc engines

Key to Fig 1:10   1 Piston   2 Piston ring, scraper
3 Piston rings, taper   4 Piston ring, parallel   5 Small-end bush
6 Gudgeon pin   7 Circlip   8 Gudgeon pin lubricating hole
9 Connecting rod   10 Cylinder wall lubricating jet
11 Connecting rod cap   12 Lockwasher   13 Bolts
14 Connecting rod bearings   15 Connecting rod and
cap marking

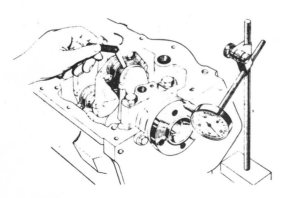

FIG 1:11 Gauging side clearance of connecting rods. The dial indicator is measuring crankshaft end float

renewed. All new shells are drilled for the oil jet previously mentioned, so that they may be fitted either to the rod or the cap.

Never file the rods, caps or bearing shells, as they at once become non-standard and can never be used to obtain new rods on an exchange basis. On the 1098 cc engines, particular note must be made of the following. Should the piston or connecting rod suffer damage or the small-end bush need renewing, the pistons and connecting rods are supplied as matched sets only. In no circumstances should the small-end bush, piston or connecting rod be renewed separately.

Pistons:

The 800 cc, 848 cc and 948 cc engines have split skirt aluminium alloy pistons with the split adjacent to the clamping bolt in the small-end.

To remove the pistons from the connecting rods, unscrew the clamping bolt from the small-end of the connecting rod, taking it out completely, and then the gudgeon pin can be pushed free. The piston has four rings, three at the top for compression sealing and the one at the bottom for oil control. The top one is plain. The next two are taper, and should be fitted with the narrow side uppermost. They may also be found to be marked with a 'T'. Oil control rings can be fitted either way up. Piston rings must always be removed upwards over the top of the piston. Use a narrow piece of thin steel inserted under one end of the ring and rotate it gently, applying slight upward pressure on the ring so that it begins to rest on the land above the ring groove, until the whole ring is out of the groove. All rings must be replaced from above after cleaning carbon from the grooves with a piece of broken ring. When in place in the bore the ring gap between the ends should be to the figure in Technical Data. This can be measured by pushing the ring 1 inch down the bore, using a piston to do so. When refitting pistons ensure that the ends of the rings are fully home in the groove. Remove cylinder bore glaze before refitting pistons.

When the engines are produced, the pistons are fitted by selective assembly because of very small variations in size. The grade number is stamped on the piston crown inside a diamond mark, and this must always coincide with a similar grading number stamped on the cylinder block face adjacent to the bore. The piston crown is also stamped 'FRONT' to show which way round it should be fitted, and oversize pistons have their size stamped in a small ellipse. This size must always be stamped on the cylinder block adjacent to the bore after every rebore.

If the piston clearances given in Technical Data are exceeded a rebore is necessary. Oversize pistons for the 800 cc, 848 cc and 948 cc engines are available in +.010 inch, +.020 inch, +.030 inch, and +.040 inch sizes, and suitable bore sizes for these are given in Technical Data.

The 1098 cc engine has oversize pistons which are only available in two sizes, namely +.010 inch and +.020 inch, complete with connecting rods. The 1098 cc pistons are detached from the connecting rods by removing both spring circlips from inside the piston bosses and pushing out the gudgeon pin. To reassemble, the gudgeon pins should be a hand push fit at a room temperature of 20°C (68°F). Replace the circlips, ensuring that they are right home in their grooves.

The clamped type of gudgeon pin should also be a hand push fit. To reassemble, line up the groove at the centre of the pin so that the clamp bolt can be inserted. The bolt must screw up freely and properly compress the spring washer. It will not do this if it is bent, in which case it must be renewed. Check the fit of the gudgeon pin by holding the piston and connecting rod assembly horizontally, when the weight of the big-end should be just sufficient to turn the pin in the piston. Oversize gudgeon pins are not available.

If it is necessary to fit cylinder bore liners this can only be done by experts with precision machinery. After the liners are fitted they are finished to the standard bore size.

1:10 Removing the crankshaft and main bearings

The forged steel balanced crankshaft is supported in the crankcase by three main bearings which have renewable shells. These shells are of the steel-backed type which do not need bedding in. The bearing surfaces are of special alloys ranging from whitemetal to copper/lead or lead/indium according to the duties of the engine, and reference should be made to Technical Data before renewing them. Do not mix different alloys in one engine.

On each side of the centre main bearing are thrust washers to control end float of the crankshaft. Before removing the bearing caps, check this end float to see whether the thrust washers need renewal, as shown in **FIG 1:11**. The bearing assembly is clearly shown in **FIG 1:12**. Now mark each bearing cap and the crankcase so that there can be no doubt about the exact location when the cap is replaced. With the rear engine mounting plate removed and the two bolts through the front mounting plate into the side of the front bearing cap unscrewed, it will be possible to take off each cap. Note the locking plates and the tubular dowels which are shown in **FIG 1:12**. The bottom halves of the thrust washers have tags on them and will come away with the centre cap. Keep the shells with their respective caps. The crankshaft can now be lifted out, the top halves of the bearing shells put with their caps in the right order, and the top halves of the thrust washers removed.

Inspect the crankshaft journals and big-end pins for scoring and ovality, comparing the sizes with those given in Technical Data. If necessary the crankshaft may be reground, but not below —.040 inch. Bearing shells are available for the undersizes, —.010 inch, —.020 inch, —.030 inch, and —.040 inch. Clean the crankshaft oilways thoroughly, particularly if any of the bearings have 'run'. Do this by forcing petrol or paraffin through the holes under pressure, following up with clean engine oil. Examine the bearing shells and renew them if they show signs of scoring or breaking away.

Never file the caps to take up wear or to reduce running clearances.

When the crankshaft is replaced the thrust washers should have their oil grooves facing outwards.

Like the big-end bearing shells, the main bearing shells will be found to have tabs which fit into notches machined in the caps and the crankcase housings.

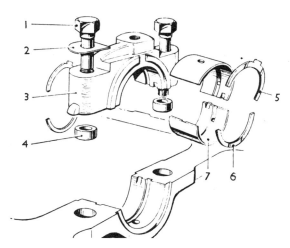

FIG 1:12 Inverted view of centre main bearing. Note tab on lower thrust washer 5

Key to Fig 1:12 1 Main bearing bolts 2 Lockwasher 3 Main bearing cap 4 Dowels 5 Thrust washer (lower) 6 Thrust washer (upper) 7 Main bearing shell

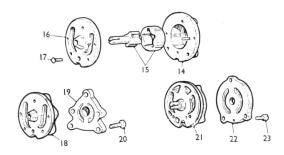

FIG 1:13 Three variations of the Hobourn Eaton oil pump. The A40 pump will be recognizable from one of these

Key to Fig 1:13 14 Body (A35) (9 and 9AB) 15 Shaft and rotor 16 Cover (A35) (9 and 9AB) 17 Screw (A35) (9 and 9AB) 18 Body (A30) 19 Cover (A30) 20 Screw (A30) 21 Body (A35) 22 Cover (A35) 23 Screw (A35)

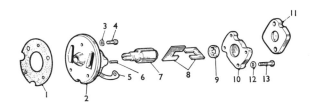

FIG 1:14 The Burman oil pump

Key to Fig 1:14 1 Joint 2 Body 3 Washer 4 Setscrew 5 Lockplate 6 Dowel 7 Rotor 8 Vanes 9 Sleeve 10 Cover (A35) 11 Cover (A30) 12 Shakeproof washer 13 Screw

1:11 The oil pump, relief valve and filter

Now that the rear engine mounting plate has been removed, the oil pump can be seen at the end of the camshaft tunnel, as shown in **FIG 1:5**. Bend back the locking tabs from the three outer bolts and unscrew them so that the pump can be withdrawn. If the pump is withdrawn with the camshaft in place, note the position of the slot in the driving shaft so that it can be lined up with its pin in the camshaft on replacement. **FIG 1:13** shows the Hobourn-Eaton pump dismantled to reveal the inner and outer rotors. Replace any worn parts, dropping the outer rotor into the body with the chamfer downwards. There is a later type of Hobourn-Eaton pump which has a cover located by two dowels and a machine screw into the front face. The Burman pump shown in **FIG 1:14** is of the sliding vane type. To remove the vanes from the spindle prise off the sleeve at the back end, next to the rear cover. If new parts are fitted, try the spindle of either pump to see that it revolves freely. It is also important to check on the condition of the gasket between the pump face and the cylinder block. It must be in perfect condition and fitted so that the inlet and outlet ports are not restricted. Some engines may be fitted with an oil pump made by Concentric. This is not meant to be dismantled and must be renewed complete. It can be recognized by the CMC mark on the cover.

Oil pressure relief valve:

This will be found on the righthand side of the cylinder block behind the distributor, as in **FIG 1:15**. This valve provides an extra return passage back to the sump if oil pressure becomes excessive when the oil is cold. As the valve lifting pressure is not adjustable it is important to check the free length of the spring and replace it if it is less than the figure given in Technical Data. Another factor which will affect the relief pressure is the position of the screwed plug, so that it is important to fit the two fibre washers, as shown in the illustration. Latest engines may have only one copper washer. Examine the seating of the valve cup for wear. If not excessive, it can be ground in using a very little fine compound, every trace of which must be removed after the operation. Oil pressure should be up to 60 lb/sq in according to model. See Technical Data.

External oil filters:

These are of two types, the early bypass as shown in **FIG 1:16** and the fullflow shown in **FIG 1:17**. The bypass filter is thrown away when clogged, but the fullflow filter has a replacement element. If these filters need attention with the engine in the car, stop the engine before unscrewing anything. To take off the bypass filter, remove the bracket setscrew, then slacken the clip screw and slide off. Unscrew the filter anticlockwise by hand. When replacing, make certain that the rubber sealing washer is sound, tighten up by hand and replace the clip and bracket securely.

To inspect the element in the fullflow filter, unscrew the centre bolt from below and take away the casing complete with element and oil by keeping the bolt head pressed upwards. Make no attempt to wash the element if it is clogged as dirt may well be forced deeper into the felt. Clean the inside of the casing, put in a new element,

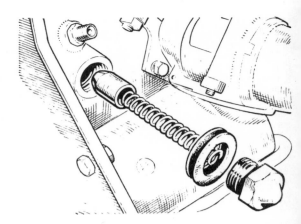

FIG 1:15 Location of the oil pressure relief valve. Note the two fibre washers. Later engines have a single copper washer

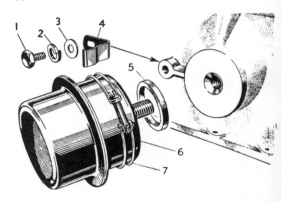

FIG 1:16 The bypass oil filter withdrawn, showing the clip and bracket assembly

Key to Fig 1:16

1 Setscrew	2 Spring washer	
3 Plain washer	4 Oil filter bracket	5 Rubber seal
6 Oil filter	7 Locking clip	

fill with oil and replace, keeping the bolt firmly in place or the oil will be lost. If leakage has been evident, replace the sealing washer in the groove under the head, and the washer on the centre bolt. Tighten just enough to make an oiltight joint, run the engine and check for leaks at once. Top up the sump. On 8AG engines with a warning light connected to a switch in the filter head, first disconnect the battery.

1:12 Reassembling the engine

To start with, it is advisable to provide a complete set of new gaskets. Clean every joint face free from old gasket material and jointing compound. Pay particular attention to such crevices as those behind the crankcase webs where swarf from reboring operations can lodge. Clean out all oil holes with a powerful jet of fluid, following up with some clean engine oil. If the auxiliaries such as the water pump distributor and mechanical fuel pump have been overhauled according to the instructions in later chapters, or are in good condition, the work of re-assembling the engine can proceed.

Stand the block on its top face and fit the top halves of the main bearing shells into the crankcase housings, in their correct order and with the locating tabs properly inserted in their notches. The top halves of the thrust washers are also fitted. These have no locating tab. Oil liberally and drop the crankshaft carefully into place. With the bottom bearing shells in their correct caps, these can be replaced and the fixing bolts inserted with a locking plate under each.

Tighten the bolts to the torque figure of 60 lb ft, starting with the centre bearing. As each cap is tightened check to see that the crankshaft will turn freely. If it does not, remove the last cap to be tightened and look for burrs or dirt under the shell. When it comes to fitting the rear cap, coat the horizontal surfaces with jointing compound. If there has been trouble with oil leakage into the clutch housing look at the rear end of the crankcase where there is the upper half of the housing which collects oil thrown off by the thrower ring on the crankshaft behind the rear bearing. It can be seen in **FIG 1 : 5** just in front of the rear mounting plate. The half-circular part must be close to, but must not actually touch, the oil return scroll cut in the crankshaft behind the knife-edged thrower ring. Before fitting the rear cap, verify that this rear cover is exactly flush with the bottom face of the block and has an even clearance all round the top half of the crankshaft. If this is not so, slacken the three fixing set-screws, tap the cover into the correct position and retighten the screws. The jointing compound on the horizontal face of the rear bearing cap will now make a good seal on this rear cover. Lastly, fix the two bolts which go through the front mounting plate into the side of the front bearing cap. There is a locking plate for these two bolts.

Replacing the camshaft, the oil pump, the flywheel and the clutch:

Oil the camshaft and slide it into the crankcase. Refit the camshaft locating plate to the front mounting plate with the small oil jet hole facing the righthand side of the engine. Replace the oil pump, using a new gasket, lining up the slot in the driving spindle with the crosspin in the end of the camshaft before pressing home. Turn the camshaft slowly to assist re-engagement. Fit the camshaft locating plate with the whitemetal side towards the cam-shaft. Lock the pump fixing bolts and then bolt the rear engine mounting plate into position, taking special care of the joint washer so that oil leaks at this point are not possible. The flywheel can now be bolted to the crankshaft, the flange being clean and free from burrs. Lock the four bolts after they have been tightened to the specified torque figure.

When the clutch is bolted to the flywheel, the centre plate must be centralized using the special arbor which is described in the Clutch chapter. Tighten the fixing bolts in the cover flange a little at a time, crossing from side to side.

1 :13 Replacing the timing gear

Put the packing washers on the crankshaft behind the small chainwheel. Assemble the two wheels inside the chain with the timing marks in the position shown in

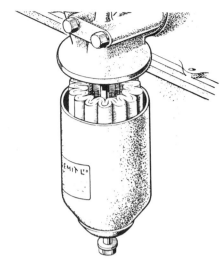

FIG 1 :17 The fullflow filter partly dismantled to show the element

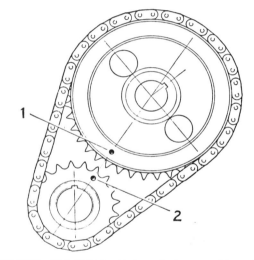

FIG 1 :18 The timing gears ready to assemble, with marks 1 and 2 adjacent

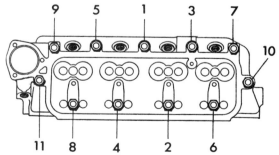

FIG 1 :19 The order of loosening and tightening the cylinder head nuts on the A40. The A30 and A35 omitted studs 10 and 11

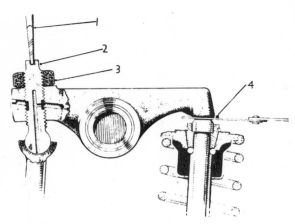

FIG 1:20 Adjusting the clearance between rocker end and valve stem

Key to Fig 1:20   1 Screwdriver   2 Adjusting screw
3 Locknut   4 Feeler gauge

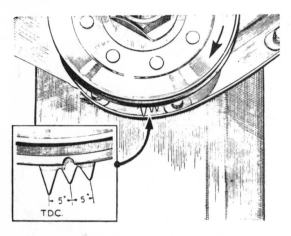

FIG 1:21 The ignition timing pointers. The inset also shows the pulley notch

FIG 1:18. Turn the crankshaft until the key is at TDC and put the camshaft key at one o'clock. Take the wheels and chain together and put the small wheel on the crankshaft until the key engages. Turn the camshaft until its key lines up with the keyway in the large wheel and press both wheels home. Check the timing marks and then secure the camshaft wheel with the lockwasher and nut. The next step is to put the dished oil-thrower on the crankshaft with the concave side facing forward as shown in **FIG 1:6.** The timing cover is best replaced with the pulley in place in the seal. Fitting a new seal has been covered in **Section 1:6.** The pulley boss is oiled and inserted into the seal and then the cover and pulley are offered up to the crankshaft. Line up the pulley keyway with the key and press into place. Screw in the cover fixing screws, tightening them gradually and evenly. The pulley securing screw is locked by a plate which engages the pulley key-

way. With the screw firmly tightened, a tab can be turned up to lock it. Use a torque wrench setting of 70 lb ft.

1:14 Fitting the pistons and connecting rods

Assuming that the rings have been fitted to the pistons and the pistons to their correct connecting rods according to earlier instructions, they can now be replaced in their original bores, unless they are new. Oil the bores first and use a spring compressor. The ring gaps should be at 90 deg. to each other and see that the word 'FRONT' on the piston crown is correctly placed. On split-skirt pistons this can be checked by observing that the split is on the camshaft side of the engine, where the gudgeon pin clamping bolt should be too. Pull the connecting rod down the bore until the top bearing shell can be pressed into place. Oil the big-end pin and fit the bottom shell into the cap. With the identifying numbers or marks aligned, the cap can be fitted and the bolts inserted with their locking plate under the heads. Tighten to the torque figure of 35 lb ft and check that the crankshaft is free to turn. Then lock the bolt heads.

The big-end bearings are offset on the connecting rods. Fit them so that the longer boss is to the rear on rods 1 and 3, and to the front on 2 and 4.

Replacing the sump:

Fit the strainer, entering the suction pipe into the tapped hole in the crankcase and then securing the bracket feet to the two rear bearing caps. Tighten the suction pipe nut. Fit new gaskets to the sump if the old ones are at all doubtful, smearing the joint faces with grease. Lift the sump into place, insert the fourteen setscrews and tighten them evenly. Each screw should have a shakeproof washer and a plain one.

1:15 Replacing the head

The block must now be standing the right way up so that the tappets can be inserted, oiling each one and replacing it where it came from. The head gasket is fitted dry, the words 'TOP' and 'FRONT' being stamped on it so that there can only be one way for it to go. See that the water bypass hose at the front end on the lefthand side is in place with the clips fitted but loose. The head can now be lowered squarely into place. Drop the pushrods into their correct holes, making sure that the lower ends enter the tappets properly. The rocker gear is then dropped over the head studs, each pushrod being carefully located under the correct adjusting screw. All the head and rocker pedestal nuts and washers are now screwed on, with the rocker shaft locking plate in position. There are four plates on later engines, one on top of each pedestal. Proceed to tighten the nuts a turn at a time in the sequence given in **FIG 1:19** where it will be seen that the rocker pedestal nuts are tightened as pairs. The torque figures are given in Technical Data. Turn the crankshaft to see that all is well and then adjust the valve clearance.

1:16 Valve rocker adjustment

These engines have been designed to run with a valve rocker clearance of .012 inch when cold and if good performance is to be maintained the correct clearance is essential. **FIG 1:20** shows a rocker with a feeler gauge between the rocker arm and the valve stem. To adjust the clearance it is necessary to ensure that the valve is closed, with the tappet on the back of the cam opposite to the peak. This can be done by observing the following sequence:

Adjust No. 1 rocker with No. 8 valve fully open.
Adjust No. 3 rocker with No. 6 valve fully open.
Adjust No. 5 rocker with No. 4 valve fully open.
Adjust No. 2 rocker with No. 7 valve fully open.
Adjust No. 8 rocker with No. 1 valve fully open.
Adjust No. 6 rocker with No. 3 valve fully open.
Adjust No. 4 rocker with No. 5 valve fully open.
Adjust No. 7 rocker with No. 2 valve fully open.

Notice that the numbers in each line add up to nine. Remembering this, it is easy to go on checking without constant reference to the table. Slacken the locknut just enough to allow the adjusting screw to be turned with a screwdriver until the feeler gauge is very slightly nipped. Then tighten the locknut, keeping the adjusting screw from turning. Always check the clearance after this in case the adjustment has been disturbed in the locking process. A point of great importance is that this clearance adjustment cannot be accurate if the rocker end is pitted through wear.

Oil leakage from the cover can only be prevented by the use of a good gasket correctly positioned. A glance at **FIG 1 : 2** will show the order for replacing the rubber bush and cup washer on the cover studs. The thermostat is now replaced at the front end of the head, assuming that it is in good condition or has been checked according to the notes in the Cooling chapter. The narrow ring gasket is dropped into the recess in the head, followed by the thermostat and then the triangular joint washer and lastly the elbow, facing to the right. Screw up the bypass hose clips to finish the head assembly.

1 : 17 Replacing the distributor and drive

Using a long $\frac{5}{16}$ inch UNF bolt in the tapped end of the distributor drive shaft, insert it into the righthand side of the cylinder block after reading the instructions for this operation in the Ignition chapter. Use a $\frac{5}{16}$ inch BSF bolt on the 800 cc A30. The greatest care is essential here, or the ignition timing will be out. With the shaft gear correctly meshed, remove the bolt. Fit the distributor housing using the special bolt and washer provided. These are used because the bolt head must not protrude above the face of the housing. Refit the distributor to the housing, and if the clamp has been disturbed, refer to the Ignition chapter for details of how to reset the timing.

The fuel pump

Replace the mechanical fuel pump, if one is fitted. Use a good joint washer and feed the rocker arm in carefully so that it is correctly positioned against the eccentric on the camshaft.

1 : 18 Valve timing

Should it be necessary to check the valve timing, look up the figures given in Technical Data for the engine concerned. It is not possible to check the timing accurately unless the normal valve clearance of .012 inch is increased to the figure shown with the engine cold. In **FIG 1 : 21** it can be seen that there is a groove in the rear flange of the crankshaft pulley and a set of three pointers on the timing cover. Turn the crankshaft until the second valve from the front is about to open. This is No. 1 cylinder inlet valve. The groove in the pulley should now be opposite the middle pointer. This indicates an inlet valve opening of 5 deg. before TDC. On early engines the pulley groove should be $\frac{13}{64}$ inch short of alignment with the arrow on the timing cover. It is most important to restore the valve clearance to the correct setting of .012 inch cold.

Replacing the rocker cover:

With the breather pipe to the front, the rocker cover can now be fitted.

1 : 19 Manifolds, water pump and generator

Manifold replacement:

If the inlet and exhaust manifolds have been parted, details of their assembly were given earlier in the chapter. Note that the four setscrews are left finger tight until the manifolds are installed on the head studs and the stud nuts tightened. Always use a new gasket.

The water pump and generator:

These are serviced by referring to the chapters on Cooling and Electrical Equipment, and if satisfactory they can be replaced. Use a new paper joint washer between the pump body and the cylinder block. Refit the generator, leaving the pivot and link bolts finger tight until the belt is put on the pulleys. With the belt in place lift the generator using a gentle hand pull only. Tighten the three bolts and check the belt. This must not be excessively tight nor so loose that the belt slips. It should be possible to move it laterally about an inch in the middle of the longest run.

The engine assembly is now complete with the exception of the carburetter and air cleaner, which are best fitted after the engine has been replaced in the car. Refill with oil and water. Do not fit the air cleaner until the engine has been run up to working temperature and the rocker clearance checked. After 100 miles tighten the cylinder head nuts to the correct torque reading and give the rocker clearance a final check.

Replacing power unit in car:

Refitting the engine and gearbox as a unit is a reversal of the removal procedure. If the gearbox was left behind in the frame, refitting needs some care to ensure that the gearbox first-motion shaft enters the clutch driven plate hub without strain. Refer to **Chapter 5** for details of the assembly so that the operation is understood. Then apply the handbrake and engage top gear to lock the first-motion shaft. As the engine approaches the gearbox, keep it square and guide the clutch driven plate hub onto the shaft. **Let no weight hang on either part.** Rotate the engine until the splines mate and then push the engine home.

1 : 20 Fault diagnosis

(a) Possible fault if engine will not start

1 Defective coil
2 Faulty condenser
3 Dirty, pitted or incorrectly set contact breaker points
4 Ignition wires loose or insulation faulty

5 Water on sparking plug leads
6 Corrosion of battery terminals or discharged condition
7 Faulty or jammed starter
8 Plug leads wrongly connected
9 Vapour lock in fuel pipes
10 Defective fuel pump
11 Over-choking
12 Under-choking
13 Blocked petrol filter or carburetter jets
14 Leaking valves
15 Valve timing incorrect
16 Ignition timing incorrect

(b) If the engine stalls

Check 1, 2, 3, 4, 10, 11, 12, 13, 14 and 15 in Section (a)
1 Plugs defective or gap incorrect
2 Retarded ignition
3 Mixture too weak
4 Water in fuel system
5 Petrol tank breather choked
6 Incorrect valve clearance

(c) If the engine idles badly

Check 1 and 6 in Section (b)
1 Air leak at manifold joints
2 Incorrect slow-running adjustment
3 Air leak in carburetter
4 Slow-running jet blocked
5 Over-rich mixture
6 Worn piston rings
7 Worn valve stems or guides
8 Weak exhaust valve springs

(d) Engine misfires

Check 1, 2, 3, 4, 5, 8, 10, 13, 14, 15 and 16 in Section (a)
Check 1, 2, 3 and 6 in Section (b)
1 Weak or broken valve springs

(e) Engine overheats (see Chapter 4)

(f) Compression low

Check 14 in Section (a); 6 and 7 in Section (c); and 1 in Section (d)
1 Worn piston ring grooves
2 Scored or worn cylinder bores

(g) Engine lacks power

Check 3, 10, 11, 13, 14, 15 and 16 in Section (a); 1, 2, 3 and 6 in Section (b); 6 and 7 in Section (c); 1 in Section (d); and Sections (e) and (f)
1 Leaking joint washers
2 Fouled sparking plugs
3 Automatic advance not functioning

(h) Valves or seats burnt

Check 14 in Section (a); 6 in Section (b); 1 in Section (d); and Section (e)
1 Excessive carbon around valve seat and head

(j) Sticking valves

Check 1 in Section (d)
1 Bent valve stem
2 Scored valve stem or guide
3 Incorrect valve clearance

(k) Excessive cylinder wear

Check 11 in Section (a), and check Chapter 4
1 Lack of oil
2 Dirty oil
3 Dirty air cleaner
4 Piston rings gummed up or broken
5 Badly fitting piston rings
6 Connecting-rods bent

(l) Oil consumption excessive

Check 6 and 7 in Section (c); and check Section (k)
1 Ring gap too wide
2 Oil return holes in piston choked with carbon
3 Scored cylinders
4 Oil level too high
5 External oil leaks
6 Ineffective valve stem oil seal

(m) Crankshaft and connecting rod bearing failure

Check 1 in Section (k)
1 Restricted oilways
2 Worn journals or crankpins
3 Loose bearing caps
4 Extremely low oil pressure
5 Bent connecting rod

(n) Internal water leakage (see Chapter 4)

(o) Poor circulation (see Chapter 4)

(p) Corrosion (see Chapter 4)

(q) High fuel consumption (see Chapter 2)

(r) Engine vibration

1 Loose generator bolts
2 Fan blades out of balance
3 Exhaust pipe mountings too tight

1:21 Modifications

These are made from time to time and as the modified parts are not always interchangeable with the originals, the following notes will be helpful.

To improve water sealing a modified cylinder head gasket has been introduced on the 948 cc and 1098 cc engines. This has ferrules round the water holes. The new gasket is interchangeable with the old. To ensure that the valve rocker screw does not work loose, a new rocker assembly has been introduced with the screwed boss increased in depth from $\frac{7}{16}$ to $\frac{9}{16}$ inch. The adjusting screw has also been increased in length from $1\frac{9}{32}$ to $1\frac{3}{8}$ inch. The old and new adjusting screws are interchangeable but the later type of rocker with the thickened boss must only be used in conjunction with the longer screw. The third ring from the piston crown on early engines was plain. A tapered ring is now fitted to improve oil consumption, so that the order is now: (1) plain, (2) taper, (3) taper, and (4) oil control. This assembly can be used on early pistons.

Shorter valve guides with a plain bore, and exhaust valves with smaller-diameter stems are fitted to the cylinder heads of later engines. The new valves and guides are interchangeable, in pairs, with the old.

Later engines may be found to have a one-piece inlet and exhaust manifold in which case the instructions dealing with the bolting together of the separate manifolds may be passed over.

CHAPTER 2

CARBURETTER AND FUEL SYSTEMS

Early cars have mechanical fuel pumps and Zenith carburetters, and later cars have electric fuel pumps and SU carburetters.

2:1 The mechanical pump

This is the AC-Sphynx Y-type, operated by an eccentric on the engine camshaft, and it will be found low down on the lefthand side of the crankcase. Some models have an external priming lever for pumping fuel by hand without running the engine. The pump is shown in section in **FIG 2:1** and an exploded perspective view is seen in **FIG 2:2**. Notice that in a later version of the same pump there is a different arrangement for the valves.

Operation:

As the engine camshaft 13 revolves, the eccentric 12 lifts the rocker arm 16 which is pivoted at 17. The arm pulls rod 1 and diaphragm 3 downwards against pressure from the spring 2. Consequent suction in chamber 4 causes fuel to be sucked into the chamber through filter 9 and inlet valve 11. On the return stroke the pressure of spring 2 pushes the diaphragm upwards, forcing fuel through the delivery valve 7 and port 8 into the carburetter. When the carburetter bowl is full and the float needle valve is shut, there is no flow of fuel from the pump until more is needed by the engine. This means that the pump chamber remains full, the diaphragm depressed and the connecting link 15 out of contact with the abutment on rocker arm 16. The arm will then reciprocate idly until a renewed demand for fuel causes the diaphragm to rise. Spring 14 keeps the rocker arm in constant contact with the eccentric to eliminate noise.

2:2 Servicing mechanical pump

Routine servicing (FIG 2:3):

To clean the gauze filter unscrew the cover retaining screw and remove the domed cover. Lift out the filter and clean it with a brush and petrol or with an air jet. Clean out the sediment chamber too. When refitting the cover use a new cork washer if the old one is broken or hard. Also see that there is a good fibre washer under the head of the retaining screw. Do not overtighten.

Dismantling:

Referring to **FIG 2:2** do the following, after scratching an alignment mark across the body flanges.
1 Unscrew bolt 1 and remove cover 3.

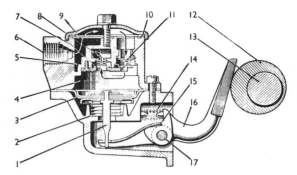

FIG 2:1 Sectional view of AC-Sphynx 'Y' type mechanical fuel pump

Key to Fig 2:1 1 Diaphragm pullrod 2 Diaphragm return spring 3 Diaphragm 4 Pump chamber 5 Sediment chamber 6 Inlet union 7 Delivery valve 8 Delivery port 9 Gauze filter 10 Cork sealing washer 11 Inlet valve 12 Camshaft eccentric 13 Camshaft 14 Anti-rattle spring 15 Connecting link 16 Rocker arm 17 Rocker arm pivot pin

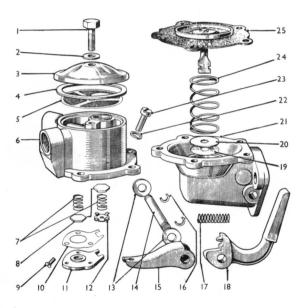

FIG 2:2 Component parts of mechanical fuel pump, type 'Y'

Key to Fig 2:2 1 Cover retaining screw 2 Fibre washer 3 Cover 4 Cork sealing washer 5 Gauze filter 6 Upper casting 7 Valve spring 8 Inlet and delivery valves 9 Valve plate screw 10 Valve plate gasket 11 Valve plate 12 Retainer 13 Packing washers 14 Rocker arm pivot pin 15 Connecting link 16 Retaining clips 17 Anti-rattle spring 18 Rocker arm 19 Fibre washer 20 Metal washer 21 Pump body 22 Spring washer 23 Upper chamber securing screw 24 Diaphragm return spring 25 Diaphragm assembly

2 Lift out filter gauze 5 and cork sealing washer 4.

3 Unscrew the five securing screws 23 and separate the pump halves 6 and 21.

4 Unscrew the screws 9 and remove the valve plate 11, the inlet and delivery valves 8, the valve plate gasket 10, the springs 7 and the delivery valve spring retainer 12.

5 Remove the diaphragm and pullrod assembly by rotating through 90 deg. and pulling out. This will release the diaphragm spring 24.

6 Remove the metal washer 20 and the fibre washer 19.

7 Remove the two retaining circlips 16 and washers 13, push out the rocker arm pivot pin 14 which will release the rocker arm 18, the link 15 and the spring 17.

Reassembling:

Before proceeding, all the valves should be swilled in clean paraffin as this not only cleans them but helps to improve their sealing.

1 Place the delivery valve 8 on its spring 7 and inlet valve 8 on the deeply recessed seating in the upper casting.

2 Put valve spring 7 on the centre of the inlet valve 8.

3 Position retainer 12 on top of the inlet valve spring 7. The retainer is a small four-legged pressing. Take care not to distort the legs.

4 Lay valve plate gasket 10 in position.

5 Locate valve plate 11 accurately and secure with the three screws 9.

6 With a piece of wire, press downwards on the inlet valve and upwards on the delivery valve to ensure that they work freely.

7 Replace the gauze filter and cover, with new gaskets if necessary.

8 Assemble link 15, packing washers 13, rocker arm 18 and spring 17 in the body 21. Insert rocker arm pin 14 through the hole in the body, at the same time engaging the packing washers 13, the link and the rocker arm. Then spring the clips 16 into the grooves at each end of the pin. The rocker arm pin must be a tap fit in the body. If wear has made it too free, burr the holes in the body slightly.

9 Fitting the rocker arm can be simplified by pushing a piece of .240 inch diameter rod through the hole in one side of the body until it engages the rocker arm washers and the link. The actual pin is then pushed in from the opposite side, removing the guide rod as the pin moves inward.

10 Fit the diaphragm assembly to the body by first inserting washer 19, metal washer 20 and spring 24 in the pump body. Place the diaphragm assembly over the spring with the pullrod downwards, and centre the upper end of the spring in the lower protector washer. The diaphragm should now be put into the position shown in **FIG 2:4**, with the locating tab at twelve o'clock. Press downwards on the diaphragm and turn the assembly anticlockwise through a quarter of a turn. The slots in the pullrod should now be engaged in the fork in the link. It is possible to push the rod down too far, so check this by measuring the distance from the flange of the pump body to the upper diaphragm protector, with the diaphragm held at the top of its stroke by the spring. This should be

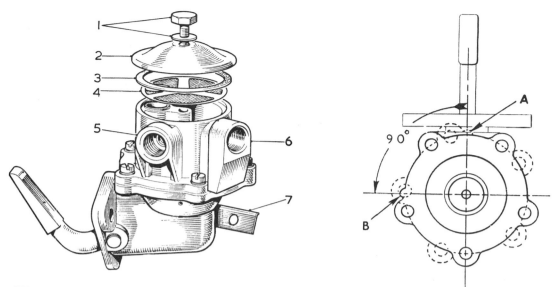

FIG 2:3 Top cover of pump removed to show filter

Key to Fig 2:3 1 Retaining screw 2 Cover 3 Cork sealing washer 4 Gauze filter 5 Delivery union 6 Inlet union 7 Priming lever

FIG 2:4 Fitting the diaphragm. Turn locating tab from 'A' to 'B' to engage pullrod

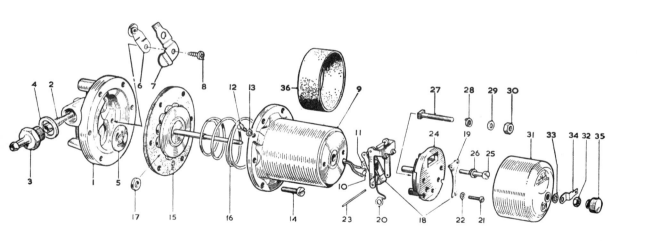

FIG 2:5 Earlier SU electric fuel pump, type SP, fitted to A40Mk II

Key to Fig 2:5 1 Body 2 Filter 3 Nozzle inlet 4 Washer for nozzle 5 Valve (outlet) 6 Valve (inlet) 7 Retainer (valve) 8 Screw for retainer 9 Housing (coil) 10 Tag (5BA terminal) 11 Tag (2BA terminal) 12 Screw (earth) 13 Washer (spring) 14 Screw (housing to body) 15 Diaphragm assembly 16 Spring 17 Roller 18 Rocker and blade 19 Blade 20 Tag (2BA terminal) 21 Screw for blade 22 Washer (dished) 23 Spindle for contact breaker 24 Pedestal 25 Screw (pedestal to housing) 26 Washer (spring) 27 Screw for terminal 28 Washer (spring) 29 Washer (lead—for screw) 30 Nut for screw 31 Cover (end) 32 Nut for cover 33 Washer (shakeproof) 34 Connector (Lucar) 35 Knob (terminal) 36 Sleeve (rubber)

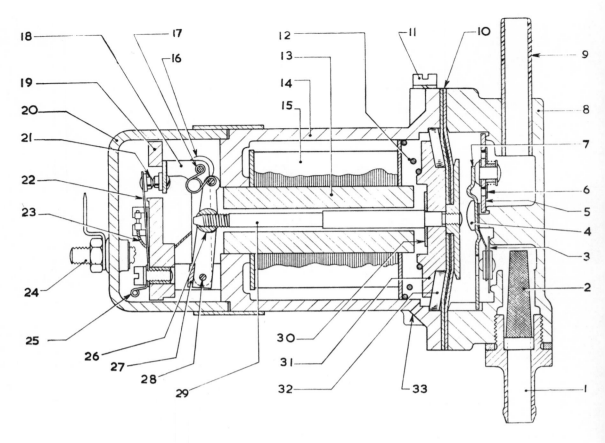

FIG 2:6   Sectional view of SU electric fuel pump, type SP

Key to Fig 2:6   1 Feed nozzle   2 Filter   3 Inlet valve   4 Screw (valve retainer)   5 Carrier plate   6 Delivery plate
7 Valve retainer   8 Body   9 Outlet connection   10 Diaphragm   11 Earth screw   12 Feed spring   13 Solenoid core
14 Coil housing   15 Coil   16 Fibre rollers   17 Toggle spring   18 Outer rocker   19 Pedestal   20 End cap
21 Contact points   22 Spring blade   23 Braided earth wire   24 Terminal screw   25 Coil lead tag   26 Trunnion
27 Inner rocker   28 Rocker hinge pin   29 Armature spindle   30 Impact washer   31 Armature   32 Brass rollers   33 Air vent

approximately $\frac{9}{16}$ inch whereas a dimension of $\frac{3}{16}$ inch shows that the link is riding on the shoulders of the pullrod.

11 Fit the two halves of the pump together by pushing the rocker arm until the diaphragm is level with the body flange. Place the upper half of the pump in position by aligning the scratch marks made before dismantling. Replace the five flange screws and lockwashers, tightening until the washers are only just engaged. Work the rocker arm several times and finally hold it fully 'up'. The diaphragm will then be right down as in **FIG 2:1** when the screws can be tightened.

Testing:

Flush the pump by immersing it in clean paraffin and work the rocker arm a few times. Empty the pump by continuing this operation clear of the paraffin. Do not immerse again, but place a finger over the union socket marked 'IN' and work the rocker arm several times. When the finger is removed there should be a distinct sucking sound. The finger is now placed over the outlet and the rocker arm pressed inwards. This will have the effect of compressing air in the pump chamber where the pressure should be held for two or three seconds. Repeat this operation with the pump immersed in paraffin and watch the diaphragm clamping flanges for signs of air bubbles which denote a leak.

Care is needed when refitting the pump to the engine to ensure that the rocker arm is correctly positioned against the eccentric, and not to one side or underneath. Run the engine and check for leaks at the pipe unions and pump flanges, after tightening the fixing bolts. Do not forget to clamp the breather pipe under one of the bolts.

2:3 The electrically operated fuel pump

There are two types of electric pump in use, the working principles for both being the same. The Austin A40 Mk II uses the SP as in **FIGS 2:5** and **2:6,** and the AUF200 as in **FIG 2:7**. The pump is located under the floor of the luggage compartment on the righthand side.

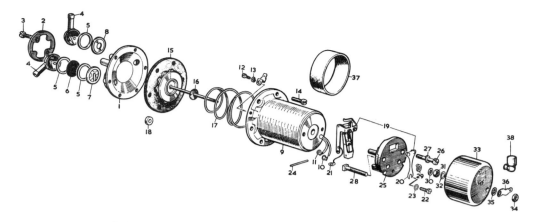

FIG 2:7   The SU pump, type AUF200, fitted to A40 Mk II (later)

Key to Fig 2:7   1 Body   2 Spring clamp plate   3 Screw   4 Nozzle (inlet/outlet)   5 Sealing washer   6 Filter
7 Valve (inlet)   8 Valve (outlet)   9 Housing (coil)   10 Tag (5BA terminal)   11 Tag (2BA terminal)   12 Screw (earth)
13 Washer (spring)   14 Screw (housing to body)   15 Diaphragm assembly   16 Impact washer   17 Spring   18 Roller
19 Rocker and blade   20 Blade   21 Tag (2BA terminal)   22 Screw for blade   23 Washer (dished)
24 Spindle for contact breaker   25 Pedestal   26 Screw (pedestal to housing)   27 Washer (spring)   28 Screw for terminal
29 Washer (spring)   30 Washer (lead—for screw)   31 Nut for screw   32 Spacer (nut to cover)   33 Cover (end)
34 Nut for cover   35 Washer (shakeproof)   36 Connector (Lucar)   37 Packing sleeve   38 Non-return valve

Operation:

FIG 2:6 shows the pump at rest with diaphragm 10 pressed to the right by spring 12. The armature spindle 29 has pulled the inner rocker 27 to the right so that spring toggle 17 forces the outer rocker to the left, keeping the contacts 21 closed. The rockers are mounted on a common hinge pin 28. The outer contact is fixed to spring blade 22.

The electrical circuit is thus from the terminal screw 24 through the coil winding to the outer spring contact. With the contacts closed, current then passes by way of the outer rocker arm and a braided copper wire to the coil housing back to earth. When the pump is switched on the solenoid winding 15 is energized, pulling the armature 31 and the diaphragm 10 towards it. The armature assembly is centralized by a ring of brass rollers 32 which allow movement to and fro. The partial vacuum to the right of the diaphragm causes fuel to be drawn into the pumping chamber of body 8 by way of inlet valve 3. Simultaneously the armature spindle 29 has moved the inner rocker to the left, causing the toggle spring 17 to flick the outer rocker over to the right and so open the contacts. The break in the electrical circuit de-energizes the coil and the pressure of the feed spring 12 forces the diaphragm to the right, pushing fuel out through the delivery valve 6. This movement of the diaphragm and its spindle means that the inner rocker goes back to the right, the outer rocker to the left, the contacts are closed and the cycle repeated.

2:4 Servicing electric pump

Routine maintenance:

Unscrew the inlet nozzle and clean the gauze filter to be found inside. The contact breaker points can be cleaned by drawing a strip of paper between them while holding them lightly together. Make sure that the electrical connections remain tight.

Dismantling:

To avoid confusion between the two models refer to **FIG 2:5** for the numbered parts.

1 Unscrew the inlet nozzle 3 and remove, together with filter and fibre washer.
2 Remove the six coil housing screws 14 and carefully separate the diaphragm from the two flanges.
3 Unscrew the valve retainer screw 8 and withdraw the retainer 7 with the two valves 5 and 6.
4 Hold the housing over a bench and unscrew the diaphragm 15 by rotating it anticlockwise. The eleven brass rollers 17 will then fall out.
5 Take off the spring 16 and the impact washer (not shown), but do not attempt to part the spindle from the diaphragm as this is serviced as a unit.
6 Remove the terminal connections and take off cap 31.
7 Unscrew the spring blade securing screw 21 and remove the long coil lead and the blade. Remove nut 30, cutting away the lead washer 29 which will be found flattened underneath it. Unscrew the two pedestal screws 25 and disconnect the braided copper earth lead which comes from the outer rocker.
8 Turn the pedestal 24 on its side and remove the remaining coil lead from the terminal screw, then remove the screw itself.
9 Push out the steel pin 23 and remove the rocker assembly. Do not remove the toggle springs on the assembly.

In the case of the later type of pump, use the following instructions, referring to **FIG 2:7** for the part numbers mentioned.

1 Unscrew the 2BA screws 3 securing the spring clamp plate 2. This holds the inlet and outlet nozzles 4 in place. The filter 6 and valve assemblies 7 and 8 can then be removed, noting the positions of the sealing washers.

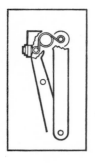
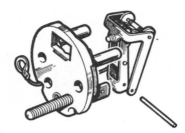

FIG 2:8 Fitting early-type rocker assembly to pedestal. Inset shows correct position of toggle spring

Inspection:

Refer to **FIG 2:5.**

1 Test each valve assembly in turn by alternately sucking and blowing at the inlet and outlet connections. The inlet valve unseats when blowing and seats when sucking; the outlet the reverse.

2 Examine the diaphragm for deterioration.

3 If the contact breaker points are badly burned and pitted, the rocker assembly and spring blade 18 must be replaced.

4 Check the strength of the feed spring 16. It should compress to a length of 1 inch under a load of $7\frac{1}{2}$ to 8 lb.

In the case of the pump shown in **FIG 2:7**, check the narrow tongues on the valve cages 7 and 8. These retain the valves and should not be distorted but allow a valve lift of approximately $\frac{1}{16}$ inch.

Assembly of the pump shown in FIG 2:5 :

1 Replace the valves and inlet connection.

2 Secure the free ends of the rocker assembly to the pedestal with the pivot pin (see **FIG 2:8**). This pin is hardened and must be replaced by a genuine SU spare part if it is worn.

3 Fit the square-headed terminal screw to the pedestal. Replace the spring washer, the short lead from the coil, a new lead washer and the nut.

4 Slip the braided earth lead from the outer rocker on to one of the pedestal screws, then a spring washer. Secure the pedestal with both screws.

5 Fit the remaining coil lead to the 4BA screw and secure the spring blade to the pedestal with the lead on top of the blade. The blade must bear against the small rib as shown by the arrow in **FIG 2:11.**

6 Adjust the blade until the points make firm contact and are a little above the points on the rocker as in **FIG 2:9.** Move the rocker arm to check that the points wipe over the centre line of each other.

7 With the outer rocker depressed, the spring blade should rest on the rib mentioned previously. If it does not, remove the blade and very lightly set it towards the pedestal. Excessive pressure will restrict the rocker travel.

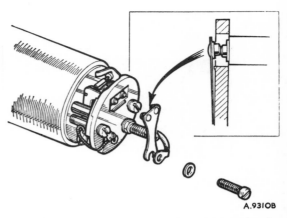

A.9310B

FIG 2:9 Setting the blade and rocker contact points for correct relative position

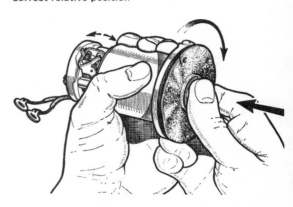

FIG 2:10 Screwing in the diaphragm until the rocker ceases to throw-over

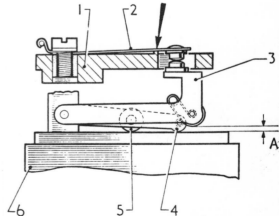

FIG 2:11 The contact gap setting on earlier-type rocker assemblies

Key to Fig 2:11 1 Pedestal 2 Contact blade 3 Outer rocker 4 Inner rocker 5 Trunnion 6 Coil housing A=.030 inch

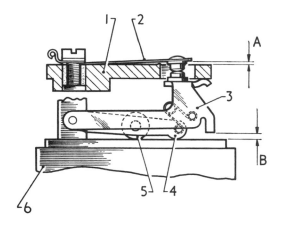

FIG 2:12 The rocker finger settings on later-type assemblies

Key to Fig 2:12 **A** .035±.005 inch **B** .070±.005 inch
1 Pedestal 2 Contact blade 3 Outer rocker 4 Inner rocker 5 Trunnion 6 Coil housing

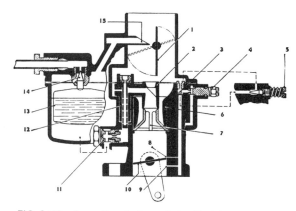

FIG 2:13 A sectional view of the Zenith carburetter, type 26 JS, fitted to early A30's

Key to Fig 2:13 1 Strangler flap 2 Inner venturi 3 Air jet
4 Slow-running jet 5 Air regulating screw 6 Choke tube
7 Deflector 8 Progression outlet 9 Slow-running outlet
10 Throttle flap 11 Main jet 12 Emulsion tube 13 Float
14 Needle 15 Air release tube

8 With the impact washer and feed spring in place, pass the armature spindle through the solenoid core and screw it into the trunnion on the inner rocker.

9 Rotate the diaphragm until the outer rocker will just not throw over and then unscrew it seven holes at the diaphragm's edge.

10 Position the brass rollers between the armature and the diaphragm, fit the body to the coil housing and tighten the six screws evenly. It is not necessary to stretch the diaphragm during this operation. **Do not use jointing compound on the diaphragm.**

11 Replace the bakelite cap, terminal fittings and the rubber sleeve.

When dealing with the pump shown in **FIG 2:7**, there are the following changes in procedure:

1 After replacing the pedestal on the coil housing, do not fit the contact blade.

2 Fit the diaphragm as in the previous instructions, and with the rollers in place fit and adjust the contacts, removing the contact blade after this. Now hold the coil housing horizontally and push the armature spindle firmly and steadily. Unscrew the diaphragm, pressing and releasing the spindle until the rocker just throws over as in **FIG 2:10**. Turn the diaphragm back (unscrew it) to the nearest hole and then a further four holes.

3 Replace the inlet and outlet valves in the following order. The valves are identical assemblies. Place the outlet valve assembly, tongue uppermost, in the recess marked 'OUTLET', follow with a joint washer and then the outlet nozzle. With the tongue downwards, place the inlet valve assembly in the deeper recess marked 'INLET', with a joint washer to follow. Now put the filter in the recess with the domed side upwards, then a joint washer and the inlet nozzle. Clamp the nozzles in place so that they will be horizontal when in position in the luggage compartment.

4 Fit and adjust the contact breaker assembly according to the following instructions.

5 With the outer rocker back against the coil housing, the contact blade should rest lightly on the small rib on the pedestal face as shown by the arrow in **FIG 2:11**. To adjust, swing the blade sideways, bend slightly and test. Over-tensioning will restrict rocker travel. Hold the blade against the rib without pressing the tip. A .030 inch feeler should now pass between the white fibre rollers and the face of the coil housing. Set the tip of the blade to correct this gap.

Later rocker assemblies are to be seen in **FIG 2:12** which shows the gaps which can be checked by feeler gauge. The lift of the contact blade above the pedestal face should be .035 inch, bending the stop at the back of the rear contact if necessary. The gap between the rocker finger and the coil housing should be .070 inch. The finger can be bent to obtain this gap.

Testing the pump:

With the pump fitted and the fuel lines connected, switch on. If the pump is noisy and operates rapidly, an air leak is probable. Check by disconnecting the fuel line from the carburetter and turning the pipe down into a jar. Keeping the end submerged with the pump switched on, the emission of continuous bubbles will confirm an air leak. Check that the inlet union to the pump is tight and that all connections from the tank to the pump are in good order. Check also that the coil housing screws securing the diaphragm flanges are evenly tightened.

If the pump operates without delivering fuel check for a serious air leak on the suction side or foreign matter under the valves, particularly the inlet. Remove the valves for cleaning.

If the pump works initially but the carburetter float chamber does not fill, look for an obstructed float needle. Disconnect the fuel line from the carburetter, switch on and check the flow from the open pipe. If it diminishes rapidly and the pump slows down, check the petrol tank

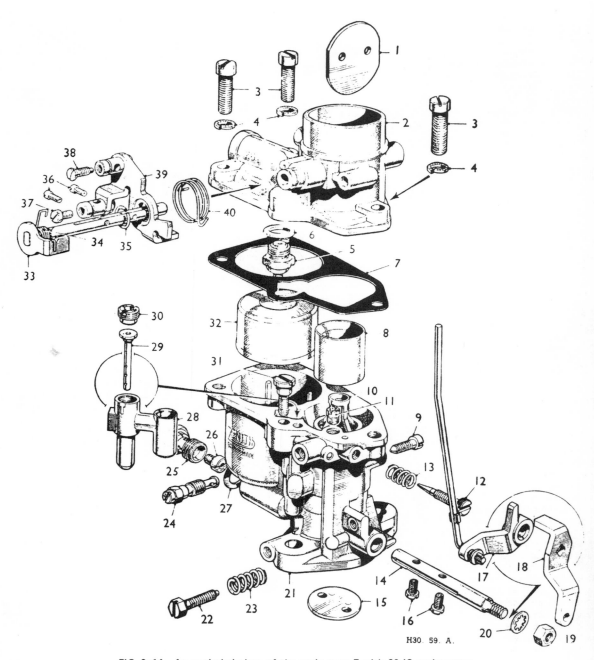

FIG 2:14 An exploded view of the early-type Zenith 26 JS carburetter

Key to Fig 2:14   1 Strangler flap   2 Strangler body   3 Strangler body to carburetter screw   4 Spring washer
5 Needle seating   6 Washer   7 Gasket   8 Choke tube   9 Choke tube fixing screw   10 Deflector
11 Slow-running air bleed jet   12 Air regulating screw   13 Spring   14 Throttle spindle   15 Throttle   16 Throttle fixing screws
17 Floating lever and interconnection rod assembly   18 Throttle lever   19 Throttle lever fixing nut   20 Shakeproof washer
21 Carburetter body   22 Throttle stop screw   23 Throttle stop screw spring   24 Slow-running jet   25 Main jet carrier
26 Main jet   27 Fibre washer for main jet carrier   28 Inner venturi   29 Emulsion tube   30 Main air jet
31 Inner venturi fixing screw   32 Float   33 Strangler spindle   34 Strangler spring   35 Strangler lever retaining clip
36 Strangler flap fixing screws   37 Interconnection swivel screw   38 Strangler swivel screw   39 Strangler lever
40 Strangler lever spring

venting by removing the filler cap. Blocked or inadequate venting causes a slow power stroke of the pump, burning the contact points.

If the reduced flow is accompanied by slow operation of the pump, check for a clogged filter at the pump inlet. If the pump operates rapidly, check for air leaks, dirt under the valves or faulty valve sealing washers where fitted.

If there is no flow check the electrical supply. If satisfactory, check the contact breaker points. With the main supply lead connected, short across the contacts with a piece of bare wire. If the pump then makes a stroke the fault is due to dirt, corrosion or maladjustment of the contacts.

If the pump will only operate with the inlet pipe disconnected, there may be a restriction in the pipe between the pump and the tank. **If compressed air is used to clear a pipeline, never pass it through the pump as the valves will be damaged.**

If all these checks fail to locate the trouble, suspect a stiffening of the diaphragm fabric or abnormal friction in the rocker mechanism. Remove the coil housing and flex the diaphragm a few times, taking care not to lose the eleven rollers under it. Assemble the diaphragm as previously instructed and use a little thin oil on the 'throw-over' spring spindles where they pivot in the brass rockers.

Renew the solenoid assembly if there is excessive sparking at the contact points. **Do not attempt to cure leakage of the diaphragm joint by applying any kind of jointing compound.**

2:5 Early Zenith carburetter

Early A30:

This downdraught carburetter is the Zenith, type 26 JS. **FIG 2:13** shows it in section, **FIG 2:14** is an exploded view.

Operation:

When starting from cold the strangler flap 1 in **FIG 2:13** is closed by the dashboard control. The interconnecting rod assembly shown in **FIG 2:14** opens the throttle flap slightly at the same time. Rich mixture will now be delivered for starting the engine. Immediately the engine fires a stronger depression will be created on the engine side of the flap, and as this is held closed only by the tension on the spindle spring, the strangler flap will open and close rapidly with pulsations from the engine suction, thus providing a weaker mixture as the engine speeds up.

When the engine is warm enough the strangler can be opened fully. With the throttle closed to the idling position mixture is supplied by the slow-running jet 4 in **FIG 2:13**, to which reference should be made for all the reference numbers. Engine suction will be concentrated on outlet 9 and then, by way of drilled passages, to the slow-running jet 4. The output from this jet is controlled by the slow-running screw 5, which acts as an air bleed. The progression outlet 8 provides more fuel as the throttle continues to open until the high depression in the choke tube 6 causes petrol to be drawn from the emulsion tube 12. This petrol joins the intake air to form an emulsion which is drawn into the engine. The emulsion tube is drilled throughout its length. As the petrol level in the tube falls, these holes are uncovered to provide compensation for the main jet 11.

2:6 Servicing the early carburetter

Dismantling the 26 JS:

Thoroughly clean the outside of the carburetter, and then refer to **FIG 2:14**.

1 Unscrew the swivel screw 37 enough to allow the strangler body 2 to be drawn off after removing screws 3. Tip out float 32 and store safely.
2 From the strangler body remove the needle seating 5 and washer 6.
3 Remove the strangler flap 1 by unscrewing the two screws 36, so that the spindle 33 can be withdrawn after unhooking spring 34. Mark the flap before removing it as the bevelled edges can only be fitted one way round. Also note the correct position of the strangler spindle and spring with reference to the strangler lever.
4 Clip 35 holds the lever 39 in position. Undo this and slip off the lever and the spring 40.
5 Close the throttle and note the relative positions of the floating lever assembly 17 and throttle lever 18. Note the way the bevelled edges of the throttle fit the bore of the carburetter, and then unscrew the two screws 16 and withdraw the throttle. Pull out the spindle 14 with the floating lever assembly and the throttle lever, leaving the washer 20 and nut 19 in position. Take out the throttle stop screw 22 and spring 23.
6 Remove the main jet carrier 25, and unscrew the main jet 26. With a screwdriver remove the air regulating screw 12, the slow-running jet 24, the slow-running air bleed 11 and the main air jet 30 which holds down the emulsion tube 29.
7 On type 26 JS-2 carburetters the screw 31 can be taken out to allow the venturi 28 to be removed. Screw 9 when detached will permit the removal of choke tube 8 and deflector 10.
8 On type 26 JS-3 carburetters the screw 31 secures the discharge nozzle, and screw 9 a modified choke tube. The inner venturi 28 and the deflector 10 are deleted.

Reassembling the 26 JS:

Clean all the parts with petrol, and clear the jets with compressed air if possible. Do not push wire through the jets. Note that all the jet sizes are clearly marked. The higher the number the larger the jet. Refer to Technical Data for correct jet sizes.

Now follow the dismantling procedure in reverse. On type 26 JS-3 carburetters ensure that the bar in the choke tube contacts the beak of the discharge nozzle before the choke tube fixing screw is fitted. Change the gasket 7 between the strangler body and the carburetter body if it is damaged. Replace the float with the word 'TOP' uppermost.

2:7 Later Zenith carburetter

On the later A30 and 948 cc A35 cars:

This is the Zenith, type 26 VME, illustrated in **FIGS 2:15** and **2:16**.

Operation:

The throttle and strangler interlinkage is similar to that on the type 26 JE carburetter, but there are many changes which will affect the sequence of operations, assuming

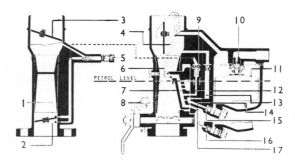

FIG 2:15 A sectional view of the Zenith 26 VME carburetter

Key to Fig 2:15 1 Progression outlet   2 Slow-running outlet   3 Strangler flap   4 Interconnecting rod 5 Air regulating screw   6 Emulsion block outlet nozzle 7 Emulsion tube   8 Throttle stop screw   9 Slow-running jet 10 Needle seating   11 Float   12 Well (slow-running) 13 Well (compensating jet)   14 Compensating jet tube 15 Compensating jet   16 Main jet   17 Main jet tube

that the engine has reached working temperature. With the throttle closed to the idling position, mixture will be supplied by the slow-running jet 9 in **FIG 2:15**. Depression will be concentrated on the outlet 2 and from there to the slow-running jet 9 where it is regulated by the slow-running screw 5. Petrol will be drawn from the well 12 beneath the jet. When the throttle is opened slightly, depression is concentrated on the larger outlet 1 to give a progressive getaway from the initial slow-running position. Further opening of the throttle will concentrate the depression upon nozzle 6. Petrol will then be drawn from passages 13 and 7 where there is a reserve of petrol for instant acceleration. When this is used the supply is from the main and compensating jets 16 and 15. When the petrol in well 13 has been consumed the top of the well is open to atmosphere and the compensating jet 15 becomes an air bleed. Petrol from the main jet 16 meets emulsified petrol from the compensating jet in a common channel 7 where it also becomes emulsified. The mixture is then drawn from the emulsion block nozzle 6. As petrol is used float 11 will fall, opening the needle valve in seating 10 to allow more petrol to enter the chamber.

Dismantling the 26 VME:

The parts can be identified in **FIG 2:16**.

1 Remove the float chamber 27 by unscrewing bolts 3 and put the float in a safe place.
2 Remove the main and compensating jet plugs 26 and 24 from underneath the float chamber. A screwdriver will take out the jets. The slow-running jet 36 and screw 37 may also be unscrewed. Take out the five screws 18 and remove the emulsion block 19, taking particular care of the joint washer 20.
3 The float needle seating 21 can be removed from the carburetter body 5. Part the strangler flap 2 from the spindle 30 by removing screws 1 and withdraw the spindle after unhooking spring 31. Note the bevels on the flap edges to ensure correct replacement, and also the position of the strangler spring with respect to lever 28.

4 Disconnect the interconnection rod 8 from its upper end. Undo clip 29 which holds the strangler lever in position. Slip off the lever and spring, noting the correct assembled position.
5 Close the throttle and take note of the relative positions of the floating lever and interconnection rod assembly 9 and 8, and the throttle lever 10. Notice that the bevelled edges of the throttle fit closely in the bore of the carburetter body before removing screws 14 and withdrawing the throttle. Take out spindle 13 with the interconnection rod assembly and the throttle lever 10, leaving behind nut 11 and washer 12.
6 Take out throttle stop screw and spring 17 and 16, also air regulating screw 6 with its spring. Detach screw 7 to remove the choke tube 4. Wash all the parts in clean petrol and blow compressed air through all drilled passages. Failing an air supply, a bicycle pump can be used.

Reassembling the 26 VME:

This is a straightforward reversal of the dismantling procedure.

Change gasket 34 between the float chamber and the carburetter body if it is damaged. Replace the float with the word 'TOP' uppermost.

Zenith carburetter adjustment (both models):

It will be impossible to obtain the best performance from the carburetter if the air cleaner is clogged, if ignition settings are incorrect, or if there is serious wear in the valve guides and air leaks at other points. These leaks can occur at the carburetter spindles if they are worn, and at any gaskets and joint faces which are damaged. Trouble is often caused by the float feed, which may be due to a worn or sticking needle or a punctured float. The float can be tested by immersing completely in hot water when bubbles will rise from a leak.

If starting is difficult and petrol is reaching the float chamber, check the strangler control and interlinkage. With the strangler flap closed, the throttle should be open a fraction, and this can be adjusted at the top end of the interlinkage rod. Assuming that the engine has started and has reached working temperature, check the idling performance. Heavy 'thumping' slow running with black smoke from the exhaust pipe indicates a rich mixture which can be corrected by turning the regulating screw in an anticlockwise direction, when the engine speed should increase, with smoother running. The speed can now be reduced to correct idling by means of the throttle stop screw, which is also turned anticlockwise. Another slight adjustment of the slow-running mixture regulating screw may be needed until the idling is smooth. Very slow idling is not necessary.

Weak mixture can be corrected by turning the regulating screw clockwise. The screw is number 12 in **FIG 2:14** and 6 in **FIG 2:16**.

2:9 SU carburetter, type HS2

This carburetter is fitted to the 848 cc and 1098 cc A35 and to the 948 cc and 1098 cc A40 Mk II. The only real difference between early and late carburetters is in the float chamber mechanism, as can be seen in **FIGS 2:18** and **2:19**.

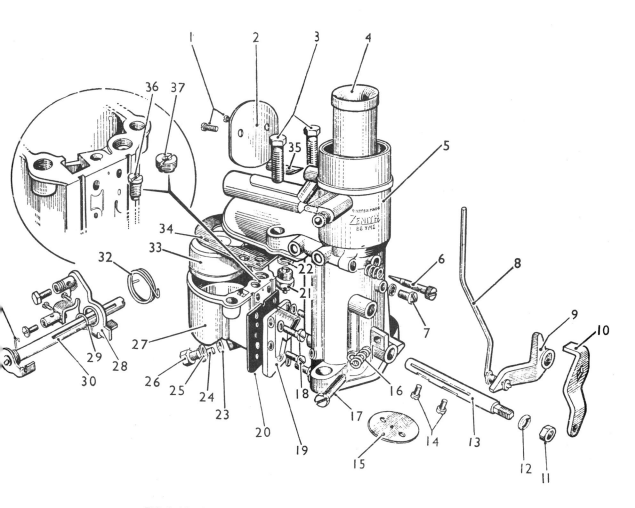

FIG 2:16   An exploded view of the Zenith 26 VME carburetter

Key to Fig 2:16   1 Strangler flap fixing screws   2 Strangler flap   3 Fixing screws (bowl to barrel)   4 Choke tube
5 Carburetter body   6 Air regulating screw   7 Choke tube fixing screw   8 Interconnection rod   9 Floating lever
10 Throttle lever   11 Throttle lever fixing nut   12 Spring washer   13 Throttle spindle   14 Throttle fixing screws
15 Throttle   16 Throttle stop screw spring   17 Throttle stop screw   18 Emulsion block fixing setscrews
19 Emulsion block   20 Gasket for emulsion block   21 Needle seating   22 Washer for needle seating
23 Compensating jet washer   24 Compensating jet plug   25 Main jet washer   26 Main jet plug   27 Float chamber
28 Strangler lever   29 Retaining clip for strangler lever   30 Strangler spindle   31 Strangler spring
32 Spring for strangler lever   33 Float   34 Gasket (bowl to barrel)   35 Air release tube   36 Slow-running jet
37 Screw over capacity well

Operation:

Using **FIG 2:17** as a guide, the SU carburetter action can be followed. The body 1 is fitted with the usual butter-fly throttle valve 29. On the air intake side of this valve is a variable choke aperture formed by piston 5 rising and falling inside a top chamber 5. This action is automatic, depending as it does upon the depression arising from throttle opening and engine load. The variable volume of intake air needs a varying flow of petrol, which is achieved by using a tapered needle 17 attached to the piston. This rises and falls in a fixed jet aperture 12 giving the greatest flow when the piston is at the top of its travel. Rapid

fluctuations of the piston are damped out by an hydraulic damper 7. Rich mixture for starting is obtained by pulling the jet downwards to a smaller diameter of the tapered needle, so increasing the area of the annulus and the flow of petrol. The spring 9 is fitted to assist gravity to return the falling piston.

2:10 Servicing SU carburetter

Removing:

Remove the air cleaner as instructed in **Section 2:11**. Disconnect the mixture and throttle controls, the ignition

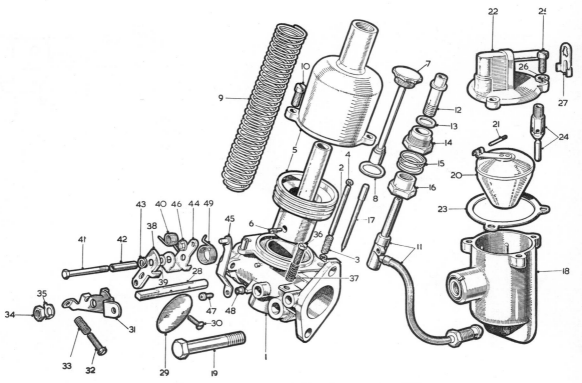

FIG 2:17 Components of SU carburetter, type HS2

Key to Fig 2:17   1 Body   2 Piston lifting pin   3 Spring for pin   4 Circlip for pin   5 Suction chamber and piston assembly
6 Needle locking screw   7 Piston damper assembly   8 Washer (fibre)   9 Piston spring   10 Screw   11 Jet assembly
12 Jet bearing   13 Washer (brass)   14 Lockwasher   15 Lockspring   16 Jet adjusting screw   17 Jet needle
18 Float chamber   19 Bolt   20 Float   21 Hinge pin   22 Float chamber cover   23 Gasket
24 Needle and seat   25 Screw   26 Spring washer   27 Baffle (overflow)   28 Throttle spindle   29 Throttle disc   30 Screw
25 Screw   26 Spring washer   27 Baffle (overflow)   28 Throttle spindle   29 Throttle disc   30 Screw
31 Throttle lever   32 Cam stop screw   33 Spring   34 Throttle spindle nut   35 Tab washer   36 Idling stop screw
37 Spring   38 Cam lever   39 Washer   40 Cam lever spring   41 Cam lever pivot bolt   42 Pivot bolt tube
43 Spring washer   44 Pickup lever assembly   45 Jet link   46 Jet link retaining clip   47 Jet link screw   48 Bush
49 Spring for pickup lever

vacuum pipe from the carburetter body and the fuel pipe from the float chamber Release the carburetter from the inlet manifold, taking careful note of the position and condition of the gaskets and the heat washer (if fitted).

Dismantling the HS2:

Before stripping anything, mark the relative positions of throttle and control levers. Scratch a line across the flanges of the body and piston chamber so that they can be mated accurately on assembly. Refer to **FIG 2:17.**

1 Remove the damper 7 and invert the carburetter to pour off the thin damper oil inside. Remove screws 10 and lift off the piston chamber and piston 5 with spring 9. This is a piece of precision engineering and must be treated with great care.

2 Remove the float chamber cover 22 looking out for the loose float needle 24 if the float hinge pin 21 is taken out. Preserve gasket 23 carefully.

3 Detach the nylon fuel pipe 11 from the float chamber which can then be released by unscrewing bolt 19.

4 The jet 11 can be pulled out, but if the assembly 12 to 16 is disturbed then the jet will need re-centring.

5 Piston lifting pin 2 is held in place by circlips 4. It is used for carburetter tuning.

With the damper still removed, check that the piston is quite free in the piston chamber. Clean carefully if there is any sign of sticking, and oil the piston rod with thin oil. There should be no metallic contact between the piston rim and the inside of the piston chamber. Do not oil any other part but the piston rod. If a needle is to be changed slacken screw 6. Correct needle sizes are given in Technical Data. Insert the new needle so that its shoulder is flush with the bottom face of the piston. Refer to **FIG 2:18** to check the position of the float, as this controls the fuel level in the jet. Insert a piece of round bar between the hinged lever and the lip of the float chamber lid. The end of the lever should just rest on the bar. If it does not, reset by bending at point 'C'. Do not bend the lever, which must be quite flat and at right-angles to the needle when it is on its seating.

The float and lever are different on early carburetters. **FIG 2:19** shows the method of setting for correct fuel level. Insert a $\frac{5}{16}$ inch round bar between the float lever and the lid. The lever fork should just touch the bar when the needle is seated. Set by bending where the fork joins the shank, as the shank must always be flat and at right-angles to the needle.

Reassembly:

Follow the dismantling process in reverse. Take care to position the keyway in the piston over the key in the body. Before replacing the damper pour in 20W oil until it is within $\frac{1}{2}$ inch of the top and check the piston for free movement. It should drop with a smart click. This check can also be done with the carburetter fitted and is necessary if the engine is reluctant to start and will not accelerate. This may be due to a sticking piston, caused by dirt or a badly centred jet, but remove the damper to check.

To centre the jet, referring to FIG 2:17 :

1 Disconnect the link between the jet lever and the jet head.
2 Remove the nylon tube from the float chamber and withdraw the jet.
3 Remove jet adjusting screw 16 and spring. Replace the jet.
4 Slacken jet locking screw 14 until the jet bearing is just free to rotate.
5 With the damper removed, press the piston down fully and tighten the jet locking nut, keeping the jet in the correct angular position for the nylon tube to be recoupled to the float chamber.
6 The piston should now fall freely with a metallic click. Fully lower the jet and check the sound. If it differs repeat the centring operation, replacing the jet adjusting screw and spring, when successful.

Carburetter adjustment on the HS2:

If the tapered needle is stationary the jet aperture can be increased by lowering the jet, and decreased by raising it. This is the basic operation when tuning an SU carburetter. Run the engine up to working temperature and then set the throttle stop screw for fast-idling (see FIG 2:21). With the jet head firmly in contact with the jet adjusting nut, turn the nut up or down until the engine runs smoothly.

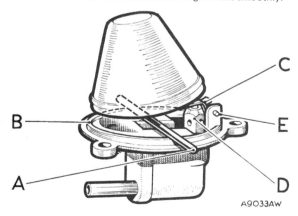

A9033AW

FIG 2:18 Checking the float lever adjustment on later SU carburetters

Key to Fig 2:18
C Angle of float lever **A** $\frac{1}{8}$ to $\frac{3}{16}$ inch **B** Machined lip
E Lever hinge pin **D** Float needle and seat assembly

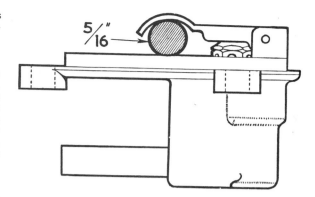

FIG 2:19 Float lever check on early SU carburetters

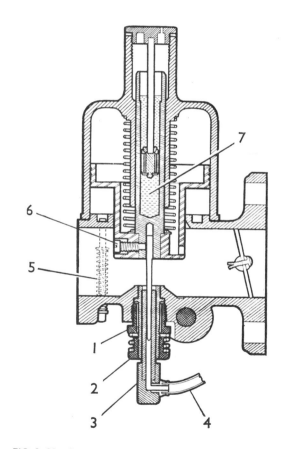

FIG 2:20 A section through the SU carburetter

Key to Fig 2:20 1 Jet locking nut 2 Adjusting nut
3 Jet head 4 Nylon fuel pipe 5 Piston lifting pin
6 Needle securing screw 7 Piston damper oil well

Check this by raising the piston about $\frac{1}{32}$ inch with a penknife blade or the piston lifting pin 5 in **FIG 2:20**. If the engine stops the mixture is weak. If the speed of the engine continues to increase with the piston raised as much as $\frac{1}{4}$ inch the mixture is too rich. If $\frac{1}{32}$ inch gives a slight momentary increase in engine speed the mixture is correct. Now set the throttle stop screw for the desired slow-running. The fast-idling screw 4 in **FIG 2:21** is adjusted by pulling on the dash panel control knob until the linkage is about to move the jets. This will be about $\frac{1}{4}$ inch. Adjust the fast-idling screw to given an engine speed of 1000 rev/min when hot.

Faulty performance:

If there is trouble on the road it may be due to a piston sticking, to a blocked jet or to flooding. Check the piston by removing the air cleaner and the piston damper, and then lifting the piston with a finger. It should rise and fall freely. If it does not, the trouble may be dirt or a badly centred jet. A blocked jet may sometimes be cleared by opening the throttle with the engine running and momentarily blocking the air intake. With the throttle still open the engine should start to race, showing that the jet has been cleared. Flooding from the float chamber may be due to dirt in the needle valve. The needle can be removed by withdrawing the float pivot pin. If the tapered end of the needle is deeply grooved, replace both needle and seating with new ones. If there is apparently a lack of fuel, disconnect the pipe to the carburetter and if the pump is working there should be regular spurts of fuel from the pipe.

2:11 Air cleaners

Two types of air cleaner have been fitted, one having an oil wetted element and the other a dry element.

Oil wetted type:

To remove, slacken the clamp bolt, disconnect the breather pipe and lift off. Wash the wire mesh in fuel and let it drain until dry. Re-oil the mesh and again let it drain before replacing on the engine.

Dry type:

This type of air cleaner must not be disturbed until a new element is to be fitted. To renew the element unscrew the wing nut, lift off the cover or body and extract the element. Remove every trace of dust from inside the body, fit the new element and reassemble. The extended air intake pipe can be positioned near the exhaust manifold during very cold weather conditions to prevent carburetter icing. Move the intake away from the manifold when warmer conditions prevail.

On both types of air cleaner, the frequency of servicing depends on road conditions. When these are very dusty, more frequent attention is required. A choked element will adversely affect carburation.

2:12 Fault diagnosis

(a) Leakage or insufficient fuel delivered

1 Air vent in tank restricted
2 Petrol pipes blocked
3 Air leaks at pipe connections
4 Pump or carburetter filters clogged

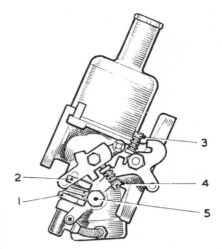

FIG 2:21 Adjustment points on the SU carburetters

Key to Fig 2:21   1 Jet adjusting nut   2 Jet locknut
3 Throttle stop screw   4 'Fast-idle' adjustment screw
5 Float chamber securing bolt

5 Pump gaskets faulty
6 Pump diaphragm damaged
7 Pump valves sticking or seating badly
8 Fuel vapourising in pipelines due to heat

(b) Excessive fuel consumption

1 Carburetter needs adjusting
2 Fuel leakage
3 Sticking controls
4 Dirty air cleaner

5 Excessive engine temperature
6 Brakes binding
7 Tyres under-inflated
8 Idling speed too high
9 Car overloaded

(c) Idling speed too high

1 Rich fuel mixture
2 Carburetter controls sticking
3 Slow-running screw incorrectly adjusted
4 Worn carburetter throttle valve

(d) Noisy fuel pump

1 Loose mountings
2 Air leaks on suction side and at diaphragm
3 Obstruction in fuel pipe
4 Clogged pump filter

(e) No fuel delivery

1 Float needle stuck
2 Vent in tank blocked
3 Electric pump connections faulty
4 Electric pump contacts dirty
5 Pipeline obstructed
6 Pump diaphragm stiff or damaged
7 Inlet valve in pump stuck open
8 Bad air leak on suction side

CHAPTER 3

THE IGNITION SYSTEM

3:1 Automatic timing

All the distributors incorporate automatic ignition timing, both by a centrifugal mechanism and vacuum control. The weights of the centrifugal device fly out against the tension of springs as engine speed rises. This advances the contact breaker cams relative to the driving shaft, giving advanced ignition according to speed. The vacuum control is operated by depression in the inlet manifold, this suction varying with engine load. At small throttle openings with no load on the engine there is a high degree of vacuum in the manifold, causing the control on the distributor to advance the ignition. When hill-climbing on large throttle openings the much-reduced vacuum means that the control will retard the ignition. The units mentioned can be seen in **FIG 3:1**.

3:2 Routine maintenance

With the rotor removed, add a few drops of oil to the cam bearing. This is point 3 in **FIG 3:2**. Do not remove the screw.

Smear the cams with a small amount of grease or a very little engine oil. Squirt a few drops of oil into the gap between the cams and the contact breaker plate, taking care that no oil gets on the plate or near the contacts.

Adjust the contact breaker points by turning the engine until they are fully opened by one of the cams, as shown in **FIG 3:2**. Slacken screw 1 and with a screwdriver in slots 2, move the fixed contact plate until the gap between the points is between .014 inch and .016 inch. Set the sparking plug gaps to an opening between .024 inch and .026 inch.

3:3 Removing distributor

1 Turn the engine by hand until the rotor arm points to No. 1 plug lead in the distributor cap. Note the position of the vacuum unit as it will simplify connecting the vacuum pipe during assembly.
2 With the low-tension lead disconnected from its terminal, and the suction pipe from the vacuum control unit, remove the two bolts securing the clamp plate to the distributor housing. This plate 3 and pinch bolt 5 can be seen in **FIG 3:5**. Do not slacken this bolt or the timing will be lost.

3:4 Dismantling distributor

1 To remove the contact breaker assembly and plate, lift off the rotor and withdraw the low-tension terminal post shown top right in **FIG 3:1**. Remove the two

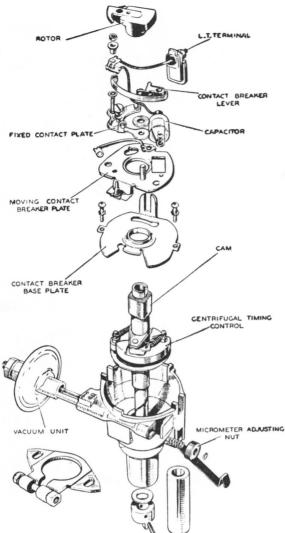

FIG 3:1 The component parts of the Lucas DM2 distributor

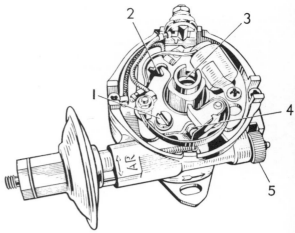

FIG 3:2 Distributor cap removed to show the contact breaker platform

Key to Fig 3:2 1 Contact adjusting screw 2 Contact adjusting slot 3 Cam and drive shaft oiling point 4 Contact points 5 Micrometer adjuster

At the top, inside the spigot which locates the rotor arm, is a screw which must be removed in order to release the cam spindle. **Before doing this, note the relative positions of the rotor arm driving slot and the driving dog at the bottom of the spindle (see FIG 3:1).** This is to ensure that the timing is not 180 deg. out when the cam spindle is re-engaged with the centrifugal weights during assembly.

3 Having removed the cam spindle, take off the centrifugal weights, each one being an assembly complete with spring and toggle.

4 To unscrew the adjusting nut and spring from the vacuum unit spindle, remove the circlip at the end.

To remove the driving spindle from the body, drive out the parallel pin which secures the driving dog. Note the position of any thrust washers.

3:5 Servicing distributor

Examine the distributor cap for cracks or signs of 'tracking'. Evidence of the latter can be seen as a thin black line between the brass segments inside the cap. The only cure is to replace the cap with a new one.

The carbon brush 1 in **FIG 3:8** should protrude slightly and move freely. It is of composite construction to give some degree of radio interference suppression, the top part being a resistive compound. Never replace this long type with a short, non-resistive brush. Clean the cap thoroughly with a dry cloth. Renew the rotor if the metal electrode is loose or badly eroded.

The faces of the contact breaker points should be clean, with a greyish, frosted look. If not too deeply burned and pitted, they can be polished by using a fine stone with a rotary motion. It is essential to keep the faces flat and square, so that they meet perfectly when fitted. Clean afterwards with petrol. The movable contact arm should be free on its pivot without being unduly slack. If there is wear of the centrifugal timing weights and pivot pins

screws securing the plate, ease up, and unhook the vacuum link.

2 Dismantle the contact breaker assembly by removing the nut and washer from the anchor pin for the moving contact spring. Now withdraw the insulating bush and the tags, noting the order and position so that they will be correctly replaced. Lift off the moving contact and the insulating washers from the anchor and pivot pins. The fixed contact plate is removed by unscrewing the single fixing screw, together with both the spring and flat washers. Remove the securing screw to release the capacitor.

renew the weights and the cam assembly. The latter must also be renewed if it is not a close sliding fit in the driving shaft. Excessive clearance causes cam wear and erratic opening of the contact points. Check the fit of the driving shaft in the body and renew the shaft and the bearings if they are worn. Immerse new bushes in thin engine oil for twenty-four hours, or for two hours in oil heated to 100°C. They can then be pressed into the distributor body.

3:6 Assembling distributor

1 Lubricate, with thin engine oil, the parts of the centrifugal advance mechanism, the drive shaft and the section of the shaft where the cam fits.
2 Assemble the parts, making sure that the cam driving pins engage with the centrifugal weights in the original position. When seen from above, the small offset of the driving dog must be on the right when the driving slot for the rotor arm is at six o'clock.
3 When replacing the vacuum control unit, turn the adjusting nut to the halfway position.
4 Adjust the contact breaker to the correct gap.

3:7 Installing distributor

1 Insert the distributor in the engine housing and turn the rotor until the driving dogs engage. Being offset, there is only one position for the dogs where this can take place.
2 Fit the two bolts securing the clamp plate and tighten them after setting the vacuum control unit to the position it occupied originally. Leave one of the bolts holding the clamp plate to the distributor housing slack, until the pinch bolt has been tightened. If the pinch bolt rotates in a fixed nut, tighten to 50 lb in. If the bolt is tightening by a rotating nut, use a torque figure of 30 lb in.
3 Fit the vacuum pipe and distributor cap and check the timing.

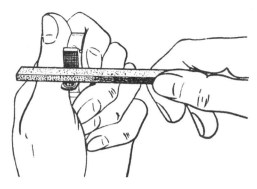

FIG 3:3 Cleaning the contact breaker points

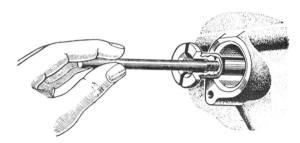

FIG 3:4 Using a piece of threaded rod to replace the distributor driving spindle

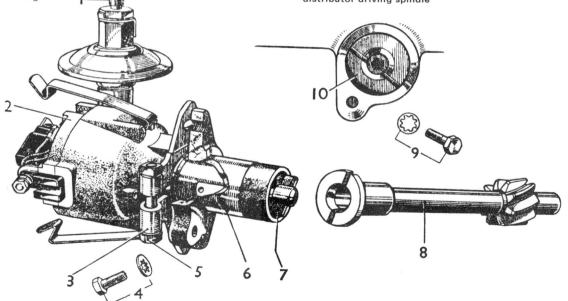

FIG 3:5 The A30 body, housing and drive shaft. The inset shows the offset slot in shaft

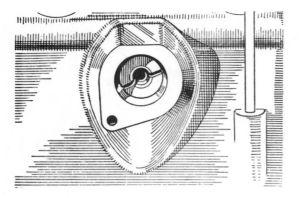

FIG 3:6 Correct position of driving slot with large offset uppermost. This applies to all models except the A30

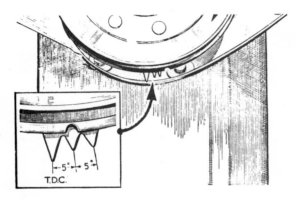

FIG 3:7 The ignition timing pointers. Note the notch in the pulley rim

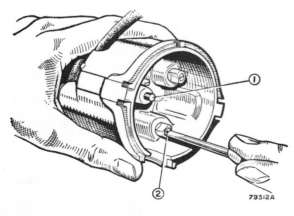

FIG 3:8 Connecting the high-tension leads on early cars. 1 is the carbon brush, 2 is the cable-securing screw

Setting the driving spindle:

The distributor is driven by a spindle which engages with a skew gear on the camshaft. If this spindle has been removed according to the instructions given in the Engine chapter, it must be accurately replaced or the ignition timing will be out.

On 800 cc A30's:

1 Screw a length of $\frac{5}{16}$ inch BSF rod, or a long bolt, into the end of the driving spindle, as shown in **FIG 3:4**.
2 Turn the crankshaft until No. 1 piston is at TDC on the compression stroke. Valves 7 and 8 will then be just rocking.
3 Insert the driving spindle into the distributor housing in the crankcase so that it meshes with the camshaft gear. When it is fully home, the slot must be at twenty minutes past ten with the small offset below and to the left. This position is clearly shown by the inset in **FIG 3:5**. The driving dog on the distributor is also offset and will mesh only in one place.

On 848 cc, 948 cc and 1098 cc A35's and A40's:

Follow the original instructions but replace with the offset slot at 20 minutes to two with the large offset uppermost as in **FIG 3:6**. The screwed rod should be $\frac{5}{16}$ inch UNF.

The distributor can now be replaced.

3:8 Timing the ignition

On A30's before engine No. 93536, the timing marks on the flywheel are not visible unless the gearbox is removed. To time the ignition without seeing the marks proceed as follows.

1 Set No. 1 piston at TDC on the compression stroke with valves 7 and 8 just rocking.
2 Slacken the distributor clamp bolt and turn the distributor body until the contact points are just about to open with the rotor pointing to No. 1 plug lead segment in the distributor cap.
3 Tighten the clamp bolt, replace the cap and test on the road.

With low octane fuel the engine should pink slightly under load in top gear from 10 to 30 mile/hr with the accelerator hard down. If pinking is violent and persists after 30 mile/hr the ignition must be retarded by small movements of the micrometer adjusting knob. If there is no pinking or it dies out early, advance the ignition.

With premium fuel there will be no pinking and the flywheel marks must be used. Turn the crankshaft to set No. 1 piston at TDC as before.

1 Turn the flywheel until the 1/4 mark lines up with the pointer on the housing.
2 Turn the flywheel backwards so that the 1/4 mark is $\frac{33}{64}$ inch away from the pointer, corresponding to $6\frac{1}{2}$ deg. of crankshaft rotation. This is the setting for fuels rated at less than 80 octane. With premium fuels set the mark $\frac{7}{8}$ inch away, corresponding to 11 deg. of rotation.
3 Slacken the distributor bolt, point the rotor at No. 1 segment in the cap, then turn the distributor until the points are just opening.
4 Tighten the clamp bolt and test on the road, making slight adjustments on the micrometer knob if necessary.

Timing on later A30's and all other models:

1 Set No. 1 piston at TDC on the compression stroke.
2 Turn the crankshaft until the notch in the crankshaft pulley is in line with the longest pointer on the timing cover. This is marked TDC in **FIG 3:7**. If the cover is off, align the timing marks on the chainwheels.
3 Turn the crankshaft backwards to the angular setting in degrees BTDC given in Technical Data.
4 Set the micrometer adjustment centrally, turn the distributor until the contact points are just opening with the rotor arm pointing at No. 1 plug lead segment in the cap.
5 Tighten the clamp plate bolt.

It is possible to use the electrical method to determine the precise moment when the contact points open. To do this, remove the vacuum pipe and turn the distributor body until the contact points are fully closed. Turn on the ignition switch, remembering that the low-tension lead must be connected to the distributor. Connect a twelve-volt lamp with one lead to the low-tension terminal and the other to earth and rotate the distributor body clockwise until the lamp lights. This is the position where the points have just opened. Now tighten the clamp bolt, check that the rotor is opposite No. 1 plug lead segment in the cap, refit the cap and vacuum pipe and test on the road. The micrometer adjustment is used for small movements only, and is intended to set the timing accurately for slightly different grades of fuel.

The adjustment nut is shown by the lower arrow in **FIG 3:9**. Turn it clockwise to retard and anticlockwise to advance the ignition, looking on the end of the threaded spindle. Each graduation at the point shown by the upper arrow represents an approximate timing movement of 5 deg. This is equal to 55 clicks on the adjusting nut.

Timing with a stroboscopic lamp:

1 Disconnect the vacuum pipe.
2 Do not allow the engine rev/min to rise higher than 600 or the centrifugal weights in the distributor will advance the ignition.

3:9 Faulty performance

Misfiring and difficult starting may be due to defective high-tension leads to the plugs and ignition coil. To renew them, remove the securing screws inside the distributor cap, as shown in **FIG 3:8**. Later cars have plug-in cables with sealing sleeves. Fill the holes in the cap with silicone grease and push the leads into place so that there is a ring of grease to form a watertight seal. Secure the leads with the pointed screw. Press carbon brush 1 to see that it moves freely. Replace the cap and leads so that the firing order is 1, 3, 4, 2, bearing in mind that the rotor moves anticlockwise. Start the engine, and if misfiring is evident and it is known that it is not due to other defects in the engine, disconnect each plug lead in turn and hold it about $\frac{3}{16}$ inch away from the cylinder head. If the spark is strong and regular, but misfiring continues when the lead is replaced, then the sparking plug is at fault. The treatment of sparking plugs is dealt with in a later section. If the spark from the lead is weak and irregular, suspect the distributor or the low-tension circuit. If the distributor, and the contact breaker points, are in good condition, test the low-tension circuit with a 20-volt voltmeter.

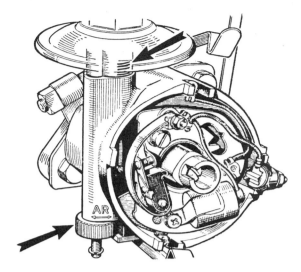

FIG 3:9 The micrometer adjusting nut. The vernier scale is shown by the top arrow

1 Switch on the ignition and turn the crankshaft until the points are fully open.
2 Check battery to starter switch cable. Connect voltmeter between the supply terminal of starter switch and earth. No reading indicates a faulty cable or connection.
3 Check cable from starter switch to fuse unit terminal 'A1'. Connect voltmeter between terminal 'A1' and earth. No reading indicates a faulty cable or connection.
4 Check control box. Connect voltmeter between control box terminal 'A1' and earth. No reading indicates a faulty control box.
5 Check cable from control box to lighting and ignition switch. Connect voltmeter between the lighting switch terminal 'A' and earth. No reading indicates a faulty cable or connection.
6 Check the ignition switch. Connect the voltmeter between the switch and earth. No reading indicates a faulty switch.
7 Check cable from ignition switch to fuse unit terminal 'A3'. Connect voltmeter between terminal 'A3' and earth. No reading indicates a faulty cable or connection.
8 Check cable from fuse unit terminal 'A3' to ignition coil. Connect the voltmeter between the ignition coil terminal SW and earth. No reading indicates a faulty cable or loose connection.
9 Check the ignition coil. Connect the voltmeter between the ignition coil terminal CB and earth. No reading indicates a faulty ignition coil.
10 Check cable from ignition coil to distributor. Connect the voltmeter between the distributor terminal and earth. No reading indicates a faulty cable or connection.
11 Check the distributor. Connect the voltmeter across the contact points. If there is no reading, remove the capacitor and test again. If there is then a reading, the

capacitor is at fault. Test the capacitor by substitution, connecting a new one between the low-tension terminal and earth. Fit a new capacitor complete with bracket, but if the capacitor alone is available, unsolder the old one from its bracket, using as little heat as possible for the re-soldering operation. The capacity is .2 microfarad.

A final test is to remove the high-tension lead from the centre of the distributor cap. Switch on the ignition and turn the crankshaft until the contact points are closed. Hold the high-tension cable about $\frac{3}{16}$ inch away from the cylinder block and flick the contact breaker lever to open the points. If there is a strong spark the ignition coil is in order, but no spark indicates a faulty coil.

3:10 Sparking plugs

Examine the deposits on the firing end to check on working conditions. The normal condition will be for a plug which is of the correct grade used for a mixed period of high-speed and low-speed driving. This leaves a deposit which is from brown to greyish tan in colour. White to yellowish powdery deposits indicate long periods of constant-speed driving or much low-speed city driving. Neither of these deposits will affect performance if the plugs are cleaned on a blasting machine and the gaps reset. File the sparking surfaces to reveal bright clean metal.

Wet black deposits can be traced to oil fouling, due mainly to cylinder bore wear, or worn pistons, rings and valve stems.

Dry, fluffy black deposits are caused by rich mixture or misfiring. Excessive idling or slow speeds will also keep plug temperatures so low that normal deposits are not burned off.

A white blistered appearance of the insulator nose, and badly eroded electrodes, indicate overheating. This can be caused by weak mixture, poor cooling, incorrect ignition timing or sustained high speeds and heavy loads.

After cleaning, which should include the sparking plug threads, set the gap between the electrodes to a figure between .024 and .026 inch. Fit new gaskets and tighten to a torque of 30 lb ft. If the plugs cannot be seated by hand, clean out the threads in the cylinder head by using a tap or an old sparking plug with three or four saw cuts down the threads.

Replacement sparking plugs must be those specified by the car manufacturers, and the correct types will be found in Technical Data.

3:11 Fault diagnosis

(a) Engine will not fire

1 Battery discharged
2 Distributor contact points dirty, pitted or out of adjustment
3 Distributor cap dirty, cracked or 'tracking'
4 Carbon brush inside distributor cap not in contact with rotor
5 Faulty cable or loose connection in low-tension circuit
6 Distributor rotor arm cracked
7 Faulty coil
8 Broken contact breaker spring
9 Contact points stuck open

(b) Engine misfires

1 Distributor contact points dirty, pitted or out of adjustment
2 Weak contact breaker spring
3 Distributor cap dirty, cracked or 'tracked'
4 Faulty coil
5 Faulty cable or loose connection in low-tension circuit
6 High-tension plug and ignition coil leads cracked or perished
7 Sparking plug loose
8 Sparking plug insulation cracked
9 Sparking plug gap incorrect
10 Ignition timing too far advanced

CHAPTER 4

THE COOLING SYSTEM

4:1 Operation of system

All the cars described in this manual have pressurized water cooling systems in which the natural thermo-syphon circulation is augmented by a centrifugal impeller mounted at the rear end of the fan spindle. This impeller receives water from the bottom tank of the radiator and passes it through the cylinder block. It then goes up into the cylinder head until it reaches a thermostat at the front end of the head. The thermostat valve remains closed while the water is cold, so that the water re-circulates round the engine and warms up rapidly. This rapid warm-up reduces the risk of severe cylinder bore wear. When the water reaches a temperature in the region of 80°C the thermostat valve opens, allowing the water to pass through the top hose into the radiator header tank. From here the hot water falls through the radiator core to the bottom tank, being cooled on its way by the external air flow through the core. The volume of cooling air is increased by a belt-driven fan.

A spring-loaded valve in the filler cap pressurizes the cooling system and so raises the temperature at which the water boils. **FIG 4:1** shows the cap removed, and the locking cams on the filler spout. When the engine is hot, unscrew the cap slowly until the resistance of the lobes at the ends of the cams can be felt. After waiting a moment until the pressure is released, the cap can be removed.

4:2 Maintenance

Overheating may be caused by a slack fan belt. With the correct tension it should be possible to move the belt laterally about 1 inch at the centre of its longest run. To adjust the belt refer to **FIG 4:2** which shows the three nuts to be slackened. Lift the generator by hand, tighten the adjusting link nut first, followed by the other two, and finally check the tension. A belt which is too tight throws an undue strain on both generator and fan spindle bearings.

The bearings in the water pump rarely need replenishment, being packed with grease, but if it is thought necessary some extra lubricant can be introduced through the large screw hole above point 'A' in **FIG 4:3**. Do not use pressure or the lubricant may reach the carbon seal and impair its efficiency. To drain the radiator and water passages, open the tap beneath the radiator and the tap at the rear of the cylinder block, as seen in **FIG 4:4**. Antifreeze can be collected, strained and used again, but if topping up with water is needed, remember that this dilution will reduce the protection. If the car is fitted with a heater, draining the engine and radiator will not drain the heater unit so that antifreeze must be used. This should be of the ethylene glycol or glycerine type conforming to Specification BS.3151 or BS.3152.

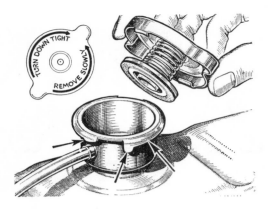

FIG 4:1 The radiator filler and pressurizing valve. If the system is hot, unscrew the cap slowly until the lefthand stop is reached, pause and then remove, protecting the hand against escaping steam

The water system should be flushed periodically to clear away the sludge and deposits which tend to clog the passages. Remove the filler cap, open the drain taps and flush the system with clean water from a hose held in the filler orifice. Extra cleaning can be given by removing the radiator, turning it upside down and flushing it through in the reverse direction. When refilling, close the drain taps, open the water tap to the heater if one is fitted and fill slowly, using soft water for preference.

4:3 Water pump servicing

The water pump fitted to early A30's is shown in **FIG 4:5**. The water seal is readily dismantled but the rear bearing needs a special tool to centralize it because it must pass through the front bearing housing on its way out. This needs the services of a well-equipped garage.

To dismantle as far as this proceed as follows:

1 Remove the radiator and slacken the top clip of the thermostat bypass hose. This is the hose clipped to the bypass tube 8.
2 Remove the generator as detailed in the Electrical chapter.
3 Unscrew the four nuts holding the pump body to the cylinder block and remove the pump with the bypass hose.
4 Remove the fan blades and the fan pulley (when detachable) from the hub.
5 Remove the spindle nut and washer and withdraw the hub. Prise out the Woodruff key 21.
6 Hold the pump body and tap out the spindle towards the rear, using a soft-faced hammer. The spindle will carry with it the impeller vane and water seal assembly, items 16 to 20. Note that parts numbered 1 to 6 and 14 and 15 are assembled and removed from the front end of the body.
7 Prise out the spring retaining ring 6 and remove the lubricant retainer 5. Bearing 4 and distance piece 3 can then be tapped out from the rear by a drift, but the rear bearing needs a special tool to remove it, as mentioned earlier.

Examine the bearing and the carbon sealing ring 16 for wear. Renew worn parts and the spring 19 if it has weakened.

Reassemble in the reverse order. After engine No. 41992 a modified seal assembly was fitted. This one-piece seal replaces items 16, 18 and 19 in the earlier water pump. The complete pump assembly is interchangeable with the old one, but the pump body 7, the water seal assembly, the distance piece 17, the spindle with vane 20 and the lubricant retainer 5 are not separately interchangeable.

Water pump, all other models:

This can be seen in section in **FIG 4:3**. It is removed from the engine according to the previous instructions and can then be dismantled.

1 Remove the fan blades and belt pulley from the hub.
2 The hub is an interference fit on the shaft and must be pulled off with an extractor.
3 Pull out the bearing locating wire through the hole in the top of the pump body just in front of point 'A'.
4 Tap the spindle gently rearwards, releasing the combined spindle and bearing assembly, with seal and vane.
5 The impeller vane is an interference fit on the spindle and can be drawn off with an extractor, enabling the one-piece water seal assembly to be removed.

Check the spindle and bearing assembly for wear. The bearings cannot be replaced if worn, so that the whole spindle assembly must be renewed. Also replace the seal if the carbon face is worn or if there is evidence of leakage. When reassembling in the reverse order make certain that the hole in the bearing body is in line with the lubricating hole 'A' before pressing the spindle and bearing assembly into the pump housing. Note when fitting the vane that the tips of the blades must clear the body by the dimension given in **FIG 4:3**. If the interference fit of the fan hub

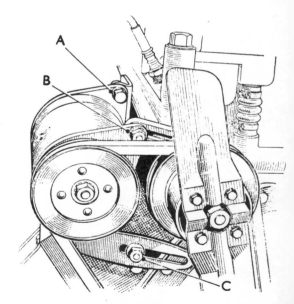

FIG 4:2 To adjust the fan belt loosen generator nuts A and B and link nut C

was impaired when it was removed from the spindle, the hub should be renewed. Take care that the face of the hub is flush with the end of the spindle as shown at point 'B' in **FIG 4 : 3**.

If the original spindle and bearing assembly has been retained and it is thought advisable to introduce some extra lubricant, do so through the screw hole above point 'A' in **FIG 4 : 3**. Do not exert undue pressure when doing this or lubricant may be forced past the seals. Fit the fan and pump assembly to the cylinder block using a new paper joint washer, and after replacing the generator and belt, adjust the latter to the correct tension.

4 : 4 Thermostat

1 To remove the thermostat drain the cooling system and remove the top hose from the outlet elbow at the front end of the cylinder head.

2 Take off the three securing nuts and spring washers and lift the elbow from the studs.

3 Remove the paper joint washer and lift out the thermostat.

4 Test the thermostat opening temperature by immersing it in hot water to the temperature given in Technical Data. If the valve does not start to open or is stuck in the fully open position, renew it, as it cannot be repaired.

Installation is the reverse of removal, but see that the joint washers are in good condition. One of them will be found in a recess in the cylinder head, under the thermostat flange.

In an emergency the engine can be run with the thermostat removed.

4 : 5 Temperature gauge

This is fitted to later A40's with bi-metal instrumentation. For details refer to **Chapter 11**.

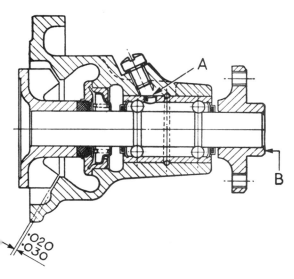

FIG 4 : 3 Sectioned water pump of later type showing lubricating hole in bearing assembly at A

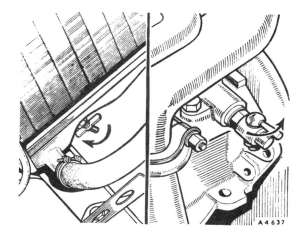

FIG 4 : 4 Radiator drain tap (left) and cylinder block drain tap (right). Arrow shows direction to open. Later engines may have a plug instead of the righthand tap

4 : 6 Antifreeze

The relatively high temperatures developed in a pressurized cooling system prevent the use of antifreeze solutions having an alcohol base, because of their high evaporation rate. For this reason only ethylene glycol or glycerine types are suitable, as mentioned under 'Maintenance'. Before adding antifreeze mixture, the radiator should be flushed through with a hose in the filler neck and the drain tap open.

Antifreeze can remain in the system for two years if the specific gravity of the solution is checked periodically and fresh antifreeze added as required. The antifreeze manufacturer can supply the equipment needed for the specific gravity check. After the second winter, drain the system, flush out and refill with fresh water and antifreeze if required.

Top up the radiator when the cooling system is at its normal running temperature to avoid losing antifreeze by expansion.

The correct solutions of antifreeze for different degrees of frost protection are given in the following table.

Solution %	Absolute safe limit	Commences freezing at
20	—19°C (—3°F)	—9°C (16°F)
25	—26°C (—15°F)	—13°C (9°F)
30	—33°C (—28°F)	—16°C (3°F)

4 : 7 Fault diagnosis

(a) Internal water leakage

1 Cracked cylinder wall
2 Loose cylinder head nuts
3 Cracked cylinder head
4 Faulty head gasket
5 Cracked tappet chest wall

(b) Poor circulation

1 Radiator core blocked
2 Engine water passages restricted
3 Low water level

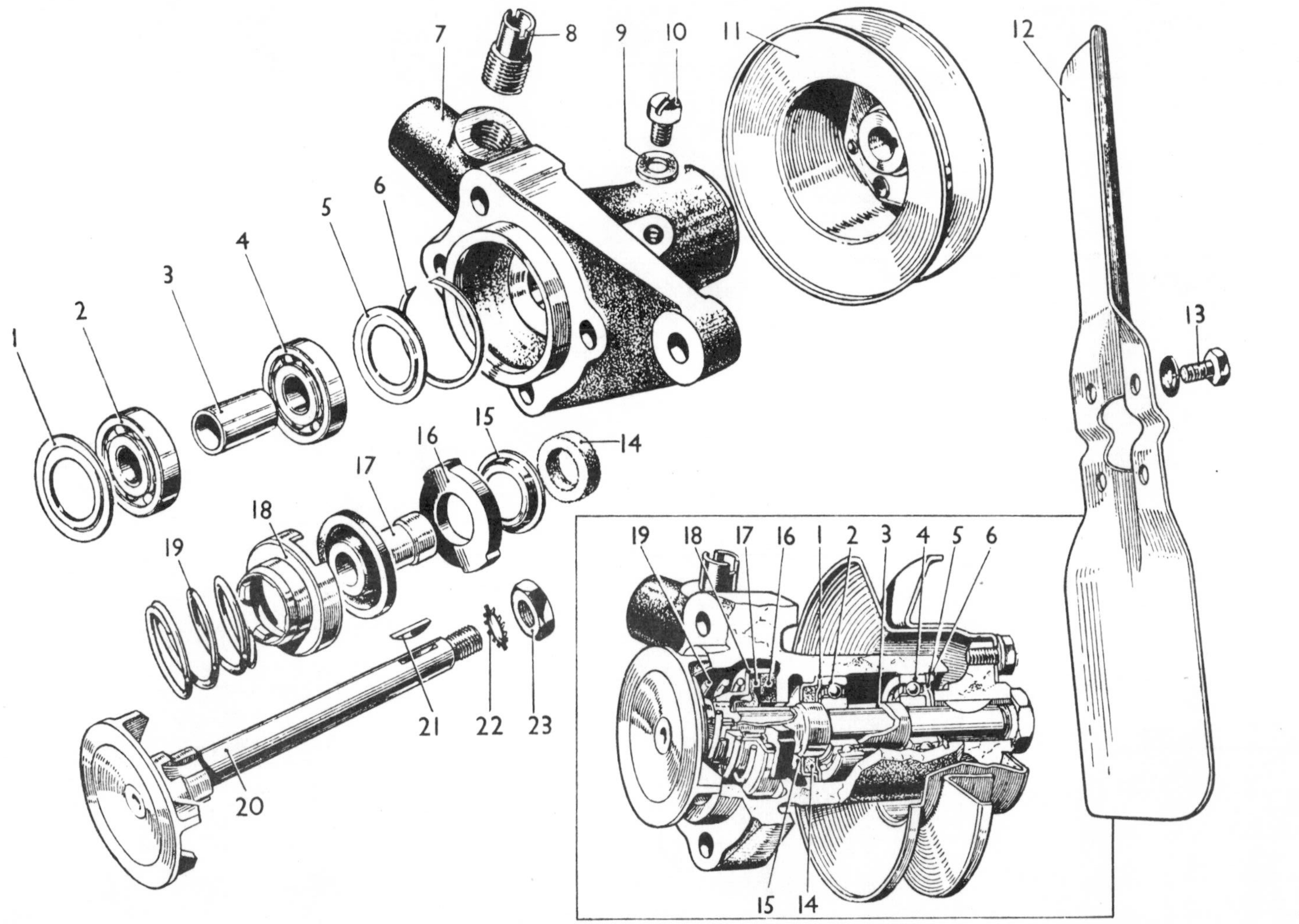

FIG 4:5 Early A30 water pump exploded

Key to Fig 4:5   1 Felt retainer (outer)   2 Bearing (rear)   3 Bearing distance piece   4 Bearing (front)   5 Lubricant retainer   6 Spring ring   7 Pump body
8 Bypass tube   9 Screwed plug washer   10 Screwed plug   11 Fan and pump pulley   12 Fan blade   13 Setscrew and washer   14 Felt ring   15 Felt retainer (inner)
16 Sealing ring   17 Rubber seal and distance piece   18 Locating cup   19 Gland spring   20 Spindle with vane   21 Woodruff key   22 Shakeproof washer

48

4 Loose fan belt
5 Defective thermostat
6 Perished or collapsed radiator hoses

(c) Corrosion
1 Impurities in the water
2 Infrequent draining and flushing

(d) Overheating
1 Check 4, 5 and 6 in (b)

2 Sludge in crankcase
3 Faulty ignition timing
4 Low oil level in sump
5 Tight engine
6 Choked exhaust system
7 Binding brakes
8 Slipping clutch
9 Incorrect valve timing
10 Retarded ignition
11 Mixture too weak

NOTES

CHAPTER 5

THE CLUTCH

:1 Operation and servicing

The clutch is shown in section in **FIG 5:1.** This ustrates the type fitted to earlier cars, but the working rinciple is the same for the later type. The clutch has a ngle driven plate to which are riveted the friction linings 3. he hub of this plate slides on splines machined on the earbox first-motion shaft, the drive from the plate to the ub being transmitted by springs to give a cushioned ke-up. The plate is sandwiched between the rear face of e flywheel 1 and a spring-loaded pressure plate 18 arried inside a cover 4 which is bolted to the flywheel. he pressure plate can be drawn backwards against the ower of the thrust springs 5 in order to free the driven ate and thus disengage the drive. This movement of the essure plate is effected by a series of levers 12 and the lease bearing 7 and 8. The release bearing derives its ovement from levers connected to the clutch pedal ther mechanically or hydraulically.

ervicing:

The clutch cover is normally serviced as an assembly, omplete with pressure plate, thrust springs and release vers. Expensive tools and gauging equipment are eded to assemble and adjust the cover accurately, and is work best left to a competent agent.

5:2 Early-type clutch

The following instructions will cover the clutches fitted to early A30 and A35 cars, and to the 948 cc A40's.

To remove the clutch, take off the gearbox as detailed in **Chapter 6.**

1 Slacken the clutch cover screws a turn at a time, working diagonally until the spring pressure is relieved, and then remove entirely.
2 The driven plate will then be completely free and should be examined for the following faults. If the plate can be used again do not touch the linings with cleaning fluids.

Looking at **FIG 5:2,** the splines in the hub 11 must not be worn nor the edges of the flange which engages the springs 10. The springs should not be broken, neither should they be weakened, so that they are free to rattle. Now examine the linings for excessive wear, loose rivets, cracks and discolouration. The polished glaze is quite normal and does not affect the ability to transmit power, but the linings should be light in colour, with the grain of the material quite clearly visible through the glaze. Evidence of oil on the linings can be seen in the much darker colour and a glazed deposit on the surface which has obliterated the grain. This will cause two defects; the clutch will stick on engagement so that it is difficult to

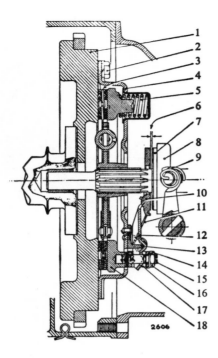

FIG 5:1 Section of the clutch fitted to 800 cc and 948 cc engines

Key to Fig 5:1 1 Flywheel 2 Holding screw 3 Driven plate 4 Cover 5 Thrust spring 6 Clearance $\frac{1}{16}$ inch 7 Graphite release bearing 8 Release bearing cup 9 Release bearing carrier 10 Release lever plate 11 Lever retainer and anti-rattle spring 12 Release lever 13 Knife-edge fulcrum 14 Tag lockwasher 15 Stud 16 Adjusting nut 17 Bearing plate 18 Pressure plate

free and yet it will slip under load. Signs of oil on the clutch can be attributed to leakage past the rear main crankshaft bearing or from the gearbox. It is not advisable to rivet new linings to an old plate. The plate may be distorted, and there may be trouble with out-of-balance effects.

Now proceed to examine the pressure plate assembly. If the friction surface of the plate 8 is ridged or pitted the assembly should be renewed. This also applies to the machined surface of the release lever plate, where it contacts the carbon release bearing 16. This face must be smooth and there must be no ridge round the outer edge due to wear.

If there has been trouble such as slip or drag, and the pressure unit is suspected, then it can be checked by an agent with the proper equipment. If it is otherwise unworn the agent will be able to look for weak or broken springs and set the release levers accurately. Otherwise the only answer is to fit a replacement unit complete.

The release bearing 16 must have a smooth polished bearing surface, without signs of cracks or pitting. The carbon block must stand proud of the cup in which it is housed by at least $\frac{1}{16}$ inch. If less than this, both cup and bearing must be renewed. The clutch withdrawal lever 15

can be rebushed if necessary. Note that the A30 lever is much longer than the one illustrated, and that it has an eye in the end for the operating rod.

Refitting:

First check the flywheel with a dial gauge for 'runout'. If satisfactory, the clutch can be fitted, but it will be necessary to use a pilot mandrel to centralize the driven plate. The reason for this can be seen in **FIG 5:1**. Notice that the splined first-motion shaft from the gearbox locates in a bush in the flanged end of the crankshaft. As it must pass through the driven plate hub to reach this bush it is evident that the two must be perfectly in-line. This is done by using the service tool shown in **FIG 5:3**.

1 Hold the clutch assembly on the flywheel and fit the bolts finger tight. Note that the longer boss to the driven plate hub has chamfered splines. These must face to the rear to facilitate entry of the first-motion shaft splines.

2 Insert the Service Tool 18G.139 through the clutch cover and the driven plate hub so that the pilot enters the spigot bearing in the end of the crankshaft. This will centralize the driven plate.

3 Tighten the clutch cover securing bolts a turn at a time in diagonal sequence to avoid distorting the cover.

4 Remove the service tool, refit the gearbox and adjust the clutch pedal free travel. This operation is covered in **Section 5:8**.

5:3 Later-type clutch

This clutch is of larger diameter to transmit the extra power of the 1098 cc engines fitted to the later A35's and A40's. It is also fitted to the 848 cc A35.

FIG 5:4 shows the clutch in section, and an exploded view of the components can be seen in **FIG 5:5**. The hydraulic slave cylinder shown as operating the release lever in **FIG 5:4** will not be correct for the A35, which is fitted with a mechanical link to the clutch pedal.

As there is no fundamental difference between this clutch and the earlier type already covered, the instructions for dismantling and refitting remain the same.

5:4 Mechanical operation

The clutch pedal linkage on the A30 and A35 cars can be seen in **FIG 5:6**, which is a view looking towards the rear of the car. Dismantle and reassemble in the following manner.

1 Detach the pull-off spring 2 and the anti-rattle spring if one is fitted. Then disconnect the operating rod 4 by removing the domed nut and locknut.

2 Remove the cotter which secures the pedal lever 1 to the shaft 5, by slackening the nut a few turns and knocking the cotter loose. This prevents damage to the cotter thread. The nut is then unscrewed. On later models the pedal is secured to the shaft by a locating screw and locknut.

3 Release the setscrews in the support flanges of the clutch pedal shaft and knock out the peg in the outer spherical bush.

4 Drive the shaft through the pedal lever towards the gearbox, which operation will release the outer spherical bush and flanges. The shaft can then be withdrawn from the supporting boss on the gearbox together with the inner bush and flange.

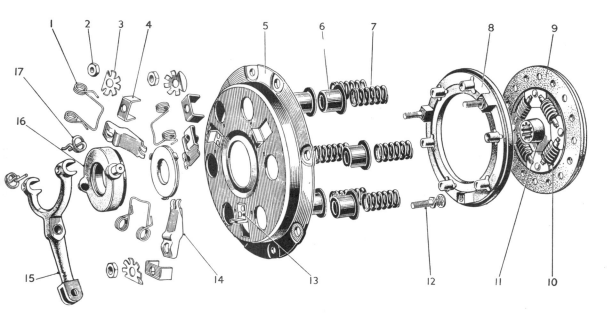

FIG 5:2   Components of the clutch fitted to early 800 cc and 948 cc engines

Key to Fig 5:2   1 Anti-rattle spring   2 Adjusting nut   3 Tab washers   4 Bearing plates   5 Clutch cover
6 Flanged cups   7 Thrust springs   8 Pressure plate   9 Clutch driven plate   10 Driven plate springs   11 Splined hub
12 Shoulder stud   13 Fulcrum   14 Release lever   15 Clutch withdrawal lever   16 Release bearing and cup assembly
17 Retaining spring

Examine the shaft and bushes for wear, renewing them if necessary. Also renew stretched springs and the rubber gaiter round the withdrawal lever if it is perished. Note that from chassis No. 13675 the inner Oilite bush was changed for *a* brass-lined rubber one.

To reassemble the parts, fit the shaft with the inner flange and bush and feed it into the gearbox boss. Now fit it with the outer bearing flange and pin the outer spherical bush to the shaft. Draw the shaft outwards until the outer support flanges can be bolted together. The pedal lever can then be refitted, and the inner bearing flange bolted up, finally hooking on the springs and adjusting the pedal clearance.

Adjusting mechanical linkage:

Press the clutch pedal with one finger, depressing it until resistance is felt. The pedal should depress and return quite freely, with a movement of no more than $\frac{3}{8}$ inch for the early clutch and $\frac{5}{8}$ inch for the later type. To adjust, slacken the locknut at the forward end of the operating rod 4 and turn the larger nut until the clearance is correct. Lock the nuts together when all is correct.

5:5 Hydraulic operation, A40

FIG 5:7 shows the components of the pedal and master cylinder assembly, but note that item 23 is not used in the clutch operation. The master cylinder piston 6 is operated by the clutch pedal 15. Pressure on the piston forces hydraulic fluid through tubing to a slave cylinder on the clutch housing. This cylinder, which is shown in section in **FIG 5:8** and can be seen at the lowest point

in **FIG 5:4,** copies the movement of the master cylinder piston.

Being coupled to the clutch release lever, the slave piston will therefore pass on the pedal movement to the release bearing and so disengage the clutch. The tube between the slave cylinder and the chassis is flexible so that engine movement has no effect on the operating fluid. Occasionally check the level of fluid in supply tank 4 and top up if necessary with Lockheed Super Heavy Duty Brake Fluid.

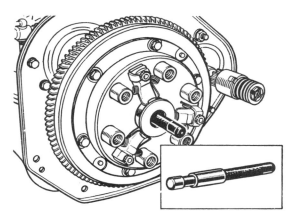

FIG 5:3   Centralizing the driven plate. The Service Tool shown is 18G.139

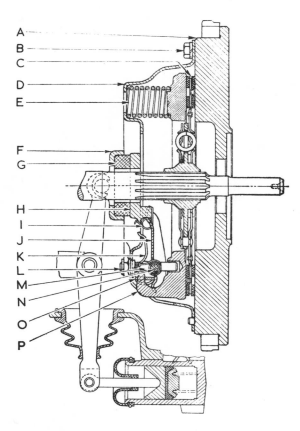

A ----
B ----
C ----
D ----
E ----

F ----
G ----

H ----
I ----
J ----
K ----
L ----
M ----
N ----

O ----
P ----

FIG 5:4 Section of the later clutch fitted to 848 cc and 1098 cc engines. The slave cylinder is shown at the bottom but is not used on 848 cc clutches

Key to Fig 5:4 A Flywheel B Securing bolt C Driven plate
D Clutch cover E Thrust coil spring F Release bearing cup
G Graphite release bearing H Release plate I Lever retainer
spring J Release lever K Anti-rattle spring L Adjusting nut
M Eyebolt N Floating pin (release lever) O Strut
P Pressure plate

5:6 Servicing master and slave cylinder

Dismantling, A40:

1 Push the hooked ends of return spring 13 off the pedal arms, remove circlip 11 and withdraw shaft 10 until the pedals are free.
2 Remove circlip 16 from pin 9 and pull out the pin.
3 Disconnect the pressure pipe union from the end plug 2, remove the securing nuts from the flange bolts and lift off the master cylinder.

To inspect the internal parts of the cylinder do the following.

1 Remove the filler cap 26 and drain out the fluid. Peel back the rubber boot 18 and remove circlip 8 from inside the cylinder mouth.
2 Invert the cylinder and tap it on a wooden surface to remove the inner assembly. This consists of the push-rod and stopwasher 7, the piston 6 and secondary

cup 19 together, the piston washer 5, the main cup 20 and the spring retainer 21 with return spring 22. Item 23 is not used in the clutch master cylinder.

3 Remove the secondary cup by stretching it over the piston with the fingers. The external metal parts can be cleaned with normal liquids, but the components inside the cylinder must not be cleaned with anything but hydraulic fluid. Examine the parts for wear, especially the cups. If there is any doubt at all, renew them.

Before reassembling be certain that everything is spotlessly clean. Then lubricate the parts with the correct hydraulic fluid and assemble them in the order shown in FIG 5:7.

The clutch slave cylinder, A40:

The cylinder is shown in section in FIG 5:8. It comprises the body 5, fitted with a pushrod 8, a rubber boot 7, a circlip 6, a piston 4, the rubber cup 3 with cup filler 2 and spring 1. There is also a bleed-screw not shown.

Dismantling:

Remove the pipe union from the cylinder, using a clean tin to catch the fluid. Take out the clevis pin connecting the pushrod to the clutch withdrawal lever, remove the bolts holding the cylinder to the clutch housing and lift away.

1 Remove the rubber boot 7, the pushrod 8 and the circlip 6.
2 It is easiest to blow out the piston 4, the cup 3 and associated components by using a compressed air supply on the pipe union hole.

The instructions for cleaning and reassembling are the same as those for the master cylinder. Disturbance of either the master cylinder or the slave cylinder means that the fluid system must be bled free from air.

5:7 Bleeding the hydraulic system

Fill the master cylinder reservoir with the correct hydraulic fluid. Attach a rubber tube to the slave cylinder bleed valve and immerse the open end in a small volume of the fluid in a clean glass jar.

With somebody to pump the clutch pedal, open the bleed screw on the slave cylinder about three-quarters of a turn. At the end of each down-stroke of the clutch pedal close the bleed-screw before allowing the pedal to return. At first there will be air bubbles appearing in the fluid in the jar, but the pumping operation must be repeated until clear fluid free from bubbles is delivered.

It is important to maintain the fluid level in the reservoir at all times and particularly while the system is being bled, as fluid is then being drawn from the reservoir in quantity. If all the fluid is used, air can enter the master cylinder bore through the small feed hole to be seen in the floor of the reservoir and this will nullify all previous work on bleeding the system.

5:8 Adjusting pedal free play

The correct amount of free movement between the master cylinder pushrod and the piston is set during manufacture, and should not need alteration. If the adjustment has been disturbed, reset the effective length of the pushrod by altering the packing under the cylinder mounting flange. Depress the pedal pad

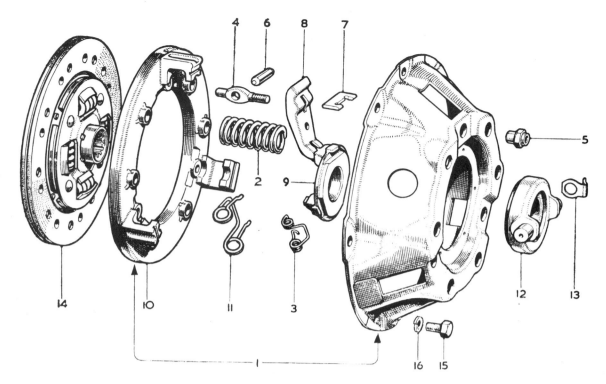

FIG 5:5   Components of the clutch fitted to 848 cc and 1098 cc engines

Key to Fig 5:5   1 Clutch assembly   2 Thrust spring   3 Release lever retainer   4 Eyebolt   5 Eyebolt nut
6 Release lever pin   7 Strut   8 Release lever   9 Bearing thrust plate   10 Pressure plate   11 Anti-rattle spring
12 Release bearing   13 Retainer   14 Driven plate assembly   15 Clutch to flywheel screw   16 Spring washer

gently until resistance is felt and adjust the pushrod until the distance required to reach this point is approximately $\frac{5}{32}$ inch. This ensures that the pushrod has a minimum free movement of $\frac{1}{32}$ inch before the master cylinder piston starts to move. There is no provision for adjustment apart from the packing pieces 24 in **FIG 5:7**

On early cars with mechanical operation of the clutch, pedal free play should be $\frac{3}{8}$ inch.

5:9 Fault diagnosis

(a) Drag or spin

1 Oil or grease on the driven plate linings
2 Bent engine backplate
3 Misalignment between the engine and the first-motion shaft
4 Leaking master cylinder or pipeline
5 Driven plate hub binding on first-motion shaft
6 First-motion shaft spigot binding in crankshaft bush
7 Distorted driven plate
8 Warped or damaged pressure plate or clutch cover
9 Broken driven plate linings
10 Dirt or foreign matter in clutch
11 Air in the clutch hydraulic system

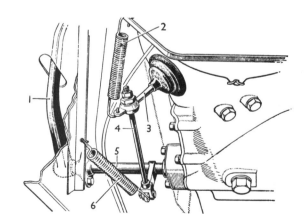

FIG 5:6   Clutch pedal linkage of the A30 and A35

Key to Fig 5:6   1 Clutch pedal lever   2 Pull-off spring
3 Clutch withdrawal lever   4 Clutch operating rod   5 Clutch pedal shaft   6 Anti-rattle spring (later models)

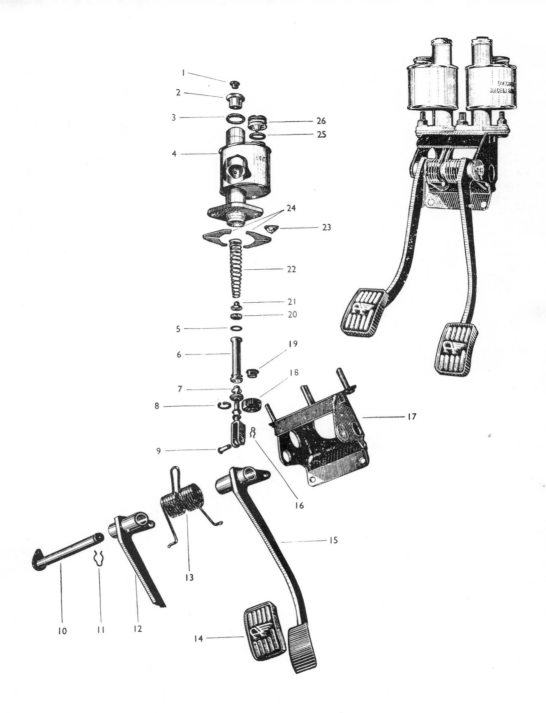

FIG 5:7 A40 master cylinder exploded

Key to Fig 5:7   1 Rubber plug (replaced by outlet union when fitted to vehicle)   2 End plug   3 Washer   4 Supply tank
5 Piston washer   6 Piston   7 Pushrod   8 Circlip   9 Clevis pin   10 Pedal cross-shaft   11 Circlip   12 Pedal arm
13 Return spring   14 Pedal rubber   15 Pedal arm   16 Circlip   17 Mounting bracket   18 Rubber boot   19 Secondary cup
20 Main cup   21 Spring retainer   22 Return spring   23 Not applicable in this installation   24 Packing pieces   25 Washer
26 Filler cap

(b) Fierceness or snatch

1 Check 1, 2, 3 and 4 in (a)
2 Worn clutch linings

(c) Slip

1 Check 1, 2 and 3 in (a)
2 Check 1 in (b)
3 Weak anti-rattle springs
4 Seized piston in clutch slave cylinder

(d) Judder

1 Check 1, 2 and 3 in (a)
2 Pressure plate not parallel with the flywheel face
3 Contact area of driven plate linings not evenly distributed
4 Bent first-motion shaft
5 Buckled driven plate
6 Faulty engine or gearbox rubber mountings
7 Worn shackles
8 Weak rear springs
9 Loose propeller shaft bolts
10 Loose rear spring clips

(e) Rattle

1 Check 3 in (d)
2 Broken springs in driven plate
3 Worn release mechanism
4 Excessive backlash in transmission
5 Wear in transmission bearings
6 Release bearing loose on fork

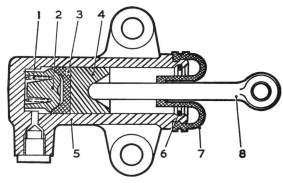

FIG 5 : 8   Section of the slave cylinder

Key to Fig 5 : 8   1 Spring   2 Cup filler   3 Cup   4 Piston   5 Body   6 Circlip   7 Boot   8 Pushrod

(f) Tick or knock

1 Worn first-motion shaft spigot or bush
2 Badly worn splines in driven plate hub
3 Release plate out of line
4 Faulty Bendix drive on starter
5 Loose flywheel

(g) Driven plate fracture

1 Check 2 and 3 in (a)
2 Drag and distortion due to hanging gearbox in plate hub

NOTES

CHAPTER 6

THE GEARBOX

6:1 Operation and lubrication

The gearboxes fitted to all the cars covered by this manual are identical with one exception. The gearlever fitted to the A30 operates directly on the selector rods. The gearbox has four forward speeds and one reverse. Synchromesh engagement is incorporated on second, third and fourth gears. Top gear is a direct drive in which the first-motion shaft 4 in **FIG 6:1** is coupled to the third-motion shaft 6 and so to the propeller shaft.

The drive to the laygear 62 and to second- and third-speed gears 16 and 20, is through single helical gears to ensure silent running. First gear and reverse are selected by sliding the spur gears 25 and 45.

The third-motion shaft is extended well to the rear and carries the propeller shaft sliding joint on splines. Metal-to-metal cone clutches are used to facilitate gear changing by synchronizing the speeds of the coupling dogs. An internal cone can be seen at the lefthand end of part 16. The coupling dogs are shown internally in part 11 and in front of the gear teeth on part 16. The coupling sleeve 11 is spring-loaded to the hub 12 by balls and springs so that when the sleeve is moved sideways by the shifting fork 31 it carries the hub with it until the cones engage. These speed up or slow down the coupling dogs until they are rotating at the same speed, the sleeve overcomes the resistance of the spring-loaded balls and further movement of the sleeve engages the dogs to complete the drive.

Lubrication:

To reach the filler plug, remove the rubber plug on the left side of the gearbox covering. Fill with the correct grade of oil to the bottom of the threads. The drain plug is underneath the gearbox casing. Drain off the old oil when it is warm and examine it for metallic particles which may be a clue to excessive wear.

6:2 Removing

All the instructions needed to remove the engine and gearbox as a unit have been given in the Engine Chapter, but it is possible to remove the gearbox without taking out the engine, as follows:

1 Disconnect the battery, and the starter cable at the starter end.
2 Remove the distributor cap and leads, all electrical connections to the engine, and also the carburetter controls.
3 Drain the cooling system and detach the top hose and heater hoses from the engine.
4 Part the exhaust down pipe from the manifold.
5 From inside the car, lift off the rubber grommet round the gearlever and after removing the three setscrews and spring washers, lift out the lever. On the A35 and A40 it will also be necessary to unscrew the top anti-rattle spring cap 7 in **FIG 6:2**. Take out the spring and

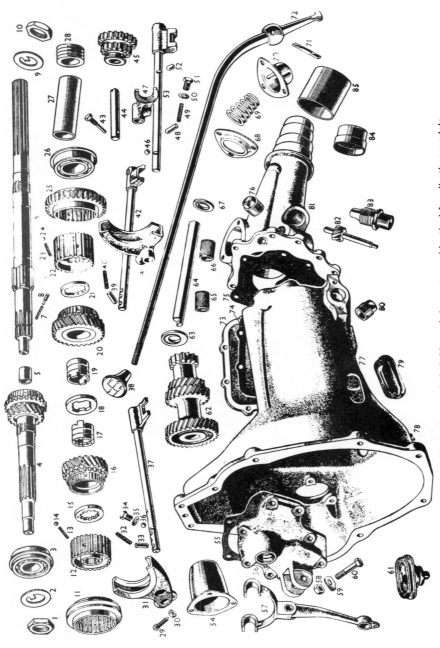

FIG 6:1   The A30 gearbox exploded. Most of the parts are identical for all other models

Key to Fig 6:1   1 1st motion shaft nut   2 Lockwasher   3 1st motion shaft lockwasher   4 1st motion shaft   5 Bush for 3rd motion shaft   6 3rd motion shaft
7 Locking peg spring   8 Locking peg   9 3rd motion shaft synchronizer   10 3rd motion shaft nut   11 Third- and fourth-speed coupling sleeve
12 Third- and fourth-speed synchronizer   13 Synchronizer coupling sleeve spring   14 Synchronizer coupling sleeve ball   15 Splined thrust washer (front)
16 Third-speed mainshaft gear and cone   17 Third-speed mainshaft gear bush   18 Interlocking ring for bushes   19 Second-speed mainshaft gear bush
20 Second-speed mainshaft gear and cone   21 Splined thrust washer (rear)   22 Second-speed synchronizer   23 Second-speed synchronizer spring
24 Second-speed synchronizer ball   25 First-speed wheel   26 3rd motion shaft bearing   27 Distance piece   28 Speedometer wheel   29 Fork locating screw
30 Locknut   31 Third- and fourth-speed fork   32 Plunger   33 Plunger   34 Plug   35 Washer   36 Ball   37 Third- and fourth-speed fork rod
38 Changespeed lever knob   39 Plunger for rod   40 Spring   41 First- and second-speed fork   42 First- and second-speed fork rod   43 Reverse shaft locking screw
44 Reverse shaft   45 Reverse wheel   46 Ball   47 Reverse fork   48 Interlock plunger   49 Spring   50 Washer   51 Plug for spring   52 Interlock plunger
53 Reverse fork rod   54 Starter pinion cover   55 Front cover joint washer   56 Front cover   57 Clutch withdrawal lever   58 Nut   59 Lockwasher   60 Bolt
61 Withdrawal lever dust cover   62 Laygear   63 Thrust washer (front)   64 Layshaft   65 Needle roller bearing   66 Needle roller bearing   67 Thrust washer (rear)
68 Changespeed lever seat (top)   69 Reverse spring   70 Changespeed lever seat (bottom)   71 Changespeed lever (peg)   72 Changespeed lever   73 Side cover
74 Joint washer for side cover   75 Joint washer for rear cover   76 Filler plug   77 Gearbox case   78 Splitpin for clutch drain hole   79 Dust cover   80 Drain plug
81 Rear cover   82 Speedometer pinion   83 Speedometer pinion sleeve   84 Oil seal assembly   85 Dust cover

60

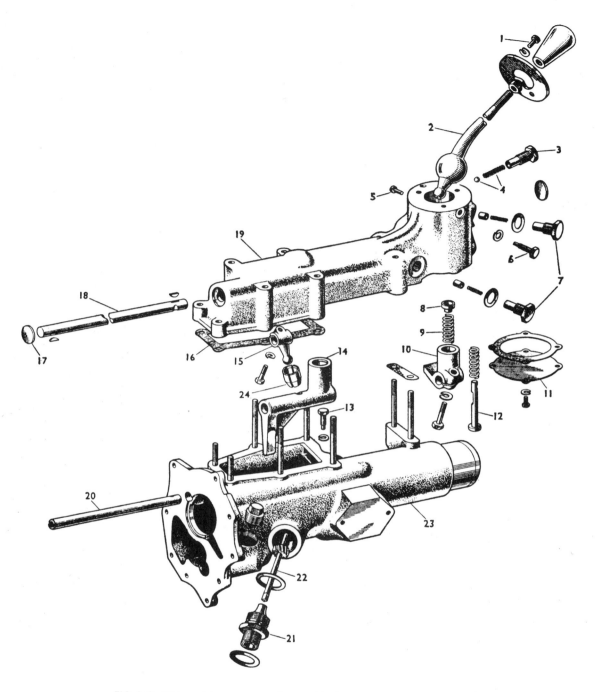

FIG 6:2 The remote gear control assembly fitted to all models except A30

Key to Fig 6:2   1 Changespeed lever cover setpin   2 Changespeed lever   3 Reverse plunger cap
4 Reverse plunger detent spring and ball   5 Reverse plunger locating pin   6 Changespeed lever locating pin
7 Anti-rattle spring caps   8 Thrust button   9 Thrust button spring   10 Selector lever rear   11 Bottom cover
12 Reverse selector plunger   13 Control shaft locating screw   14 Control lever   15 Selector lever front   16 Joint washer
17 Welch plug   18 Remote control shaft   19 Remote control housing   20 Control shaft   21 Speedometer pinion sleeve
22 Speedometer pinion   23 Gearbox rear cover   24 Tapered bush

plunger and after removing the gearlever collect the thrust button 8 and spring 9.

6 Jack up the front of the car with the rear wheels raised on blocks to avoid damage to the exhaust pipe.

7 Uncouple the propeller shaft from the rear axle after marking the flanges.

8 On the A30 and A35, release the clutch pedal pull-off spring and remove the two nuts from the front end of the operating rod. On the A40 remove the slave cylinder instead.

9 Free the exhaust pipe and tie it to one side.

10 Disconnect the speedometer cable from the gearbox.

11 On the A30 and A35 release the two setscrews in the inner, and the two nuts and bolts from the outer clutch pedal shaft support flanges, press out the pin in the outer spherical bush and slide the shaft away from the gearbox to free it.

12 Support the engine with a jack under the rear end of the sump.

13 On the A40, lift the carpets and take out the two set-screws which pass through the transmission tunnel from inside the car, into the gearbox crossmember, releasing the crossmember from below. Do the same on the A30 and A35, removing the two setscrews from the clamping plate under the gearbox rear cover.

14 Lower the jack so that the engine pivots on the front mountings until there is clearance for the bell-housing flange when drawn backwards.

15 Drain the gearbox and draw out the propeller shaft.

16 Remove the bolts and setscrews from the bell-housing flange noting their positions. Remove the starter.

17 Pull the gearbox straight back until the first-motion shaft is clear of the clutch. Take the weight of the gear-box all the time. It must never be allowed to hang in the hub of the driven plate or the plate will be distorted with disastrous results on clutch operation.

18 Replacement is a simple reversal of the dismantling sequence, but if the clutch is disturbed it will be necessary to centralize the driven plate according to the instructions given in **Chapter 5** on the clutch. Do not forget the earthing strap between the bell-housing and the car body, making it a clean, tight connection.

6:3 Dismantling

Remove the remote control assembly from the A35 and A40 gearboxes in the following manner, referring to **FIG 6:2** for details.

1 Remove the eight nuts securing the remote control housing 19 and lift off.

2 Unscrew the nine setscrews and spring washers to release the rear cover 23 from the gearbox.

3 Pull the rear cover back slightly and turn it in an anti-clockwise direction viewed from the rear. This enables the control lever 14 to clear the fork rod ends and allow the rear cover to be removed.

4 Remove the control shaft locating screw 13 and screw it into the tapped front end of the control shaft 20. Slight pressure on the screw will enable the shaft to be removed, the control lever 14 slipping off the end.

5 Remove the bottom cover 11, then unscrew the locating pin 6. Shake out the anti-rattle springs and plungers after unscrewing the caps 7.

6 Release the setscrews in the front and rear selector levers 15 and 10. Remove the welch plugs 17 at each end of the housing and drift out the shaft 18. Take care of the Woodruff keys.

7 The circlip round the front selector bush 24 is removed and the bush halves will then fall apart.

8 To remove the reverse selector plunger 12 unscrew cap 3 and shake out the detent ball and spring 4.

From now on the instructions will cover the gear-boxes on all the cars.

9 Referring to **FIG 6:1**, unscrew the speedometer pinion sleeve 83 from the left side of the gearbox rear cover 81. Collect the joint washer and remove the pinion 82.

10 Remove the clutch release bearing from the lever 57 by levering out the two retaining springs.

11 Remove the clutch withdrawal lever by unlocking the tab washer 59 and unscrewing nut 58. The bolt is screwed into the support bracket and is reached by a box spanner passed through the hole blanked off by dust cover 79.

12 Pull off the front cover 56 after removing the eight set-screws or nuts. Take care of the paper joint and packing shim.

13 Remove the side cover 73 and tilt the gearbox until the two springs and plungers fall out of the holes in the front edge of the joint face.

14 Remove the two plugs near the bell-housing on the side-cover side of the gearbox. Each has a fibre washer, and the lower plug covers the reverse plunger and spring. The other plug has a long shank and covers the interlock ball between two of the selector rods.

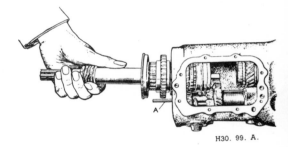

H30. 99. A.

FIG 6:3 Withdrawing the third motion shaft. The laygear is lowered on to dummy layshaft **A**

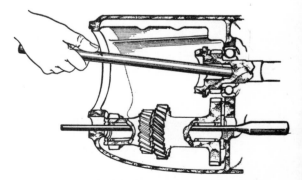

FIG 6:4 Drifting out the first motion shaft

15 Select neutral by aligning the slots at the rear ends of selector rods 37, 42 and 53. With the side cover aperture upwards, unlock and remove the reverse-fork locating screw, locknut and shakeproof washer from the fork 47. These can be reached through the drain plug hole. Also remove the similar screws, nuts and washers from the other two forks 31 and 41.

16 Tap the third- and fourth-speed selector rod 37 from the front end and withdraw it rearwards. Do the same to the first- and second-speed rod 42 and the reverse rod 53. As the rods are drawn out remove the two interlock balls from the holes at the front of the gearbox case, and the double-ended plunger 52 from the rear end. The three forks may now be lifted out.

17 Tap the layshaft 64 out of the front of the gearbox with a soft drift. When the drift is removed the laygear 62 and the thrust washers 63 and 67 will drop to the bottom of the box.

18 Draw the mainshaft assembly rearwards out of the gearbox case, then insert a long soft metal drift through the main shaft opening in the rear of the casing and drive out the first-motion shaft (see **FIGS 6:3** and **6:4**. The laygear cluster and the thrust washers may now be removed.

19 Take out the reverse shaft locking screw 43 and push on the slotted end of the shaft 44 with a screwdriver, turning at the same time until the shaft is free and the gears 45 can be removed.

6:4 Dismantling the mainshaft

1 Slide off the third and fourth gear synchronizer assembly and separate the coupling sleeve 11 by finger pressure. Wrap the assembly in a cloth during this operation to trap the three balls and springs 13 and 14 which will be released.

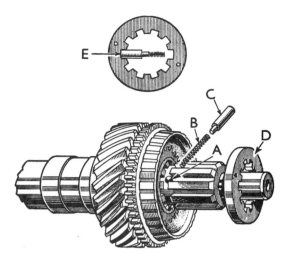

FIG 6:5 Securing the third motion shaft gears

Key to Fig 6:5 A Hole in shaft for locking plunger **B** Spring **C** Locking plunger **D** Locking washer **E** Locking washer with plunger engaged

2 **FIG 6:5** will help the operator to follow the next step. Depress the small spring-loaded plunger 'C' which locks the splined thrust washer 'D' at the front end of the mainshaft. Turn the washer with a peg spanner until one of its splines holds down the plunger. Then slide the washer and third-speed gear off the shaft, removing the plunger and spring. Slide off the bush 17, the interlocking ring 18 and the second gear 20.

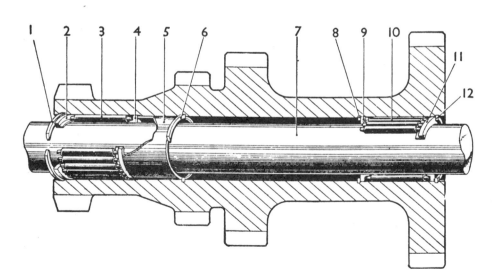

FIG 6:6 Section through laygear showing needle roller bearing assemblies

Key to Fig 6:6 1 Spring ring (outer) * 2 Outer race * 3 Needle rollers * 4 Inner race * 5 Distance piece *
6 Spring ring (inner) * 7 Layshaft * 8 Spring ring (inner) ** 9 Inner race ** 10 Needle rollers ** 11 Outer race **
12 Spring ring (outer) ** * *Small end* ** *Large end*

3 Remove the splined rear thrust washer 21, and the first-speed wheel 25 with the second-speed synchronizer assembly can be withdrawn off the end of the mainshaft. Separate the synchronizer as described in paragraph 1.

4 At the other end of the shaft unlock and remove nut 10 enabling the speedometer wheel 28 and the distance piece 27 to be removed. Draw off the ballbearing 26 in its housing and drift the bearing out.

6:5 Dismantling the laygear

Twenty-three needle rollers are fitted into each end of the laygear. They are held in place by stepped races and spring rings as in FIG 6:6.

1 Remove the spring rings from each end and take out the rollers and inner and outer races.

2 Remove the inner spring rings and distance piece.

6:6 Inspection

The first- and third-motion shaft bearings 3 and 26 become worn after long service. Try to rock the outer races sideways and if there is any looseness the bearings must be renewed.

The synchronizer cones will also be worn after much use, and this is evident if gear changing has become noisy, with none of the usual resistance to gearlever movement which shows that the cones are working. Replacement of the gear and cone assembly is then called for.

The third-motion shaft bush 5 is fitted inside the rear end of the first-motion shaft and should have a running clearance of .002 to .003 inch with the spigot on the third-motion shaft. Excessive clearance may need renewal of the bush and possibly the shaft. The second- and third-speed gear bushes 17 and 19 have an extremely low tolerance of .0025 to .0015 inch with the shaft. If there is any appreciable wear between these bushes and the third-motion shaft, they must be renewed.

6:7 Reassembling

The first-speed wheel 25 and the third- and fourth-speed coupling sleeve 11 are lapped in with their synchronizers and only mated pairs should be fitted. The hub splines of both synchronizers are also lapped with the mainshaft. Consequently, if an odd synchromesh assembly or mainshaft is fitted, it must be lapped with the part(s) concerned.

1 There is a spring ring on the outer race of the third-motion shaft bearing 26. Press the bearing into the housing (not illustrated) with the spring ring and the larger diameter of the housing on the same face. With the spring ring to the rear, press the bearing on to the mainshaft, fit the distance piece 27, the lockwasher 9 and the nut 10. Tighten the nut securely and lock.

2 When assembling the first-speed wheel 25 to the second-speed synchronizer 22, ensure that the side of the wheel with the chamfered teeth faces towards the second-speed mainshaft gear 20 when assembled on the mainshaft. With some assistance, replace the three sets of springs and balls into the synchronizer 22 and fit the first-speed wheel. Push this assembly on to the mainshaft with the protruding boss of the synchronizer towards the bearing. Follow up with thrust washer 21.

3 Next fit the bush 19 with its legs away from the thrust washer and slide the second-speed gear 20 over the bush with its cone to the rear. Oil all the parts liberally during assembly. Locate the bronze interlocking ring 18 on the legs of bush 19 and mate the legs of bush 17 in the other pair of splines in the locking ring.

4 Place the spring and plunger 7 and 8 in the hole in the mainshaft, depress the plunger and draw the third-speed mainshaft bush 17 slightly forward to keep the plunger depressed. Then slide the third-speed mainshaft gear 16 on to the bush with its cone away from the interlocking ring. Fit the steel thrust washer 15, pushing it on as far as it will go. Slip a tube over the shaft and lightly tap the washer, turning it until the plunger is released and locks it.

5 Slide the third- and fourth-speed synchronizer assembly 11 and 12 on to the shaft with the boss on the hub away from the thrust washer.

Reassembling the laygear:

1 Press the spring ring into the small end of the laygear, following it with the distance piece, which is drifted right home against the ring.

2 Assemble the needle roller bearings in the order shown in FIG 6:6.

Reassembling the first-motion shaft:

1 A new self-lubricating bush can be fitted inside the gear end of the shaft by driving it in with a drift.

2 If the bearing 3 has been removed from the shaft, refit it with the spring away from the geared end.

Reassembling the gearbox:

1 Replace the reverse gear 45, aligning the hole in the shaft 44 with the hole in the casing and locking with screw 43 fitted with a spring washer.

2 FIG 6:7 shows the use of a dummy layshaft, which is Service Tool 18G.471. This makes fitting the layshaft easier, but in the absence of such a tool it might be possible to fashion a similar device from a piece of wooden dowel rod. Insert the thin end of the dummy shaft through the clutch housing and place the large thrust washer 63 on it. Fit the laygear with the large end forward and as the dummy shaft emerges slip on the small thrust washer 67. The laygear must now have an end float between .001 and .003 inch. Various small thrust washers are available to give the required end float, their thicknesses going up in .001 inch steps from .125 inch to .131 inch. Let the laygear hang on the thin part of the dummy shaft.

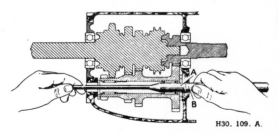

H30. 109. A.

FIG 6:7 Lifting the laygear into position. Dummy layshaft **A** pilots actual layshaft **B**

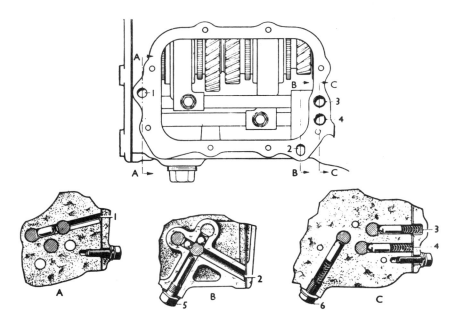

FIG 6:8 Location of balls and plungers

Key to Fig 6:8   1 Hole for interlock plunger between reverse and first- and second-speed fork rods   2 Hole for ball between reverse and third- and fourth-speed fork rods   3 Hole for first- and second-speed fork rod plunger   4 Hole for third- and fourth-speed fork rod plunger   5 Plug for first- and second-speed, and third- and fourth-speed ball hole   6 Plug for reverse plunger hole   **A, B** and **C** are scrap views of sections **AA, BB** and **CC** respectively, looking in the direction of the arrows

3 Insert the third-motion shaft into the back end of the gearbox and drift the bearing housing into its recess until the flange is flush.

4 Turn the gearbox about until the laygear teeth are clear of the first-motion shaft housing and then drift the shaft into position from inside the clutch housing. The spring ring on the bearing must register properly in the recess.

5 Draw the dummy layshaft rearwards slightly and lift the laygears into mesh. Oil the layshaft and push it into place keeping contact with the dummy shaft all the way so that the thrust washers do not drop out of place.

6 Put the reverse fork 47 in position with its tapped hole facing the drain plug hole. Fit the fork 41 over the first-speed wheel 25, and the fork 31 over the third- and fourth-speed coupling sleeve 11.

7 With the side cover uppermost, push the reverse fork rod 53 through the lowest hole in the back of the gearbox casing, through the reverse fork and then through the clearance hole in the fork 31. Align the hole in the reverse fork with the hole in the rod and fit the locking screw through the drain plug hole, using the nut and shakeproof washer to lock the screw when tight.

8 Using **FIG 6:8** as a guide, drop the double-ended plunger 52 into the hole 1. Push the first- and second-speed fork rod 42 through the uppermost hole in the back of the casing, through the fork and into the front of the casing, locking the fork to the rod with the screw as before.

9 Fork rod 37 goes into the third hole, through the fork 31 until it just enters the hole in the front of the gearbox casing. Drop a ball down hole 2 in the side cover joint face. See that it goes between the reverse rod 53 and third and fourth fork rod 37 by looking from the clutch housing end. Using a piece of rod down hole 2, press hard on the ball to centralize the slot in the selector rod. If this is not done the ball will be in the way when the third and fourth fork rod is pushed home.

Turn the gearbox so that the drain plug is uppermost and drop a ball into hole 5 which will be in-line with the drain plug hole. See that it goes between the first and second rod 42, and the third and fourth fork rod 37. Centralize the slot in the same way and push the third and fourth fork rod home, locking it in position. If an obstruction prevents the rods from being pushed right in, do not use a hammer but check that the balls are seating correctly in their slots. The correctly assembled position is shown in **FIG 6:9**.

10 Put the reverse plunger 48 into the lower hole on the drain plug side with the rounded end foremost, follow it with the spring and screw in the plug 51 fitted with a fibre washer (see position 6 in **FIG 6:8**). The upper hole is blocked by the long-shanked plug and fibre washer shown in position 5. Positions 3 and 4 show the holes in the side cover joint face which take the two remaining plungers 33 and 39 which are inserted with the rounded ends first. Follow up with the springs.

AAB

11 Replace the side cover and its paper joint washer using the eight nuts and spring washers, or the set-screws used on early gearboxes. Tighten evenly by diagonal selection.

12 Position the front cover joint washer 55, and stick the packing shim into the front cover bearing recess with grease. Secure the cover with the seven nuts and spring washers.

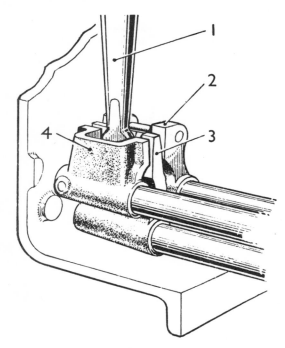

FIG 6:9   Position of selector rods

Key to Fig 6:9   1 Control lever   2 Reverse rod
3 Third- and fourth-speed rod   4 First- and second-speed rod

Note: Although a .006 inch shim is normally sufficient, use the following method to shim both front and rear covers 56 and 81. Measure the depth of the cover recess and the amount by which the bearing outer race protrudes from the gearbox casing. Tighten the cover with only the paper joint washer in place. Take off the cover and measure the thickness of the compressed paper washer. Add this thickness to the depth of the cover recess and subtract the amount by which the bearing protruded. The result gives the thickness of shims required. They are available in various thicknesses, but use the least number to achieve the desired result.

13 Replace the clutch withdrawal lever 57, using a lock washer on the bolt. Insert the bolt from the left-hand side and screw it into the bracket until it is tight enough to eliminate side play in the lever. Lock the bolt with the nut and spring washer and then bend up the tab of the lockwasher. Fit the rubber dust cover 61 and press the flat cover 79 into the opposite hole.

14 Fit the rear cover 81 using a sound paper washer. Place a .006-in shim in the recess machined to accommodate the projecting part of the rear bearing, but use the method suggested in paragraph 12 to check for the correct thickness of shimming. The shims are available in thicknesses of .004, .006 and .010 in.

15 Replace the remote control assembly in the reverse order to the instructions given for dismantling, then flush the gearbox with flushing oil and replace the drain plug. Do not forget to fill with oil of the correct grade. On all the cars, the gear lever is replaced after the gearbox is refitted into the chassis.

6:8 Modifications

The later type of third- and fourth-speed synchronizer 12 has three spring holes which are equally spaced, there are no lightening holes and the cone angles are altered. Interchangeability is affected as follows:

1 A new type third-motion shaft 6 can be used to replace an old one.

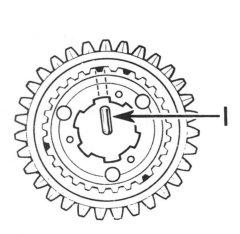

FIG 6:10   Correct position for first and second gear assembly and hub, 1098 cc cars. The plunger is shown at 1

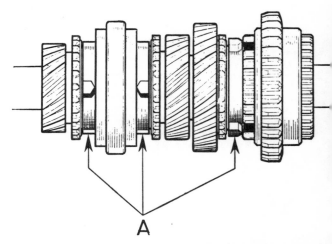

FIG 6:11   The mainshaft showing the baulk rings **A**. 1098 cc cars only

2 A new type second-speed mainshaft gear 20 with a new synchronizer 22 can replace their old counterparts, but they are not interchangeable separately.

3 A new type first-motion shaft 4 cannot be used to replace an old type, unless the following new parts are also fitted.

(a) Third-motion shaft gear with cone 16.

(b) Bush 17 for the third-speed mainshaft gear.

(c) Third-motion shaft front thrust washer 15.

(d) Third- and fourth-speed synchronizer 12.

New fork rods with modified notches can be interchanged with old ones in sets. Speedometer drive pinions of nylon were fitted on later gearboxes, and these are interchangeable with the original steel pinion and spindle. Nylon pinion bushes were also introduced in place of the brass bushes. The oil feed hole in the nylon bush is smaller to reduce the oil flow to the speedometer cable. When removing or replacing a nylon bush use a socket spanner to avoid damage to the hexagon. The copper sealing washer and the pinion oil seal retaining ring are not required with the nylon bush. Interchangeability is not affected.

6:9 Baulk rings

These are fitted to the second-, and to the third- and fourth-gear synchronizers on 1098 cc cars. The positions are clearly shown in **FIG 6:11**.

Note: If the first- and second-speed gear assembly has been dismantled it is most important to assemble the gear on the hub in the correct position, otherwise it will be impossible to select first gear. **FIG 6:10** shows the gear and hub correctly assembled with the plunger 1 aligned with the cutaway tooth in the gear assembly.

6:10 Fault diagnosis

(a) Jumping out of gear

1 Broken changespeed fork rod spring

2 Excessively worn fork rod groove

3 Worn coupling dogs

4 Fork rod securing screw loose

(b) Noisy gearbox

1 Insufficient oil

2 Excessive endplay in laygear

3 Damaged or worn bearings

4 Damaged or worn teeth

(c) Difficulty in engaging gear

1 Incorrect clutch pedal adjustment

2 Worn synchromesh cones

(d) Oil leaks

1 Damaged joint washers

2 Damaged or worn oil seals

3 Front, rear or side covers loose or faces damaged

NOTES

CHAPTER 7

PROPELLER SHAFT, REAR AXLE AND SUSPENSION

7:1 Universal joints, lubrication and removing

The front and rear universal joints on the propeller shaft are of Hardy-Spicer manufacture. The four journals on each spider run in needle roller bearings, as shown in **FIG 7:1.** The half coupling of the front joint is splined to the gearbox mainshaft and is free to slide. This accommodates the fore and aft movement of the propeller shaft as the rear springs deflect. Each spider journal has an inner shoulder which locates a metal retainer holding a cork sealing ring. The inner open ends of the bearing cups seal against the cork rings to prevent loss of lubricant and the ingress of dirt. These seals are marked 6 in the illustration.

Lubrication:

Use the correct grade of grease when lubricating. Access to the front nipple is through a hole on the left side of the propeller shaft tunnel, normally closed by a rubber plug, but on later models by a metal plate. Oil from the gearbox lubricates the sliding splined joint. Smear the splines with oil when refitting the propeller shaft.

Removing:

The joints can be tested for wear before removing the shaft. Try to lift each joint up and down. Slackness will indicate wear of the thrust faces on the spiders, and those

inside the bearing cups. If the joints can be partially rotated it is a sign that the bearings are worn. Two pointers to trouble are often seen under the spring rings 7. A bright ring on the bearing cup shows that it has been rotating, and rust indicates a lack of grease.

After scribing a line across the flanges of the rear joint to ensure correct reassembly, separate them. Place a tray under the rear end of the gearbox to catch any oil which drains out, take the weight of the shaft and draw the front splines out of the box. On some of the cars it is easier to remove the shaft over the lefthand side of the rear axle.

7:2 Dismantling joints and reassembling

Clean all dirt and enamel from the snap rings 7 and remove them by squeezing the ends together. Tap the yoke with a lead or copper hammer as shown in **FIG 7:2** when the top bearing cup should start to appear. Some support for the other yoke may help in this operation. If the bearing cup sticks it is permissible to tap on the inner lip of the cup if it is exposed, using a screwdriver or thin drift, but with the greatest care not to damage it. Pull the cup out vertically downwards to keep the rollers intact. Remove the opposite bearing, then the spider can be detached from the yoke. Repeat the operation on the remaining two bearings.

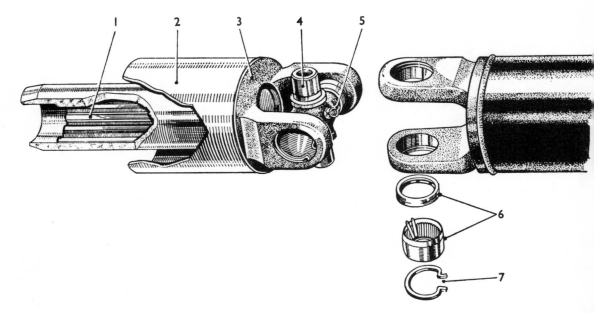

FIG 7:1 Exploded view showing the front universal joint

The spiders and bearings are available in sets. If the eyes in the yokes are worn oval, the bearing cups will no longer be a light drive fit, so that the yokes will need renewal.

Reassembling:

It is advisable to renew the cork washers and retainers 6. Coat the shoulders on the spider with shellac and press the retainers into position. Fill the holes in the spider with grease and insert in the yoke. Stick the needles in a cup with vaseline, fill with grease and tap into position. Fit the spring ring and repeat the assembly on the other side. If the spider binds tap the yoke with a soft-faced mallet after the spring rings are fitted.

Refitting the completed shaft is a reversal of the removing procedure, but clean the rear flange faces and the register thoroughly. Line up the marks previously made on the flange edges and tighten the securing bolts diagonally and evenly.

7:3 The rear axle and lubrication

FIG 7:3 shows the axle cut away to expose the internal mechanism. From this it can be seen that the bevel pinion is carried in a pair of taper roller bearings, with an oil seal immediately behind the universal joint flange. The large flange integral with the outer end of the axle shaft is bolted to a hub carried on a large ballbearing which is also backed by a seal to prevent loss of lubricant. Note that the inner splined ends of the shafts engage with splines in the hubs of the two driven gears in the differential cage. When both axles are pulled out, the whole gear assembly can be withdrawn from the banjo casing by unscrewing the ring

of nuts on the housing flange. At this point it would be as well to point out that there is very little an amateur can do to renew worn parts in the gear assembly.

For example, fitting a new crownwheel and pinion involves four operations: (1) Setting the position of the pinion, (2) Adjusting the bearing preload, (3) Adjusting the differential bearing preload, (4) Adjusting the backlash between the gears. As numerous special tools and gauges are needed to carry out such accurate settings, the services of a competent agent are essential.

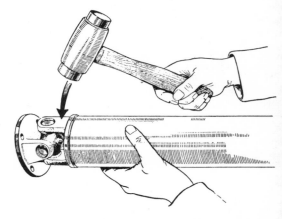

FIG 7:2 Extracting a bearing

70

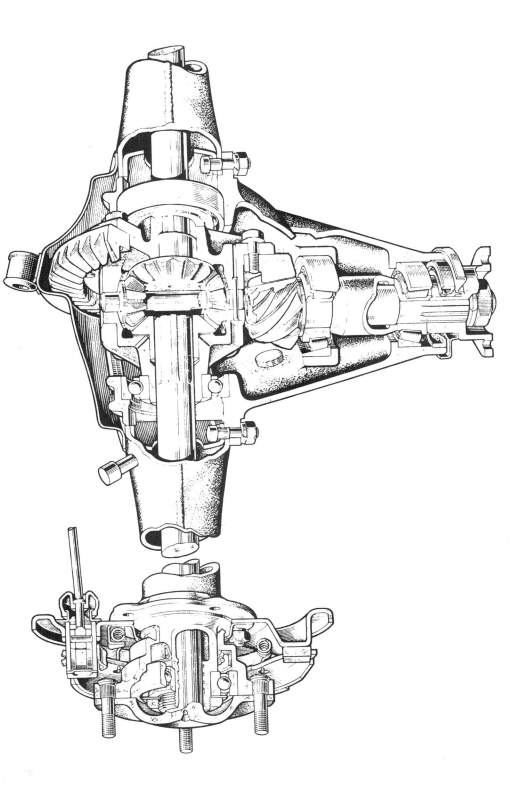

FIG 7:3   A cutaway view of the rear axle

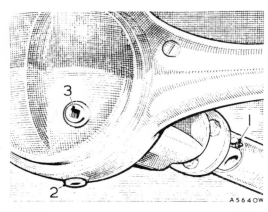

FIG 7:4 Location of rear universal joint nipple **1**, drain plug **2** and filler-level plug **3** (later models)

Lubrication:

FIG 7:4 shows the location of the filler and drain plugs. The filler plug is also a level indicator, and if no lubricant flows when the plug is removed, then fresh hypoid oil of the correct grade must be added. On early cars the filler plug will be found on the righthand side of the gear carrier (see **FIG 7:5**).

7:4 Axle shaft servicing

Removing axle shafts:

1 Jack-up the appropriate side of the car and remove the wheel, chocking the others for safety.
2 Unscrew the brake drum locating screw, release the handbrake and tap off the drum. Now drain the rear axle.
3 Looking at **FIG 7:5**, remove screw 24 from the axle shaft flange and draw out the shaft. If tight, strike the shaft with a hide hammer until a gap shows between the flanges. Lever the shaft away with a screwdriver, renewing the paper joint washer on assembly if it is damaged.

Replacing shaft:

1 Press and rotate the shaft until the splines enter. The paper joint must be about .010 inch thick if it is hand-made. Anything thinner will inevitably lead to oil leaks.
2 The screw holding the axle shaft to the hub flange must be put in the countersunk hole so that it finishes up flush.
3 Finally restore the brake drum and fixing screw, readjust the shoes on both sides and replace the wheel.

7:5 Hub servicing

1 After the axle shaft is withdrawn, knock back the keyed lockwasher 22 and remove it after unscrewing nut 23.
2 The hub is drawn off using an extractor bolted to the wheel studs, the extractor screw pressing on a pad located on the axle casing end.
3 The bearing 21 and oil seal 20 can be drifted out. The bearing is not adjustable and must be renewed if worn.

The oil seal is easily damaged and a tubular drift needed when replacing it. It is an operation best left t an agent equipped with the special tool required. During reassembly, pack the hub with grease.

7:6 Servicing springs

The springs are semi-elliptic with silent-bloc bushes the spring eyes and shackles, except that on early ca the shackle bearing on the body is of bronze and need periodical lubrication.

Maintenance:

1 Examine the spring-to-axle U-bolts and tighten th nuts if necessary. Refer to **FIG 7:6**.
2 Wipe the damper filler plugs free from dirt, check th fluid level and top up if required (not telescopic).
3 Clean the springs and wipe with an oily rag.
4 Examine each spring leaf for breaks, and the bushes f wear.

Removing springs:

1 Jack-up the car on the side from which the spring is t be removed.
2 Take out the brake cable clevis pin.
3 Put blocks under the chassis rear crossmember, a near to the rear anchorage of the spring as possible.
4 Jack-up the centre of the spring to relieve the tension
5 Remove the wheel.
6 Unscrew the four self-locking nuts from the U-bolt holding the axle to the spring.
7 Unscrew the nut on the inside of the upper rea shackle, and the locknut and spring washer from th inside of the lower rear shackle.
8 Remove the inner shackle link and remove the oute link together with the two shackle pins.
9 At the front end of the spring, unscrew the inner nu and washer and drive the pin clear.
10 Upon removing the jack, the spring will come away

Dismantling springs:

1 Place the spring on its side and grip in a vice near th centre bolt.
2 Prise open the leaf clips, then unscrew the nut from th centre pin and drive out the pin.
3 Open the vice so that the spring leaves separate. Reverse the proceedings to reassemble.

Replacing:

1 Ensure that the head of the spring centre bolt register with the hole in the axle casing.
2 The rear upper shackle pin self-locking nut must not b fully tightened but the pin allowed freedom to move i its bronze bush. Rubber bushes were fitted on late models.
3 Do not tighten the other shackle pin nuts until th springs have been deflected under a normal workin load. The bushes will then be subjected to equal torsio in each direction during service. Unequal loading lead to excessive torsion in one direction, causing rapi deterioration.

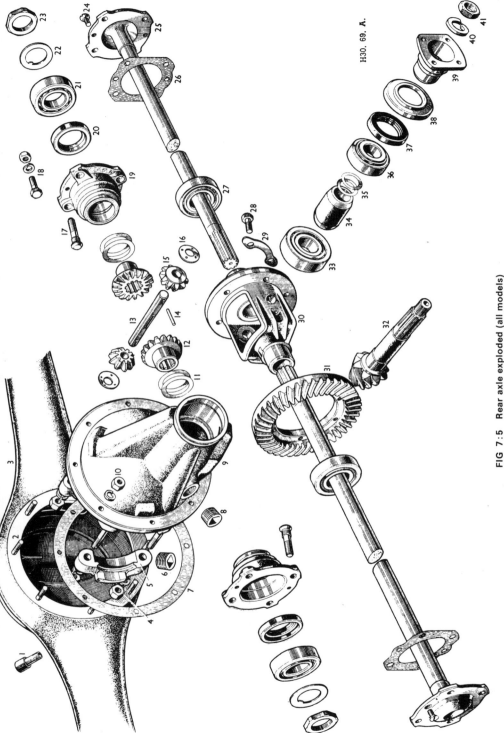

H30. 69. A.

FIG 7:5 Rear axle exploded (all models)

Key to Fig 7:5   1 Axle breather   2 Gear carrier stud   3 Axle case   4 Differential bearing cap nut and washer   5 Differential bearing cap   6 Drain plug
7 Gear carrier joint washer   8 Filler plug (earlier models)   9 Gear carrier   10 Gear carrier nut and washer   11 Differential bearing packing shims   12 Differential wheel
13 Differential pinion shaft   14 Differential shaft dowel pin   15 Differential pinion   16 Pinion thrust washer   17 Wheel stud   18 Backplate bolt, nut and washer
19 Hub casing   20 Hub oil seal   21 Hub bearing   22 Hub lockwasher   23 Hub securing nut   24 Axle shaft screw   25 Axle shaft   26 Joint washer
27 Differential bearing   28 Crownwheel setscrew   29 Lockwasher   30 Differential cage   31 Crownwheel   32 Bevel pinion   33 Bevel pinion rear bearing
34 Pinion bearing distance piece   35 Bevel pinion shims   36 Bevel pinion front bearing   37 Oil seal   38 Oil seal housing   39 Bevel pinion flange
40 Bevel pinion spring washer   41 Bevel pinion nut

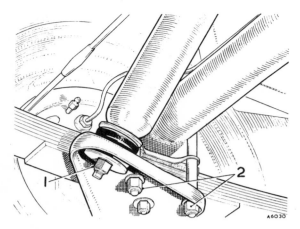

FIG 7:6   Rear telescopic damper mounting

Key to Fig 7:6   1 Damper nut   2 Retaining plate nuts

7:7 Removing axle

Austins A30, A35 and A40, Mk I:

1 Chock the front wheels, release the handbrake and disconnect the brake cable at the balance lever.
2 Disconnect the propeller shaft at the rear end.
3 Detach the damper links where they are secured to the axle by nuts and spring washers.
4 Jack-up the car on both sides. Remove the four U-bolt nuts under each spring retaining plate and tap the U-bolts clear. The axle can then be removed, looking out for the pad on top of the spring.

To refit the axle reverse these proceedings. The pad just mentioned fits over the head of the spring centre bolt which holds the leaves together. Locate this carefully so that the bolt head will enter the hole in the axle mounting bracket.

Austin A40, Mk II:

Telescopic dampers are fitted to the later A40's making some difference to the method of removing and replacing the axle.
1 Block the wheels, release the handbrake, disconnect the brake cable at the balance lever and disconnect the hydraulic pipeline.
2 Disconnect the propeller shaft at the rear end and the nuts and washers 1 from the lower end of the dampers (see FIG 7:6).
3 Jack or block up the car under the frame and remove both wheels. Unscrew nuts 2, detaching the spring plate and the U-bolts.
4 Remove the axle sideways, taking care of the pad on top of the spring.

Reverse the order of dismantling when replacing the axle, being careful to fit the pad so that the centre pin of the spring fits up into the hole in the axle mounting bracket. Finally, reconnect the brake pipeline and bleed the brakes.

7:8 Dampers—all cars except the Austin A40, Mk II

These are the Armstrong double-acting hydraulic type with access for topping up. The A30 and A35 have a stabilizing bar attached to the damper arms.

Testing:

There is no provision for adjustment, but it is possible to test the dampers by removing them and gripping the mounting lugs in a vice. Move the arm steadily up and down, when a moderate resistance should be felt throughout each stroke. If the resistance is erratic, with free movement of the arm noticeable, it may indicate lack of fluid. If there is no improvement after fluid has been added a new or replacement unit must be fitted. If the arm proves to be immoveable it is again a case of renewing the unit.

When dampers are removed from the car it is important to keep them as upright as possible to prevent trouble from aeration of the fluid.

Topping up:

Use Armstrong Super (thin) Shock Absorber Fluid for replenishment. If this is not available a good-quality mineral oil to Specification SAE 20/20W is acceptable, although it is not suitable for low temperatures and is deficient in other ways. While adding fluid, work the arm through full strokes to expel air. Fill to the bottom of the filler plug hole.

Access to the filler plugs can be gained by removing the rear seat cushion and then the two rubber plugs near each wheel arch.

Refitting:

The rubber bushes integral with both ends of the damper-to-axle connecting links cannot be renewed, so the whole link must be replaced.

On cars fitted with a stabilizing bar, always fit the bar first and then attach the connecting links. Leave all connections loose until everything is in place and then tighten up.

Dampers—Austin A40, Mk II:

These are telescopic as shown in FIG 7:6. They cannot be adjusted or topped up, so that defective dampers must be replaced by new ones.

Removing:

Unscrew the nut and washer 1. Jack-up the rear of the car under the frame on the side concerned. The damper spigot will then disengage from the spring retaining plate. After removing the top mounting nut and washer the damper can be detached. Testing should reveal the same kind of steady resistance found with the earlier type of damper.

7:9 Fault diagnosis

(a) Noisy axle

1 Insufficient or incorrect lubricant
2 Worn bearings
3 Worn gears

(b) Excessive backlash

1 Worn gears, bearings or bearing housings
2 Worn axle shaft splines
3 Worn universal joints
4 Loose or broken wheel studs

(c) Oil leakage

1 Defective seals in hub
2 Defective pinion shaft seal
3 Defective seals on universal joint spiders

(d) Vibration

1 Propeller shaft out of balance
2 Worn universal joint bearings

(e) Rattles

1 Rubber bushes in damper links worn through
2 Dampers loose
3 Spring U-bolts loose
4 Loose spring clips
5 Worn bushes in spring eyes and shackles
6 Broken spring leaves

(f) 'Settling'

1 Weak or broken spring leaves
2 Badly worn spring bushes and shackle pins
3 Loose spring anchorages

NOTES

CHAPTER 8

FRONT SUSPENSION

8:1 Operation and construction

Each front suspension unit consists of a pair of links which are pivoted at their inner ends. The outer ends are connected by a swivel pin carried on trunnion bearings, the pin passing through a swivel axle on which the brake and wheel are mounted. The lower link is a wide-based triangle to give stiffness against road shocks and braking stresses. The upper link is actually the arm of a double-acting hydraulic damper which is bolted to the car body. Between the lower link and a body abutment is a heavy-duty spring.

FIG 8:1 shows a unit exploded into its component parts. The lower link is carried on fulcrum pins 20 which pass through brackets on the body. The bearings are rubber bushes 21 and 23. The swivel pin 32 is cottered to fulcrum pin 27 and has a trunnion link 7 bolted to it at the top end. The trunnion is flexibly connected to the damper arm by pin 8 and rubber bushes 6. Turning on the swivel pin is the bushed swivel axle 36, partial rotation being imparted to it by steering arm 3. The stub of the swivel axle carries the brake mechanism and the road wheel. Spring seat 17 is bolted to the lower link and locates spring 16.

8:2 Lubrication and checking

FIG 8:2 shows the three grease nipples which need regular attention. A fourth nipple on the steering tie rod ball joint lies behind the suspension. There are two nipples on each swivel axle pin which are best lubricated when the weight of the car has been taken off the suspension by means of a jack. This allows grease to penetrate all round the bushes.

Checking for wear:

To check for wear of the swivel pin and bushes, jack-up the car until the front wheels are off the ground. Grip the tyre at the top and bottom and try to rock the wheel by pushing at the top and pulling at the bottom, then reverse the process. Any free movement indicates wear.

The pivot shaft in the damper is tested for wear by dismantling the suspension so that the arm can be moved freely.

The rubber fulcrum pin bushes slowly deteriorate and must be renewed if they show signs of softening or permit side movement.

AAB

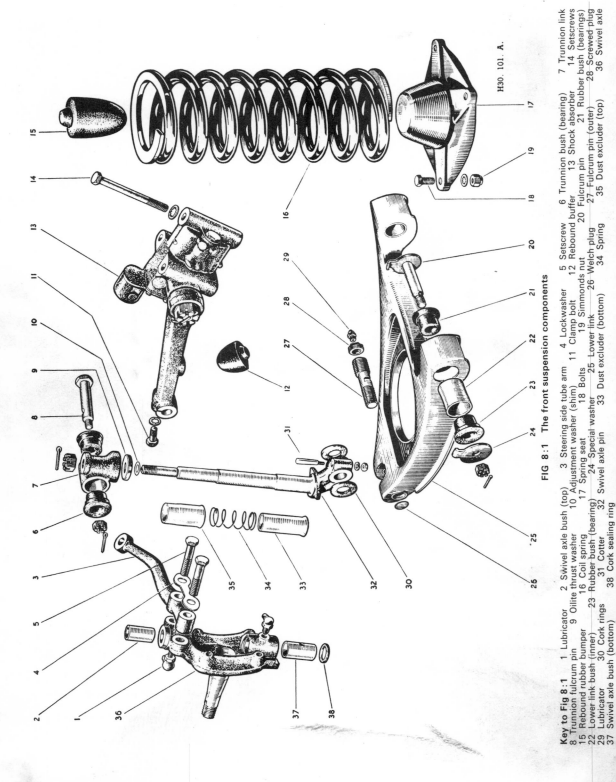

FIG 8:1 The front suspension components

Key to Fig 8:1 1 Lubricator 2 Swivel axle bush (top) 3 Steering side tube arm 4 Lockwasher 5 Setscrew 6 Trunnion bush (bearing) 7 Trunnion link
8 Trunnion fulcrum pin 9 Oilite thrust washer 10 Adjustment washer (shim) 11 Clamp bolt 12 Rebound buffer 13 Shock absorber 14 Setscrews
15 Rebound rubber bumper 16 Coil spring 17 Spring seat 18 Bolts 19 Simmonds nut 20 Fulcrum pin 21 Rubber bush (bearings)
22 Lower link bush (inner) 23 Rubber bush (bearing) 24 Special washer 25 Lower link 26 Welch plug 27 Fulcrum pin (outer) 28 Screwed plug
29 Lubricator 30 Cork rings 31 Cotter 32 Swivel axle pin 33 Dust excluder (bottom) 34 Spring 35 Dust excluder (top) 36 Swivel axle
37 Swivel axle bush (bottom) 38 Cork sealing ring

The lower fulcrum pin runs in threaded bushes. Excessive play at this point may be due to a worn pin, which can be renewed. If the bushes are worn the whole lower link must be replaced as the bushes cannot be extracted.

8:3 Removing springs

1 Place a hard wood or metal block $1\frac{1}{8}$ inch thick under the damper arm to keep it off the rubber rebound buffer when the car is jacked-up.
2 Jack-up the car on the side concerned.
3 Prepare two high-tensile bolts $4\frac{1}{2}$ inches long, threaded all the way. Take out two diametrically opposite bolts from the spring seat and replace them with the slave bolts which must be screwed up tight as in **FIG 8:3**. Remove the two remaining bolts and slacken off the nuts on the slave bolts until the spring is fully expanded and capable of being removed.

Reverse these operations to refit the spring if it is found to be without cracks and conforms with the dimensions given in Technical Data. Shortening is a sign of weakness.

8:4 Servicing suspension

1 Jack-up the car and remove the wheel and coil spring, as already explained.
2 Disconnect the steering side rod from the arm 3 in **FIG 8:1**. If the tapered shank of the ball pin is tight in the steering arm, slacken the nut a turn or two and tap the eye of the arm smartly on the side with a hammer, holding up on the other side with another hammer or a block of steel. This should jar the pin loose.
3 Disconnect the flexible brake hose at the inner end.
4 Remove the splitpins and nuts from the fulcrum pins 20 at the inner end of the lower link. Take away the pin and the outer pair of rubber bushes 23, thus freeing the lower part of the suspension.
5 At the upper end, remove the clamp bolt 11 and shake-proof washer from the damper arm. Take off the split-pin and nut on the fulcrum pin 8, tap the pin out and withdraw the rubber bushes 6. The suspension unit will now be free.

It is assumed that the brake drum and front hub have already been removed. Instructions for this operation are given in a later section. Now proceed to dismantle the suspension as follows.

Dismantling:

1 Remove the brake back plate from the swivel axle 36. Release the steering lever 3 by knocking back the lock-washer 4 and removing the bolts 5.
2 Remove the nut and splitpin from the top of the axle pin 32. Take off the trunnion 7 and thrust washer 9. The shims 10 should be put in a safe place ready for reassembly.
3 Lift off the swivel axle 36 together with the dust excluder tubes 33 and 35, and their spring 34. At the bottom there is a cork sealing ring 38.
4 Slacken the nut on cotter pin 31 and tap the cotter loose. Remove the nut, spring washer and cotter.
5 Unscrew the lower fulcrum pin plug 28 and the pin 27. Swivel pin 32 will then come away with the cork sealing rings 30. If necessary, knock out the welch plug 26.

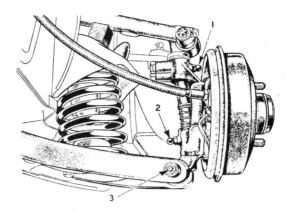

FIG 8:2   Lubrication points

Key to Fig 8:2   1 Swivel pin top bush   2 Swivel pin bottom bush   3 Lower link outer bushes

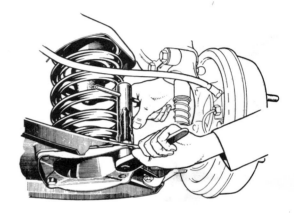

FIG 8:3   Using a pair of slave bolts to remove or replace a spring

Examination:

1 Using a micrometer, check the swivel pin for wear. The bushes 2 and 37 are also subject to wear. The bushes can be renewed, but they will then need individual broaching, which is an operation best done by someone with the necessary service tools as the bushes must be kept in perfect alignment.
2 Test the fit of the fulcrum pin 27 in the lower link threaded bushes. If a worn pin is replaced by a new one and end play is still apparent, then the bushes are worn and the whole of the lower link assembly must be replaced as the bushes cannot be renewed separately. The larger bushes 22 are renewable and can be fitted and brazed into position.
3 Examine the damper for leaks, particularly round the cross-shaft bearings. If the shaft can be moved up and down or to the side, it is worn and the complete damper will need renewal. Remove it by unscrewing bolts 14. Check the damping effect by moving the arm up and

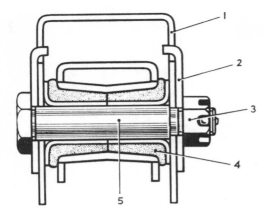

FIG 8:4   Inner end mounting of lower link

Key to Fig 8:4   1 Mounting bracket   2 Special washer
3 Castellated nut   4 Rubber bush (bearing)   5 Fulcrum pin

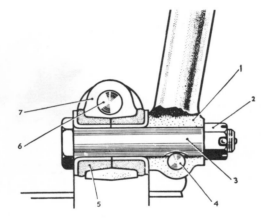

FIG 8:5   Trunnion link to damper arm assembly

Key to Fig 8:5   1 Damper arm   2 Castellated nut
3 Fulcrum pin   4 Clamp bolt   5 Rubber bush (bearing)
6 Swivel axle pin   7 Trunnion link

down steadily through full strokes. Resistance should
be even in both directions. Erratic movement could
mean that the fluid level is low. Try topping up with
correct damper fluid to just below the filler plug
opening, moving the arm through several strokes to
expel air. If there is then no improvement the damper
must be renewed as it is not adjustable.

Reassembling suspension:

The sectioned illustrations in **FIGS 8:4** and **8:5** show
the lower and upper link mountings respectively. The
correct assembly of the rubber bushes and fulcrum pins is
clearly shown.

1 If any of the parts are new, check that the fulcrum pin is
not tight in the threaded bushes nor in the lower
trunnion of the swivel pin.

2 Position the cork rings 30 in the lower link, protecting
their inner faces with very thin metal discs. Slide the
swivel pin 32 into place with the cotter hole inside. The
metal discs will prevent damage from the sharp edges
of the swivel pin bosses. When the pin is located, draw
out the discs with a pair of thin-nosed pliers.

3 Screw the fulcrum pin 27 into place in the lower link,
the small end entering the larger threaded bush first.
Line-up the cotter pin slot with the hole in the swivel
pin and tap the cotter home. If it proves difficult then
check the alignment of the slot and hole. Secure the
cotter.

4 Replace the threaded plug and nipple 28 and 29. Fit a
new welch plug in the other end if the old one was
removed. Treat the edges with jointing compound, fit
with convex side outwards and flatten the dome with
a large punch until the plug is firm and no more. Test
for tightness by pumping oil through the grease nipple.

5 Slip a new cork sealing ring 38 over the swivel pin with
the chamfered side downwards, then smear the pin
with oil.

6 Fit the dust excluders 33 and 34 and the spring 35 in
the order shown.

7 Screw the two grease nipples into the swivel axle 36
so that they will face to the rear. Slide the axle over the
pin and check for full lock in both directions.

8 Replace the thrust washer 9 and the shim 10 followed
by the trunnion 7 with its cross-bore outwards.
Replace and tighten the castellated nut. When the axle
is moved from lock to lock there should be slight
resistance with no sign of vertical slackness. This condition is reached by putting on or taking off shims 10.
These are available in thicknesses of .008 inch and
.012 inch.

9 Fit the brake backplate assembly with the flexible hose
to the front and the bleed nipple pointing upwards at
the rear. Fit the hub and brake drum either now or after
the suspension unit is back on the car.

Replacing:

1 If new rebound bumpers are to be fitted, wet the spring
bumper and push it into the hole in the bottom of the
damper mounting plate and the damper arm buffer 12
in the top.

2 Wet two of the large rubber bearings 21 and put one
inside each lower link boss. Lift the link into position on
the car and insert the pins 20 from the inside so that
the tab registers. Replace the outer pair of rubber
bushes 23, then the special washer 24 followed by the
castellated nut, which is splitpinned when tight. See
Note at the end about Nyloc nuts.

3 With the dismantling block still under the damper arm,
connect the top end. Insert the two small rubber
bearings 6 in the trunnion eye 7. Tap the fulcrum pin 8
from the rear so that it goes through both bearings and
the damper arm, being careful to keep the clamp bolt
notch at the top. Tighten the castellated nut on the
fulcrum pin until the notch is in-line with the clamp
bolt hole in the damper arm, then splitpin the nut.
Now tighten the clamp bolt on a shakeproof washer.

4 Replace the coil spring and road wheel. Lower the car
off the jack so that the packing block can be removed
from under the damper arm. Connect the flexible hose
and bleed the brakes.

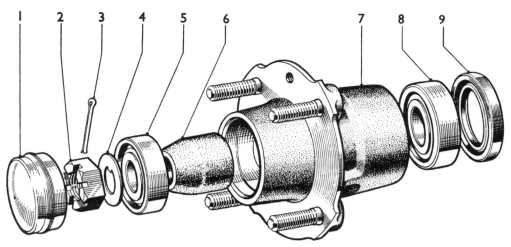

FIG 8:6 Front hub assembly

Key to Fig 8:6   1 Hub cap   2 Castellated nut   3 Splitpin   4 Locating washer   5 Outer bearing   6 Distance piece
7 Hub   8 Inner bearing   9 Oil seal

8:5 Servicing hubs

The front hub bearings are not adjustable and slackness may indicate wear and the need for replacements. Check by jacking-up the car until the wheel concerned is clear of the ground.   Grasp the wheel vertically and try to rock it.   Any movement between the hub and the swivel nut shows that the bearings are worn.

Dismantling:

The hub assembly is shown in **FIG 8:6.** Refer to this when using the following instructions.
1 Jack-up the car, remove the wheel and brake drum.
2 Take out splitpin 3 and unscrew nut 2. Use an extractor to pull off the hub.
3 Knock out each bearing by using a drift inserted in the opposite end. The oil seal 9 will precede the inner bearing 8.

If the bearings feel rough and there is noticeable slackness between the inner and outer races they must be renewed. Also renew the oil seal if leakage at the inner end has been troublesome.

Assembling:

1 Press the outer bearing into the hub with the face marked 'thrust' entering first.
2 Turn the hub over, pack it with the recommended grease and place the distance piece 6 in position with the reduced end towards the outer bearing. This distance piece is accurately made to such a length that the bearings are preloaded when the axle nut is tight. Do not interfere with the piece nor use packing.
3 Press the inner bearing into place, again with the face marked 'thrust' towards the distance piece. Replace the oil seal 9 with its lipped end towards the inner bearing as can be seen in the illustration.

4 Replace the hub on the swivel axle, using a tubular drift which spans the face of the outer bearing so that the pressure is evenly distributed. A piece of thin-walled tubing over the axle threads will protect them from damage during this operation.
5 Replace washer 4 with the peg located in the axle slot and screw on nut 2.
6 Put on the brake drum and tighten the screw in the countersunk hole. Tighten a pair of wheel nuts on diametrically opposite studs and check that the drum revolves freely.
7 Tighten the castellated nut 2 to the torque wrench figure of 50 to 55 lb ft. Insert the splitpin to lock the nut. Do not back-off to align hole and slot.
8 Wipe grease round the face of the outer bearing, do not put any in the hub cap 1 and replace the cap.
9 Fit the wheel and wheel nuts, lower the car and then tighten the nuts fully. Replace the wheel cap.

8:6 Dampers

These are hydraulic double-acting types and the instructions given for servicing the same type of damper used on the rear suspension can be followed, see preceding chapter.

Removing:

1 Jack-up the car and put blocks under the body in safe positions. Remove the road wheel and place a jack under the outer end of the lower link arm, raising it until the damper arm is clear of the rebound buffer.
2 Remove the damper arm clamp bolt and the castellated nut on the fulcrum pin. Withdraw the pin and the rubber bushes in the trunnion link.
3 Unscrew the three long bolts holding the damper body to the car.

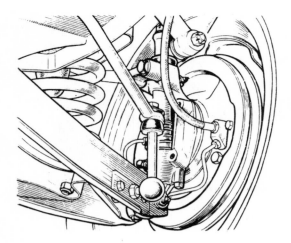

FIG 8:7 The stabilizer bar mounting on A40 Mk II

Note: The jack must be left in place under the lower link while the top arm remains disconnected so that the coil spring is kept securely in position, and no strain is put on the steering connections.

Reassembly:

Reverse the dismantling procedure but attend to the following points.
1 Do not tighten the damper mounting bolts beyond a torque wrench loading of 30 lb ft as over-tightening may affect the performance of the damper.
2 Before fitting the uper fulcrum pin, work the damper arm three or four times through its full travel to expel any air. At all times keep the damper as near as possible to its normal working position to avoid such aeration.
3 Renew the rubber bushes in the trunnion link if they have softened and allow excessive side movement.

8:7 Stabilizer bar

This is fitted to the A40 Mk II, and the mounting to the lower link is shown in **FIG 8:7**. The bar itself turns in bushes held in brackets attached to the body side-members. All the earlier instructions for removing and replacing the suspension system are correct, but the bar must be removed first. To do this remove the nuts and washers securing each end of the bar to the lower links. Remove the four bolts and washers holding the brackets to the sidemembers and lift the bar away. Refit the bar last in every case.

8:8 Settings

There are three angles in the front suspension geometry which have an important effect upon the steering and riding qualities of the car. If the suspension has been damaged these angles cannot be restored by adjustment. They must be checked against the manufacturer's figures to see whether new parts are needed. The correct angles are given in Technical Data.

FIG 8:8 should be studied to understand the three angles.

Castor angle:

This is shown at 'A' and is the tilt of the swivel pin when viewed from the side of the car. This could be affected by damage to the upper and lower links.

Swivel pin inclination:

The centre illustration at 'B' shows the tilt of the swivel pin when viewed from the front of the car. This too is most likely to be affected by damage to the links. Check with an alignment gauge.

Camber angle:

This is the outward tilt of the wheel as shown at 'C'. It can be roughly checked in the following way. Put the unladen car on a piece of level ground and ensure that the tyres are uniform and have the same pressure. Hang a plumb line from the outside wall of the tyre vertically above the hub. Measure the distance from the line to the outside

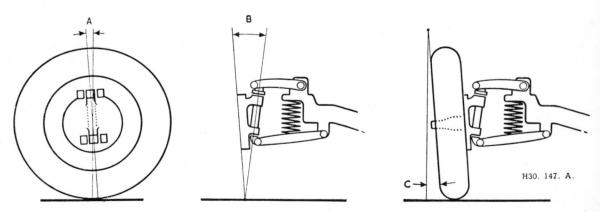

H30. 147. A.

FIG 8:8 Front suspension settings: **A** castor angle, **B** swivel pin inclination, and **C** camber angle

wall of the tyre vertically below the hub. This distance must be the same for both wheels. Damage to the links and general wear will affect this angle.

8:9 Modifications

On later chassis the lower link inner fulcrum pins are secured by Nyloc self-locking nuts. These replace the castellated nuts and splitpins formerly used. If the Nyloc nuts are removed at any time, **new** nuts must be used on reassembly.

8:10 Fault diagnosis

(a) Wheel wobble
1 Unbalanced wheels and tyres
2 Slack steering connections
3 Incorrect steering angles
4 Excessive play in steering gear
5 Broken or weak front springs
6 Worn hub bearings

(b) Wander
1 Check 2, 3 and 4 in (a)
2 Front suspension and rear axle mounting points out of alignment
3 Uneven tyre pressures
4 Uneven tyre wear
5 Weak dampers or springs

(c) Heavy steering
1 Check 3 in (a)
2 Very low tyre pressures
3 Insufficient lubricant in steering box
4 Unlubricated steering connections
5 Wheel out of track
6 Incorrectly adjusted steering gear
7 Misaligned steering column

(d) Tyre squeal
1 Check 3 in (a) and 2 in (c)

NOTES

CHAPTER 9

THE STEERING

9:1 Description and maintenance

Two kinds of steering gearbox will be covered by this Chapter, the cam-and-peg type as fitted to the A30, A35 and A40, and the worm-and-nut type fitted to the A30 and A35 as an alternative.

There is no difference in the steering layout of the cam and peg, or the worm and nut types, and **FIG 9:1** shows it as viewed from the front of the car. From this it can be seen that sideways movement of lever 4 is transmitted to the side rod 2. This in turn moves the steering arm of the righthand road wheel. The same motion is also passed by cross-tube 3 to lever 5 and so to the other side rod 2. This will then turn the lefthand wheel through the second steering arm.

Lever 4 is splined to the rocker shaft in the steering gearbox, the shaft being number 4 in **FIG 9:2**. This illustration shows the component parts of the cam and peg gearbox, and the numbers are used in the following description. Peg 3 on the arm of the rocker shaft 4 engages in the spiral groove of cam 20. The cam is attached to the steering column, and rotation of the cam will cause the arm of the rocker shaft to move in an arc. This motion is repeated by lever 23 which is splined to the shaft at its lower end.

A similar action is produced by the worm and nut gearbox featured in **FIG 9:3**. Rotation of worm 21 causes

nut 22 to slide to and fro. Peg 6 fits into a slot in the top of the nut and consequently travels in an arc as the nut slides.

Maintenance:

Accurate steering can be maintained only by regular lubrication. There are six grease nipples on the side rods and the cross-tube, as shown in **FIG 9:1**, unless the ball joints are found to be without nipples in which case they are self-lubricating. There are four nipples for the swivel axle bushes and two on the lower fulcrum pins. These can be located by reference to the previous Chapter on the front suspension.

Using the specified grades of oil, top up the steering gearbox and the idler to the level of the filler plug openings.

Toe-in:

The correct figure for toe-in is given in Technical Data. Adjustment to toe-in is made by turning cross-tube 3 in **FIG 9:1**, after releasing the locknuts at each end.
1 Bring the car to rest after a forward movement so that the wheels are in the normal running position. Have the tyres inflated equally.

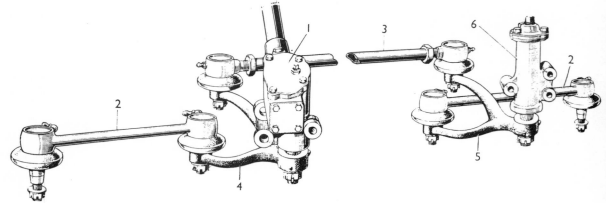

FIG 9:1   The steering layout

Key to Fig 9:1   1 Steering box   2 Side tubes   3 Cross tube   4 Steering side and cross-tube lever
5 Steering side and cross-tube lever   6 Steering idler

2 Measure the distance between the tyres or the rims at wheel centre height at the front. Mark the points of measurement and roll the car forward for exactly half a revolution so that the marks are at the rear.

Measure again between these points. The difference between the measurements is the amount of toe-in or toe-out.

9:2 Adjustment

End play—cam and peg:

FIG 9:2 shows the cam 20 and its bearings 16 with shims 17 for adjusting end play in the column. Proceed as follows:

1 Disconnect the side rod and cross-tube from lever 23.
2 Turn the steering partly to the right or left lock and have a second operator to hold the steering wheel rim without exerting end pressure on the column.
3 Try to move the lever 23 from side to side. If there is end play the steering wheel will be seen to move up and down.
4 Remove the end cover 18, having a tray handy to catch the oil draining from the box.
5 Add or remove shims until there is no play but the steering wheel will nevertheless move freely when held lightly at the rim with the thumb and forefinger. On assembly refill the gearbox with oil.

End play—worm and nut:

FIG 9:3 shows the steering column bearing assembly in the top righthand corner. The parts 10, 11, 12 and 13 are fitted over the top end of the column in the order shown. To take up end play, follow the sequence 1, 2 and 3 in the previous section, then:

1 Slacken the locknut and turn the adjustable cup 11 until there is no float and yet the steering wheel is quite free. Tightening the locknut while holding the cup 11 with a second spanner may have a tendency to tighten the bearing unduly and it is advisiable to slacken the cup back a little to allow for this.

In each case do not forget to reconnect the side rod and cross tube.

Adjusting rocker shaft:

This adjustment is done in the same way on both types of steering gearbox, the cam and peg, and the worm and nut.

1 With the side rod and cross-tube still disconnected, slacken the adjusting screw locknut 9 in FIG 9:2 and 2 in FIG 9:3. Turn the screw in to take up backlash.
2 Check the adjustment in the straight-ahead position. The reason for this is that the cam or the worm was designed so that a slight amount of backlash would be present on either lock. This compensated for the extra wear on the parts in the straight-ahead position. The adjustment is correct when a 'tight' spot is barely apparent when the steering wheel is moved past the centre position.
3 Reconnect the side rod and cross-tube.

9:3 Removing steering unit

On the A30 and A35:

1 Prise out the emblem cap from the steering wheel hub, unscrew the wheel securing nut and draw the wheel off the column. On later models a retaining ring, instead of a machined shoulder, is inserted and pinned into a corresponding recess in the wheel.
2 Remove the road wheel on the steering side, and take out the distributor.
3 Detach the side rod and cross-tube from the steering lever, release the nut securing the lever and draw it off its splines.
4 From inside the car remove the two screws which hold the lighting switch strap to the column. Also withdraw the strap which fastens the column beneath the glove box.
5 From inside the bonnet take out the three setscrews which hold the steering box bracket to the body. Withdraw the column and box complete through the bonnet opening.

On the A40:

1 Remove the parcel tray, and the battery.
2 Spring out the horn push and remove the steering wheel nut. Pull off the wheel with an extractor.

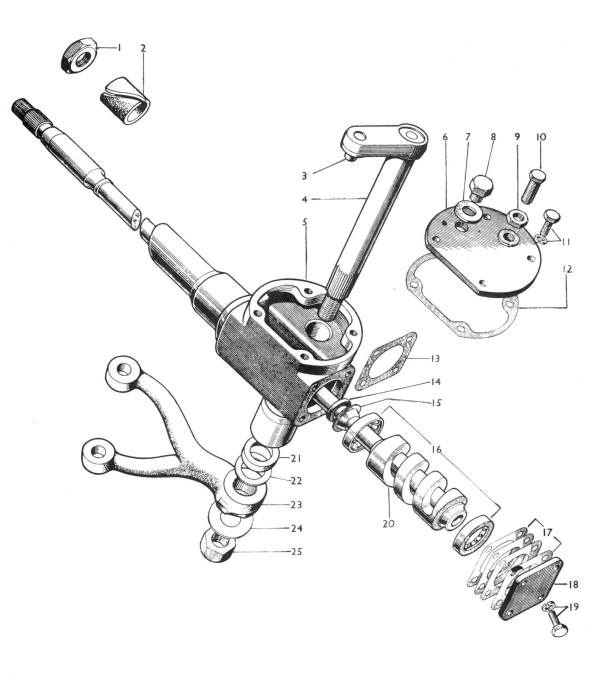

FIG 9:2 Components of the cam and peg steering unit

Key to Fig 9:2   1 Steering wheel securing nut   2 Felt bush for inner column   3 Peg for rocker shaft   4 Rocker shaft
5 Housing for gear   6 Side cover   7 Washer for oil filler plug   8 Oil filler plug   9 Thrust screw locknut   10 Thrust screw
11 Cover setscrew and washer   12 Side cover joint washer   13 End cover joint washer   14 Rubber ring for top bearing
retaining cup (for assembly only)   15 Top bearing retaining cup (for assembly only)   16 Bearing ball cups and balls
17 Shims for adjustment   18 End cover   19 Setscrew and washer   20 Cam and inner column   21 Cork sealing washer
22 Retaining disc   23 Steering side and cross-tube lever   24 Plain washer   25 Nut

Note: Item 25 replaced by a castellated nut and splitpin on later chassis

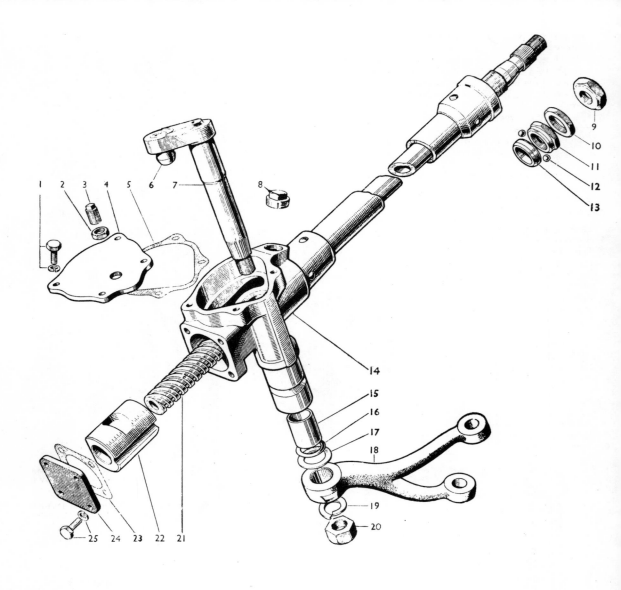

FIG 9:3 Components of the worm and nut steering unit

Key to Fig 9:3   1 Setscrew and washer for top cover   2 Locknut   3 Thrust screw   4 Top cover   5 Joint washer
6 Rocker shaft peg   7 Rocker shaft   8 Oil filler plug   9 Steering wheel securing nut   10 Adjustable cup locknut
11 Adjustable cup   12 Balls for top bearing   13 Fixed ball cup   14 Steering box and outer column   15 Bush for rocker shaft
16 Oil seal   17 Washer for oil seal   18 Side and cross-tube lever   19 Washer   20 Nut or castellated nut and splitpin
21 Inner column and worm   22 Worm nut   23 End cover joint washer   24 End cover   25 End cover setscrew and washer

Note: The worm nut 22 has not been shown in its correct position for assembly. The internally-threaded end should be towards the filler plug, and the groove which runs the length of the nut must be away from the rocker shaft.

3 Remove the two screws from the column support bracket.

4 Disconnect the snap connectors to the light switch bracket. Take out the four screws holding the switch housing to the column and remove the switch.

5 Release the side rod and cross-tube from the steering lever.

6 Take out the three setscrews from the steering box mounting flange.

7 Pull out the column and box through the bonnet opening, turning the column so that the steering lever is upwards to clear the radiator.

8 When refitting simply reverse the process.

9:4 Dismantling and reassembling

Dismantling—cam and peg:

Looking at **FIG 9:2**, do the following:

1 Remove the cover plate 6.

2 Turn the box over and support the face so that the rocker shaft 4 can be driven out with a soft metal drift. Do not remove the peg 3 unless it is badly worn, as it is a drive fit.

3 Release the end cover 18, removing the shims 17 and joint washer 13. Take out the lower ball cup and the balls 16. Turn the column vertically with the box upper-most and bump the column on a block of wood. The inner column can then be drawn out, taking care to retrieve the balls from the upper cup 16.

4 Using a strong wire hook, pull out the felt bush 2 from the top of the column. Examine the parts for wear and renew them if necessary. The top felt bush 2 is fitted by smearing the new one with heavy oil and pushing it into place. To renew the oil seal 21, use a scraper to remove the metal which has been 'peened' over the retaining disc 22, prise it out, renew the parts and 'peen' over again.

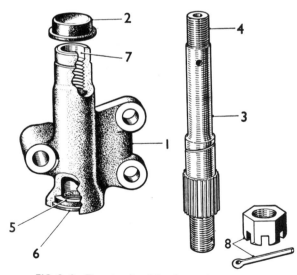

FIG 9:4 The steering idler for early models

Key to Fig 9:4 1 Idler body 2 Rubber cap 3 Idler shaft
4 Retaining thread 5 Oil seal 6 Retaining washer
7 Oil reservoir 8 Castellated nut and splitpin

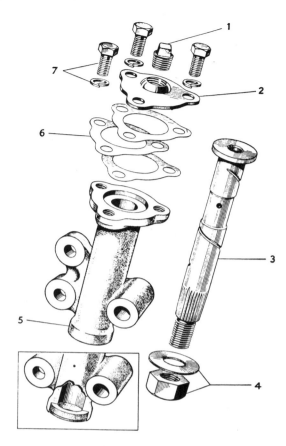

FIG 9:5 The steering idler for later models. Inset shows oil seal and retaining washer. Item **4** was replaced by a slotted nut and splitpin

Key to Fig 9:5 1 Idler filler plug 2 Cover 3 Idler shaft
4 Nut and washer 5 Idler body 6 Joint washer
7 Setscrew and washer for cover

Reassembling—cam and peg:

Reverse the dismantling procedure, using the shims 17 to adjust the end play in the column. This must turn freely after the adjustment, as the bearings will be damaged by excessive pressure. Turn back adjusting screw 10 before refitting the cover plate 6, carrying out the final adjustment of the rocker shaft according to the instructions in an earlier section.

There is a clamping bolt in the steering box mounting bracket which must not be overtightened as it may lead to stiffness and possible seizure of the rocker shaft. Use a torque wrench reading of 23 to 25 lb ft.

Dismantling—worm and nut:

Using **FIG 9:3** as a guide follow this sequence.

1 Remove the top cover 4 and tap out the rocker shaft 7 as in the cam and peg instructions.

2 Remove the end cover 24 and joint washer 23.

3 At the top, unscrew the locknut 10 and the adjustable cup 11, collecting the loose balls.

4 Bump the top end of the inner column on a block of wood to withdraw it, together with the nut 22. Retrieve the fixed ball cup 13.

Reassembling—worm and nut:

After replacing worn parts as detailed in the cam and peg instructions, reassemble the column first and adjust the top bearing so that there is no end play, yet without preloading the bearing. Complete the assembly in the same way as for the cam and peg type.

9:5 Steering idler

A glance at **FIG 9:1** will show the idler as part 6. This has been fitted in two forms, the early type being illustrated in **FIG 9:4** and the later in **FIG 9:5**.

Removing:

1 Disconnect the side rod and cross-tube from the idler lever.

2 Unscrew the three setscrews holding the idler body to its mounting bracket and lift the idler and lever clear. Draw off the lever.

Dismantling—early type:

1 Remove rubber cap 2.

2 Unscrew the idler shaft 3 by turning in a lefthand direction.

Replace worn parts. The oil seal 5 can be renewed by removing the burr which has been 'peened' over the retaining washer 6, and then prising out the washer. Insert a new seal followed by the washer and 'peen' over again to lock in place.

Assembling—early type:

1 Screw the idler shaft right home after smearing with oil

2 Fill oil reservoir 7 and replace cap 2.

Replace the idler in the car.

Note: Having fitted the complete idler it is important to turn the shaft 3 back by two complete turns from the uppermost position as assembled. This allows the shaft to turn freely on both locks without binding.

Dismantling—later type:

1 Remove top cover 2, noting that the joint washers 6 are also an adjustment for end float of the shaft.

2 Draw the lever off the splines at the lower end of the shaft 3 and withdraw the shaft.

If there has been leakage from the oil seal at the lower end of the body, replace it by following the instructions given for the early type of idler.

Assembling—later type:

1 Oil the shaft and replace in the body.

2 Fit the cover 2 and the joint washers 6, checking the end float of the shaft after screws 7 have been fully tightened. Adjust by adding or removing joint washers until the shaft will turn freely without end float.

3 Fill with oil to the level of the filler plug opening. Replace in the car.

Note: The plain nut 4 has been replaced by a castellated nut and splitpin. The later type of idler is interchangeable with the early type as an assembly. The component parts are not interchangeable.

9:6 Steering connections

There are three types of ball end connections which have been fitted, the latest being a nylon type which is

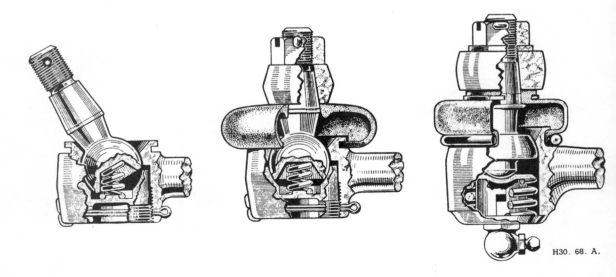

H30. 68. A.

FIG 9:6 Steering connections. (Left and centre) the Austin adjustable type. (Right) the Lockheed non-adjustable type sealed for life and needs no lubrication. On this one, should a rubber boot become damaged in service, both boot and joint must be renewed. If, however, the boot is damaged during dismantling and the joint remains quite clean, a new boot only is required. Before fitting it, smear the area adjacent to the joint with Dextagrease Super GP. The other two joints are illustrated in **FIG 9:6.**

Early Austin type:

This is shown by the central and lefthand sections in **FIG 9:6.** It can be seen that the lower ball socket is threaded for adjustment. Locking the socket is done by a splitpin in castellations and splitpin holes, the latter being drilled at a different pitch to the castellations so that fine adjustment is possible. To make an adjustment remove the splitpin and tighten the socket. Then turn it back until the ball just moves freely with a castellation and a splitpin hole in line. Insert the pin and replace the rubber boot snugly in its groove. Remember that accurate adjustment will be quite impossible if the ball pin is worn, in which case it must be replaced.

Later type:

This is the Lockheed joint shown on the right in **FIG 9:6.** It is self-adjusting and needs no other attention than regular lubrication.

The ball pins of all types have tapered shanks fitting into the various steering levers. To remove them, slacken the castellated nut a turn or two and tap the boss of the lever on the side, with a smart hammer blow, holding up on the other side with another hammer or a block of steel. This will jar the taper loose.

When replacing the joints in the cross-tube, ensure that they are in-line with each other horizontally before tightening the locking nuts.

9:7 Fault diagnosis

(a) Wheel wobble

1 Unbalanced wheels and tyres
2 Slack steering connections
3 Incorrect steering geometry
4 Excessive play in steering gear
5 Broken or weak front springs
6 Worn hub bearings

(b) Wander

1 Check 2, 3 and 4 in (a)
2 Front suspension and rear axle mounting points out of line
3 Uneven tyre pressures
4 Uneven tyre wear
5 Weak dampers or springs

(c) Heavy steering

1 Check 3 in (a)
2 Very low tyre pressures
3 Neglected lubrication
4 Out of track
5 Steering gear maladjusted
6 Steering columns bent or misaligned
7 Steering column bushes tight

(d) Lost motion

1 End play in steering column
2 Loose steering wheel, worn splines
3 Worn steering gearbox and idler
4 Worn ball joints and swivel axle.

NOTES

CHAPTER 10

THE BRAKING SYSTEM

10:1 Systems and operation

The following tables give details of the type of braking system used on each car under review. The particulars for hydraulic front and rear brakes are those for a single brake only.

HYDRAULIC FRONT BRAKES

A30, A35	...	...	...	Two cylinders, two leading shoes, clicker wheel adjustment.
A40 Mk I	...	...	...	Two cylinders, two leading shoes, screw (Micram) adjustment.
A40 Mk II	...	...	...	Two cylinders, two leading shoes, screw (Micram) adjustment.

MECHANICAL REAR BRAKES

A30, A35	...	...	...	One hydraulic cylinder operating linkage to mechanical brakes, clicker wheel adjustment.
A40 Mk I	...	...	...	One hydraulic cylinder operating linkage to mechanical brakes, clicker wheel adjustment.

HYDRAULIC REAR BRAKES

A40 Mk II	...	...	...	One cylinder, two pistons, leading and trailing shoes, backplate adjuster.

HANDBRAKE

A30, A35	...	...	...	Part of hydro-mechanical linkage to rear brake.
A40 Mk I	...	...	...	Part of hydro-mechanical linkage to rear brake.
A40 Mk II	...	...	...	Cable and rods to rear brakes.

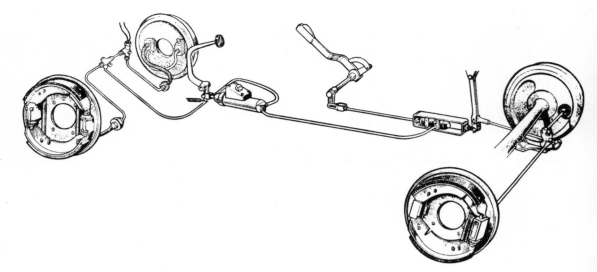

FIG 10:1 Layout of the A30 and A35 braking system

The operating principle behind all the hydraulic systems is the same. It can be followed by examining **FIG 10:1** which shows the layout of the braking system on A30's and A35's. Note, however, that the hydraulic cylinder to be seen in the middle of the handbrake linkage is peculiar to these cars and to the A40 Mk I. Later cars have a hydraulic cylinder inside each rear brake. The brake pedal is connected to the piston of a master pumping cylinder (see **FIG 10:16**). This is connected by pipes to the brake shoe operating cylinders (see item 8 in **FIG 10:4**), the whole system being full of fluid. Depressing the brake pedal causes the master cylinder piston to force fluid along the pipelines into the wheel cylinders. Here, other pistons are thrust outwards, pushing the brake shoes into contact with the drums. When the pedal is released strong springs across the shoes push the brake pistons back into their bores thus forcing the fluid back into the master cylinder.

10:2 Maintenance and adjustment

Topping up:

Never let the fluid level in the master cylinder reservoir fall too low or air may enter the system, making it necessary to bleed it. Air is compressible and gives a 'spongy' feeling to the brakes.

The filler cap is on top of the master cylinder reservoir. Clean all round it before unscrewing. Fill to within $\frac{1}{4}$ inch of the bottom of the filler neck, using Lockheed Super Heavy Duty Fluid only. If this is not available, no other fluid is permissible except one which conforms with Specification SAE 70R3. A substitute will seriously affect the working of the system.

Adjustment—front brakes—A30 and A35:

When adjusting brakes, do the complete set and not just one brake alone.
1 Apply the handbrake, jack-up a wheel and remove the hub cap.

2 Spin the wheel and apply the footbrake firmly to centralize the brake shoes.
3 Align the holes in wheel and drum with one of the clicker wheels 10 in **FIG 10:2**. With a screwdriver, turn the clicker wheel clockwise relative to the cylinder until the brake shoe is hard against the drum. Back off two or three clicks until the drum is just free. Repeat on the second cylinder.

Adjustment—front brakes—A40 Mk I and II:

Repeat 1 and 2 in preceding instructions.
3 Find the screw of one of the 'Micram' adjusters shown in **FIG 10:3** and turn it clockwise until the shoe locks the drum. Back off one notch. Repeat on the second cylinder of the same brake.

Adjustment—rear brakes—A30, A35 and A40 Mk I:

1 Place chocks under the front wheels and release the handbrake. Jack-up one of the rear wheels and remove the hub cap.
2 Turn the single clicker wheel as for the front brake (see **FIG 10:7**), but back off a little more as this adjusts the clearance of two shoes. The clicker wheel is item 4 in **FIG 10:5**. Repeat on the other brake. This adjustment sets the handbrake too, and normally no other adjustment is needed.

Adjustment—rear brakes—A40 Mk II:

1 Repeat 1 in the previous section.
2 Locate the adjuster shown in **FIG 10:6** and turn it clockwise to lock the brake drum. Back off until the drum is just free when rotated.

10:3 Preventive maintenance

BMC recommend the following procedure to guard against the effects of wear and deterioration in the braking system. For safety's sake it is vital that every part of the system is free from defects.

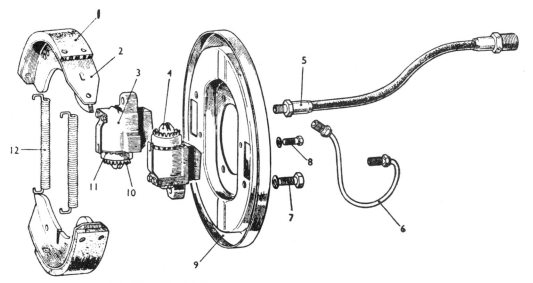

FIG 10:2 The lefthand front brake assembly on the A30 and A35

Key to Fig 10:2   1 Brake lining   2 Brake shoe   3 Wheel cylinder   4 Slotted adjusting screw   5 Flexible brake hose
6 Cylinder interconnecting bridge pipe   7 Cylinder fixing bolt (large)   8 Cylinder fixing bolt (small)   9 Backplate
10 Clicker wheel   11 Dust cover   12 Pull-off springs

1 Never use any fluid but the recommended one. Substitutes may seriously affect the rubber parts.
2 Do not leave fluid in unsealed containers as it is liable to absorb moisture. This can be dangerous.
3 It is best to discard fluid bled or drained from the system.
4 When working on the system maintain the highest standards of cleanliness, particularly when dealing with fluid and with internal parts.
5 Examine brake linings, hoses and pipes at intervals no longer than those laid down in the Passport to Service.
6 Change brake fluid completely every 18 months or 24,000 miles whichever is the sooner.
7 Examine all fluid seals and flexible hoses and renew if necessary every 3 years or 40,000 miles whichever is the sooner. At the same time check the working surfaces of pistons and cylinder bores for wear, pitting or corrosion and renew if necessary.

10:4 Servicing hydraulic systems

Before describing the dismantling of the various hydraulic systems, a few general points will be mentioned here to avoid too much repetition.

Leakage past the pistons in hydraulic cylinders is prevented by rubber seals. These have a raised lip which presses firmly against the polished cylinder bore. As the lip faces fluid pressure, the greater the pressure the stronger the seal. From this, it will be appreciated that the seals and the bores must be in perfect condition and also spotlessly clean. To ensure this, it is necessary to remove all outside dirt before dismantling any hydraulic parts. After dismantling, wash the rubber parts in clean brake fluid and no other liquid. If metal parts are washed in solvent liquids such as petrol, all traces must be dried off before reassembling.

It is advisable to replace all old seals with new ones, and most certainly if there has been leakage. To avoid damage, remove and replace the seals with the fingers.

Start reassembly by lubricating all the parts with correct brake fluid and assemble wet.

When replacing the rubber seals in the cylinder bores, enter the raised lip first and make sure that it is not trapped or turned back on itself.

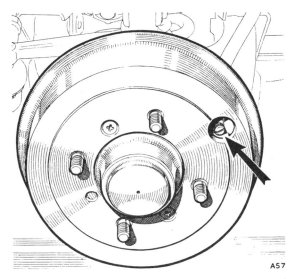

FIG 10:3 One of the two front brake adjusters, A40 Mk I and II

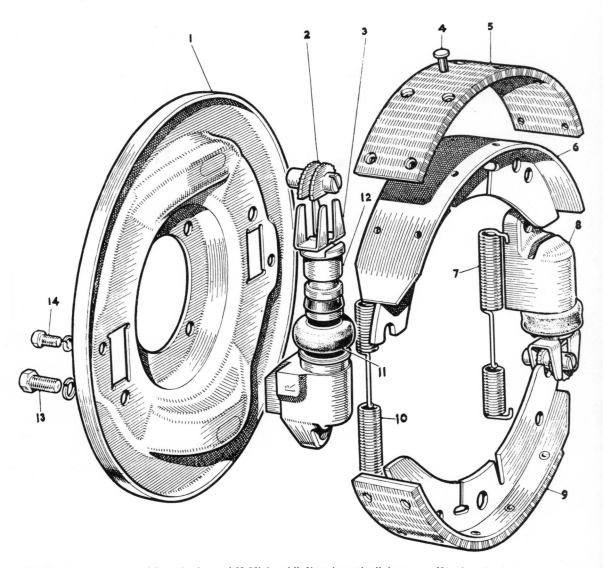

FIG 10:4 Components of front brake on A40 Mk I and II. Note how the linings are offset lengthwise on the shoes

Key to Fig 10:4   1 Backplate   2 'Micram' adjuster   3 Adjuster housing   4 Lining rivet   5 Shoe lining
6 Brake shoe   7 Return spring   8 Wheel cylinder   9 Shoe lining   10 Return spring   11 Rubber dust cover
12 Piston   13 Setscrew (large)   14 Setscrew (small)

If the brake shoes are removed from the backplate at any time, be very careful not to depress the footbrake pedal or the wheel cylinder pistons will be forced out of the bores. It is a good idea to prevent this by wiring the pistons or by fitting a clamp over them.

Removing flexible hose:

This type of hose is common to all models and there is a correct sequence for removing it if damage is to be avoided. Never start by attempting to unscrew the outer end from the brake cylinder. First unscrew the union nut on the metal pipeline, seen as item 1 in **FIG 10:8**. Hold the hexagon on the flexible hose and unscrew the locknut 2 which secures the hose to its mounting bracket. With the inner end now free the hose can be unscrewed from the wheel cylinder where it protrudes through the backplate. Always refit in the reverse order.

10:5 Servicing front brakes

Dismantling—A30 and A35:

1 Jack-up the car, remove the wheel, back off all adjustment and take off the drum.

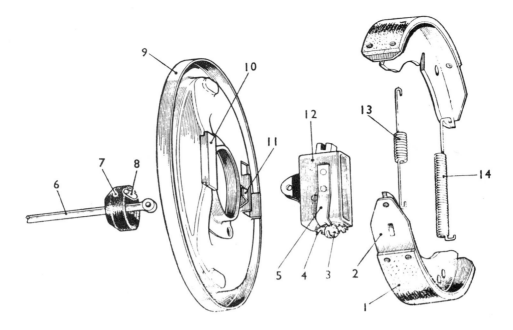

FIG 10:5   Lefthand rear brake assembly on the A30, A35 and A40 Mk I

Key to Fig 10:5   1 Brake lining   2 Brake shoe   3 Slotted adjusting screw   4 Adjuster wheel   5 Clicker spring
6 Pullrod   7 Rubber boot   8 Pin   9 Backplate   10 Abutment pad   11 Spring guide   12 Expander unit
13 Pull-off spring (short coil)   14 Pull-off spring (long coil)

2 Pull one of the shoes 2 outwards against the load of springs 12, as seen in **FIG 10:2**. Disengage the shoe from the slots in adjuster screw 4 and from the other wheel cylinder. The tension on the springs can now be eased and the other shoe removed. Unscrew the flexible hose 5.

3 Dismantle the cylinders using **FIG 10:9** for reference. Remove screws 5 and clicker spring 4. Withdraw piston 3 complete with adjusting screw 9, clicker wheel 1, dust cover 2 and tapered seal 7.

4 Clean all the parts as suggested in the notes at the beginning of the section on dismantling. Then reassemble, screwing in adjuster 9 all the way.

5 Refit the cylinders to the backplate. Attach the springs to the shoes in the position shown in **FIG 10:2**. Engage the lower shoe in the slots of the adjuster and the cylinder, tension the springs by pulling the other shoe and allow it to return into the second pair of slots.

6 Refit the hose and bridge pipe. Bleed the system.

Dismantling—A40 Mk I and II:

1 Reaching the point where the drum has been removed, pull one of the brake shoes against the load of springs 7 and 10 in **FIG 10:4** until it is clear of the abutment slot on cylinder 8. Slide the 'Micram' mask 3 off the piston cover of the opposite cylinder, release the tension on the springs and take away both shoes.

2 Remove the flexible hose, detach the bridge pipe, unscrew the cylinder bolts and remove the cylinders from the front.

3 Dismantle the cylinders by removing the dust cover 11, withdrawing the piston 12, the sealing cup, the filler and the spring. The parts may differ on some models but the principle remains the same.

4 To reassemble, follow the sequence given for the A30 and A35.

10:6 Servicing rear brakes
Dismantling—A30 and A35:

The internal mechanism of these brakes is purely mechanical, as can be seen from **FIG 10:5**. The pull-rod 6 is connected to a lever in the expander unit 12. Pulling the rod moves a slotted lever outwards (see item 1 in **FIG 10:10**). In the slot is the toe of one of the brake shoes, the heel resting in the abutment 10. The heel of the lower shoe rests in the slotted head of the adjuster screw 3. The expander unit is free to float in a slot in the backplate. When the slotted lever forces the top shoe against the drum, the expander unit reacts downwards to apply the lower shoe.

Dismantle the shoes as instructed for the front brakes, tap out pin 8 and withdraw the expander unit. Dismantle it as follows:

1 Tap out pin 7 in **FIG 10:10** and withdraw outer lever 6 and inner lever 1. Hold back the clicker spring and unscrew the adjuster screw 11 and wheel 12.

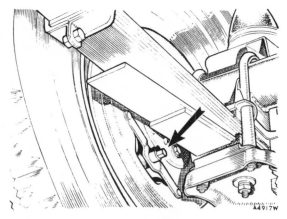

FIG 10:6　Rear brake adjustment, A40 Mk II

FIG 10:7　**A** indicates the rear brake adjuster on all models except the A40 Mk II

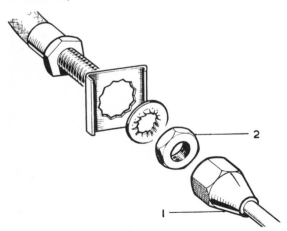

FIG 10:8　Removing flexible hoses. Unscrew union **1**, then nut **2** from inner end, finally unscrew hose at outer end

Reassembling unit:

1　Smear the parts with Lockheed Expander Lubricant.
2　Assemble the outer lever 6 and inner lever 1 on the bench, securing the parts with pin 10. Insert the assembly in the body, fitting pin 7. Replace the adjuster screw in the adjuster wheel, screwing it right home, then hold back the clicker spring and insert in the body.

Reassembling—rear brakes—A30, A35 and A40 Mk I:

1　Locate the expander unit in the backplate with the clicker spring facing inwards. Replace pin 8.
2　Assemble the shoes and springs according to **FIG 10:5**. Note that the expander unit fits in the slot behind spring guide 11 to engage the ends of the shoes farthest away in the illustration. The sharply tapered toe of one shoe faces the blunter heel of the other. The toe of the upper shoe will now enter lever 1 in **FIG 10:10**, the heel of the other shoe dropping into the slot of adjusting screw 3 in **FIG 10:5**. The opposite ends fit in abutment 10. Spring 14 must be located within guide 11. The coil of spring 13 faces inwards.

Dismantling—A40 Mk II:

FIG 10:11 shows the rear brake components for these later cars. The single hydraulic cylinder is shown 'ghosted'. It carries two working pistons back to back. These push outwards on the ends of the brake shoes. Unlike the floating cylinder on the earlier models, this cylinder is secured to the backplate. The adjuster 25 is screwed into the backplate and has a tapered end. When the adjuster is screwed in, the taper expands the ends of the shoes through the agency of tappets 24.

1　Follow the instructions for dismantling the earlier type described in the previous section, but after detaching the flexible hose, unscrew and remove the bleed screw. Take off circlip 31 and dished washer 30 from the cylinder boss where it protrudes through the backplate. Dismantle the cylinder as already described.

10:7　Brake linings

As it is possible to buy replacement shoes with new linings properly fitted it is really not advisable to attempt the relining process. Specialist facilities are needed to ensure that the linings are concentric with the drums. If the linings are not tightly bedded down on the shoes there can also be trouble from 'spongy' brakes.

Always fit complete sets, using the specified grade of lining material or there will be out-of-balance braking effects.

Do not attempt to clean oily linings as nothing permanent can be done. When fitting shoes which have new linings, turn the adjusters to the fully 'Off' position first, and release the handbrake.

10:8　Bleeding the brakes

This operation is necessary if any of the hydraulic pipelines or unions have been disconnected, or if the fluid level in the master cylinder reservoir has fallen so low that air has entered the system. The presence of air is usually shown by a 'spongy' feeling of the brake pedal and loss of braking power. After complete dismantling, more than one reservoir full of fluid may be needed to refill the system. The operator should therefore have sufficient fluid

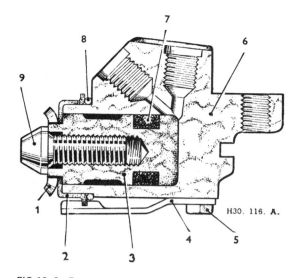

FIG 10:9 Front wheel cylinder in section, A30 and A35

Key to Fig 10:9 1 Clicker wheel 2 Dust cover 3 Piston
4 Clicker spring 5 Screws 6 Body 7 Taper seal
8 Dust sealing ring 9 Slotted adjusting screw

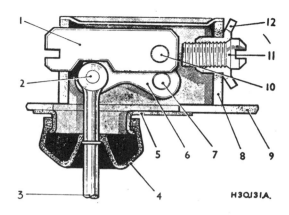

FIG 10:10 Rear brake expander unit, A30, A35 and
A40 Mk I

Key to Fig 10:10 1 Inner lever 2 Pullrod pin 3 Pullrod
4 Rubber boot 5 Dust cover 6 Outer lever
7 Pin (lever to body) 8 Expander body 9 Backplate
10 Inner and outer lever securing pin 11 Slotted adjuster screw
12 Adjuster wheel

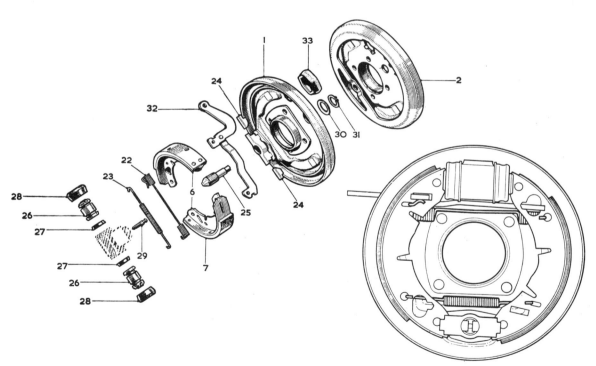

FIG 10:11 Components of rear brake on A40 Mk II. The righthand view shows the correct assembly of shoes and return
springs. Note how the linings are not symmetrically secured to the shoes

Key to Fig 10:11 1 Backplate (righthand) 2 Backplate (lefthand) 7 Lining (with rivets) 22 Return spring (cylinder end)
23 Return spring (adjuster end) 24 Adjuster tappet 25 Adjuster wedge 26 Piston 27 Seal or cup 28 Boot
29 Bleed screw 30 Belleville washer 31 Circlip 32 Handbrake lever 33 Lever boot

available to keep the reservoir topped up throughout the process of bleeding. If the fluid level in the reservoir drops so low that air can enter the system, it will be necessary to make a fresh start.

1 With every hydraulic connection secure and the supply reservoir topped up with the correct grade of fluid, remove the rubber cap from the rear bleed nipple farthest from the master cylinder (see item 29 in **FIG 10:11**). The bleed nipples will always be found behind the backplate, where the flexible hose or bridge pipe is connected. If there is no rubber cap, clean the nipple thoroughly before the next operation.

   Fit a rubber or plastic tube over the nipple and immerse the free end in a small quantity of fluid in a clean jar.

2 Unscrew the nipple part of a turn and get a second operator to depress the brake pedal steadily through a full stroke. Fluid and air bubbles will be seen coming out of the tube in the jar. Continue the slow steady strokes, pausing when the pedal is right back to allow the master cylinder to fill. Do this until fluid without a trace of air bubbles is seen to emerge into the jar. Then, during a down stroke of the pedal, tighten the bleed-screw moderately. Excessive force is undesirable.

3 Repeat the process on the other three brakes, finishing at the wheel nearest to the master cylinder. On the A30, A35 and A40 Mk I, there are no bleed nipples on the rear brakes, but a single one on the operating cylinder under the car (see item 17, **FIG 10:12**).

Keep checking the fluid level in the master cylinder reservoir so that it never becomes empty at any time. Finally, top up to the required level.

Fluid which has been bled into the jar will be dirty and aerated and should not be used again. If its cleanliness is beyond dispute it can be de-aerated by leaving it to stand for twenty-four hours.

10:9 Rear brake cylinder—A30, A35 and A40 Mk I

This hydraulic cylinder operates the rear brakes through a linkage which also forms part of the handbrake mechanism. The layout for the A30 and A35 is shown in **FIG 10:12**, the cylinder being item 17. **FIG 10:13** shows the layout for the A40 Mk I. In this, the cylinder is shown in section in the bottom lefthand corner, and again in **FIG 10:14**. The cylinder is bolted to a bracket on the underside of the car body. A pushrod 4 is fixed to stirrup 23 (see **FIG 10:12**), so that depression of the brake pedal moves both pushrod and stirrup forward to apply the rear brakes through a mechanical linkage. A slot in the hand-brake linkage can be seen in item 15, **FIG 10:12,** and as an inset in **FIG 10:13**. This allows the footbrake mechanism to work without affecting the handbrake. When the handbrake is applied the closed end of the slot pulls the linkage in the same direction as it would if the footbrake pedal had been used. The diagrammatic views in **FIG 10:15** show this principle clearly.

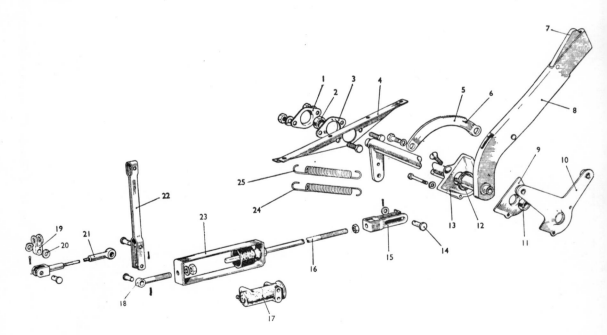

FIG 10:12 Handbrake assembly on A30 and A35

Key to Fig 10:12　1 Flange for spherical bush　2 Spherical bush　3 Flange for spherical bush　4 Cross-shaft support bracket
5 Quadrant　6 Stop peg　7 Trigger　8 Handbrake lever　9 Outer bush flange　10 Quadrant bracket　11 Spherical bush
12 Felt washer　13 Support flange　14 Sliding link joint pin　15 Sliding link　16 Handbrake rod　17 Rear cylinder body
18 Eye-rod for stirrup　19 Link to balance lever　20 Felt washers　21 Rear brake cable　22 Rear brake link　23 Stirrup
24 Rod pull-off spring　25 Lever pull-off spring

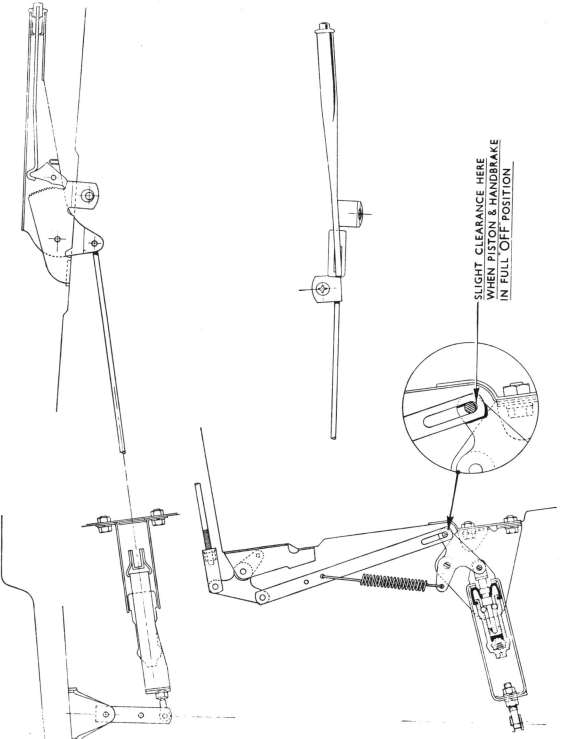

SLIGHT CLEARANCE HERE WHEN PISTON & HANDBRAKE IN FULL "OFF" POSITION

FIG 10:13   Handbrake linkage for A40 Mk I. Inset shows clearance required

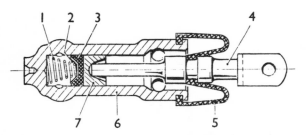

FIG 10:14 Rear brake cylinder in section, A30, A35 and A40 Mk I

Key to Fig 10:14   1 Expander spring   2 Cup expander
3 Rubber cup   4 Pushrod   5 Rubber boot   6 Body
7 Piston

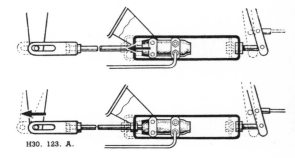

H30. 123. A.

FIG 10:15   Rear brake action on A30, A35 and A40 Mk I. (Top) brake pedal operation. (Bottom) handbrake operation

Dismantling:

1 Disconnect the cylinder from the body bracket and from the stirrup and linkage. Unscrew the pipe connection.
2 Peel back the boot 5 in **FIG 10:14** and remove it together with the pushrod 4. Blow out the piston parts 1, 2, 3 and 7 with gentle air pressure.

Reassembling:

1 Insert spring 1 with large end first. Follow with expander 2 and rubber cup 3 with lip leading. Take care not to trap or turn back this lip.
2 Insert piston 7 with its flat surface leading. Fit the small end of the boot to the pushrod, insert the rod in the bore and fit the large end of the boot to the groove in the body.
3 Refit the cylinder, drawing the pushrod back a little to allow the fixing bolts a clear passage through the body.

4 Adjust the linkage by working on the stirrup linkage so that all slackness is taken out without actually operating the rear brake expander rods. Too close an adjustment may cause the rear brakes to drag. It is essential that there is a clearance of approximately $\frac{1}{16}$ inch in the handbrake sliding link. This is shown in the inset to **FIG 10:13**.

10:10 Servicing master cylinder

The working principles and internal parts of the various master cylinders are much the same throughout. There are differences in location but the instructions for working on the internal parts will do for all models. The action of the cylinder can be seen by examining **FIG 10:16**. Pushrod 6 is connected to the brake pedal and moves inwards when the pedal is depressed. This pushes piston 10 up the bore. Fluid leakage past the piston is

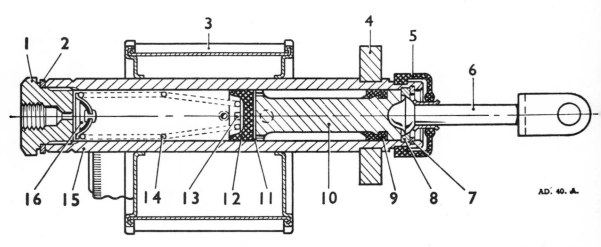

FIG 10:16   Section view of A40 master cylinder

Key to Fig 10:16   1 End plug   2 Washer   3 Supply tank   4 Mounting flange   5 Rubber boot   6 Pushrod   7 Circlip
8 Stop washer   9 Secondary cup   10 Piston   11 Piston washer   12 Main cup   13 Spring retainer   14 Return spring
15 Body   16 Valve assembly

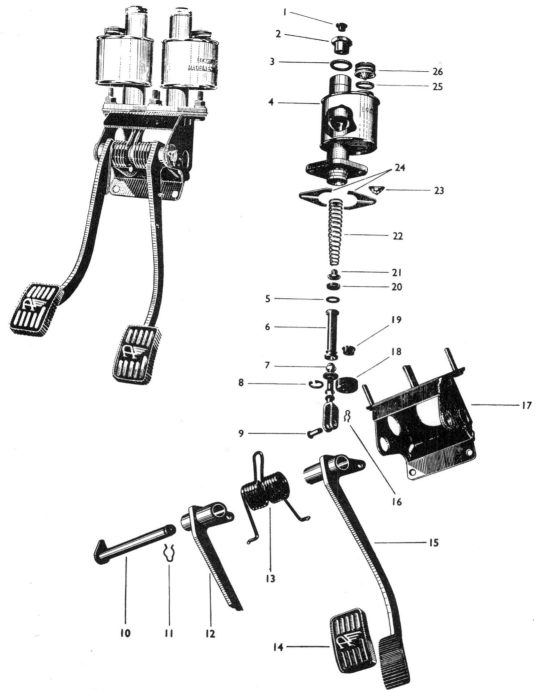

FIG 10:17 Components of master cylinder and pedal assembly on A40

Key to Fig 10:17   1 Rubber plug (replaced by outlet union when fitted to vehicle)   2 End plug   3 Washer   4 Supply tank
5 Piston washer   6 Piston   7 Pushrod   8 Circlip   9 Clevis pin   10 Pedal cross-shaft   11 Circlip   12 Pedal arm
13 Return spring   14 Pedal rubber   15 Pedal arm   16 Circlip   17 Mounting bracket   18 Rubber boot
19 Secondary cup or seal   20 Main cup or seal   21 Spring retainer   22 Return spring   23 Valve assembly
24 Packing pieces   25 Washer   26 Filler cap

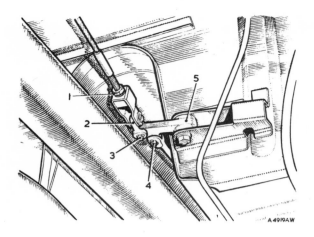

FIG 10:18 Handbrake adjuster and lubricating points, A40 Mk II

Key to Fig 10:18 1 Cable adjuster 2 Cable joint pin 3 Linkpin 4 Rod joint pin 5 Intermediate lever pivot pin

prevented by rubber seals 12 and 9. The supply tank 3 contains the main supply of fluid and the bore of the cylinder and the whole of the system is kept full of fluid by entry through a small hole to be seen just in front of the lip of seal 12. This hole is cut off as soon as the piston starts to move inwards. Fluid is forced along the bore and into the braking system past a valve assembly 16. This valve normally opens when fluid flows in both directions. Its function is to prevent fluid pumped into the system during the operation of bleeding the brakes from returning into the master cylinder, which will then take a fresh charge of fluid from the supply reservoir.

Removing master cylinder—A30 and A35:

1 The cylinder is under the floor behind the brake pedal. Disconnect the two pipes from the rear end of the cylinder.
2 Unscrew the pedal pad. Release the fixing nuts and remove the pedal and cylinder assembly.

Removing master cylinder—A40 Mk I and II:

1 The clutch and brake master cylinders are mounted separately under the bonnet and over the pedals. Check carefully which cylinder is used for the brakes and then remove the circlip 11 which secures the pedal cross-shaft. An illustration of the pedal assembly will be found in **FIG 10:17.**
2 Push off the hooked ends of the pedal return spring 13. Take out the cross-shaft and then detach the pushrod from the pedal arm 12.
3 Disconnect the pipe from the top of the cylinder, remove the securing nuts and withdraw the cylinder complete.

Dismantling master cylinder—all models:

The following instructions are based on the A40 master cylinder shown in **FIG 10:16.** The A30/A35 master cylinder differs slightly in design but not in principle, and most of the parts will be recognizable. The most obvious

difference is in the valve 16. This is hat-shaped in the A30/A35 and seats on a rubber washer at the bottom of the cylinder bore. The length of the pushrod is adjustable unlike that on the A40. Proceed as follows, working in the cleanest conditions possible:

1 Drain the fluid from the supply tank. The A40 rubber boot 5 can be removed with the fingers. The A30/A35 boot is held in place by inner and outer spring rings. These must be prised off so that the boot can be pulled out of the way to gain access to the circlip.
2 Use the pushrod to press the piston slightly down the bore to relieve the pressure on circlip 7 and remove the circlip with long-nosed pliers. The pushrod and stop washer can then be removed.
3 Invert the cylinder and tap it on a wooden surface to extract the internal parts. Very gentle air pressure can be used to blow them out in cases where they are reluctant to move. Do not forget, on A30/A35 cylinders, that there is a rubber washer at the bottom of the bore.
4 Follow the instructions in **Section 10:4** to clean and service the parts. It is always advisable to obtain a kit of rubber seals to renew those which were removed. Also refer to **Section 10:3** for advice on the renewal of parts.

Reassembling master cylinder:

1 Use the fingers to fit secondary cup or seal 9 to the piston. Work it about until it is correctly seated. On the A30/A35, press the valve seating washer down to the bottom of the bore and fit the rubber cup into the recess in the valve, then fit the valve to the large end of the spring. On both types fit the retainer to the small end.
2 Drop valve 16 into the bore, followed by spring 14, large end first. Then introduce the main cup 12, taking the greatest care not to turn back the lip. Washer 11 must be fitted with its curved edges facing the cup.
3 Fit piston 10 with the drilled face leading. Again take special care with the lip of the secondary cup. The rest of the assembling is the reverse of dismantling.
4 Fill the supply tank with the correct grade of fluid and test the assembly by pushing the piston down the bore. It should return unassisted and after a few strokes fluid should be ejected from the outlet port(s).
5 Refit the master cylinder in the reverse order to removing.

10:11 Handbrake removal and adjustment

On the A30 and A35:

1 Refer to **FIG 10:12** and release the rear end of rod 16 from the stirrup. Remove springs 24 and 25 and clevis pin 14.
2 From inside the car remove the countersunk screw from flange 13 and remove the setscrews from the same flange from under the car.
3 Slacken the fixings of flanges 1 and 3 but do not remove. From inside, remove the setscrew and washer from the rear end of quadrant 10. Release the front end from under the car. Remove the quadrant 5 from the slit in the lever.
4 Remove the setscrews securing parts 13, 9 and 10 to the body. Remove the lever through the hole in the floor. Remove the quadrant bracket and bronze

bush 11. Remove felt washer 12. This has to be cut during reassembly. Further dismantling can be readily understood by reference to the illustration.

5 Reassemble in the reverse order. Assemble bracket 4 as one unit, leaving the bolts loose until everything is in place. The flange of the bracket faces to the right. Stop peg 6 on the quadrant must also face to the right. During assembly, when the stirrup 23 is fitted to the frame cylinder it will be necessary to adjust the linkage. Do this at the stirrup, altering the length of the pullrods until all slackness is removed from the linkage without actually operating the rear brake expander pull-rods. If these are being pulled there may be drag in the rear brakes. There must be a clearance of $\frac{1}{16}$ inch in sliding link 15.

On the A40:

The handbrake is connected by cable to a compensator mounted on the rear axle, as shown in **FIG 10:18**. Non-adjustable transverse rods connect the compensator to the rear brake levers on the backplates. The handbrake linkage is shown in **FIG 10:13** where the necessary clearance in the linkage is indicated in the inset. The pull-rods are adjustable to achieve this setting.

Normally no adjustment to the linkage is necessary but a complete overhaul may make it necessary. To adjust, proceed as follows:

1 Lock the rear brake shoes to the drums by means of the adjusters on each backplate.
2 Apply the handbrake slightly and just remove any cable slackness by means of the adjustments shown in **FIG 10:18**. Lubricate the balance lever by means of the nipple on top and oil the clevis pins and joints of the transverse rods and cable fork. The cable grease nipple is just forward of the rear axle.

10:12 Brake pedal clearance

The correct amount of free movement between the master cylinder pushrod and the piston is set during manufacture and should not need alteration. If the adjustment has been disturbed, reset the effective length of the rod connecting the piston to the pedal. Adjust until the pedal pad can be depressed about $\frac{5}{32}$ inch before the piston begins to move. This clearance can be felt if the pedal is depressed by hand. It is most important that the pushrod should have a minimum free movement of $\frac{1}{32}$ inch before the piston starts to move. There is no adjustment on the pushrods of flange-mounted single master cylinders, but adjustment is possible by the use of packing washers under the flange (see item 24 in **FIG 5:7**).

10:13 Modifications

On the A40 Mk I system which has a cylinder for operating the rear brakes, a modification was introduced to exclude the possibility of corrosion. From Car No. 22523, copper packings were added between each side of the cylinder and its mounting bracket. They were also fitted under the mounting bolts and nuts. Plain washers under the nuts face on to the new packings and the bolts were increased in length.

10:14 Fault diagnosis

(a) 'Spongy' pedal

1 Leak in the system
2 Wear of the master cylinder and bore
3 Leaking wheel cylinders
4 Air in the system
5 Gaps between the underside of linings and the shoes

(b) Excessive pedal movement

1 Check 1 and 4 in (a)
2 Excessive lining wear
3 Very low fluid level in supply reservoir
4 Too much free movement of pedal

(c) Brakes grab or pull to one side

1 Brake backplate loose
2 Scored, cracked or distorted drum
3 High spots on drum
4 Unbalanced shoe adjustment
5 Wet or oily linings
6 Worn or loose rear spring fixings
7 Front suspension or rear axle anchorages loose
8 Worn steering connections
9 Mixed linings of different grades
10 Uneven tyre pressures
11 Broken shoe return springs
12 Seized handbrake cable

NOTES

CHAPTER 11

THE ELECTRICAL SYSTEM

11:1   The system

All the models covered by this manual have 12-volt electrical systems in which the positive battery terminal is earthed. There is a regulator in the control box which gives compensated voltage control of the charging circuit to prevent damage to the battery by overcharging.

Both headlamps use the double-filament dipping system and later headlamps have sealed beam units.

There are wiring diagrams in the Technical Data section to enable those with some electrical experience to trace and correct wiring faults.

Serious mechanical and electrical defects in the generator and starter motor are best cured by fitting new units on an Exchange basis, but instructions for those adjustments which can be made by a reasonably competent engineer have been included in this Chapter. To carry out such adjustments to the electrical control gear demands the use of precise measuring instruments. Unreliable instruments will make accurate adjustment impossible.

11:2   The battery

This is a 12-volt lead/acid type using dilute sulphuric acid as an electrolyte. The life of a battery is a hard one and it will be considerably shortened by the lack of regular maintenance. An obvious sign of trouble is corrosion of the terminals and surrounding parts. This causes both electrical resistance and electrical leakage. Clean off the corrosion by washing with dilute ammonia then dry the parts and smear the terminal posts with petroleum jelly. Use anti-sulphuric paint on adjacent metal parts such as the battery bolts, the strap and the tray. The top of the battery must always be dry and clean. Dampness encourages the spread of corrosion and provides a path for electrical leakage.

The electrolyte:

The level must be maintained just above the tops of the separators. Never add acid but top up with distilled water. The condition of the battery can be checked by measuring the Specific Gravity of the electrolyte in each cell with a hydrometer. The indications are as follows:

For climates below 27°C or 80°F

Cell fully charged   — Specific Gravity 1.270 to 1.290
Cell half-discharged — Specific Gravity 1.190 to 1.210
Cell fully discharged— Specific Gravity 1.110 to 1.130

These figures are for an electrolyte temperature of 16°C or 60°F. Add .002 to, or subtract .002 from the hydrometer readings for each 3°C or 5°F rise or fall from that temperature.

All six cells should read approximately the same. If one cell differs radically from the rest it may be due to an internal fault or possibly there has been spilling or leakage of the electrolyte. If it has been spilled, add more with the same Specific Gravity. This can be made by adding sulphuric acid to distilled water. It is highly dangerous to add water to acid.

If the battery is in a low state of charge, take the car for a long daylight run or put it on a charger at 4 amps until it gasses freely, taking out the vent plugs and refraining from using a naked light when it is gassing.

If the battery is unused for long periods, give a freshening-up charge every month. Never leave it in a discharged condition.

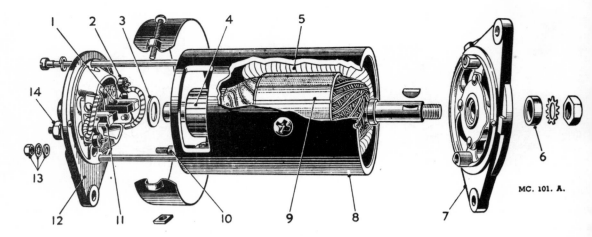

FIG 11:1   The A30 generator exploded

Key to Fig 11:1   1 Brush   2 Brush spring   3 Thrust collar   4 Commutator   5 Field coil   6 Distance collar
7 Driving end bracket   8 Yoke   9 Armature   10 Field terminal   11 Brush holder   12 Commutator end bracket
13 Field terminal nut and washers   14 Terminal

11:3   The generator. Lubrication. Output

The A30 generator is shown exploded in **FIG 11:1**. This is a two-brush type with 'windows' in the yoke. These are covered by a band which can be unclamped to give access to the brushgear. There is a plain bearing at the commutator end and a ballbearing at the driving end.

For all practical purposes the other models are covered by **FIG 11:2**. This shows that the yoke is without windows so that the end cover must be removed to get at the brushes. Again there is a plain bearing 3 at the commutator end and a ballbearing 9 at the driving end. There is a Lucar 'tag' type connector for the field terminal post 13 on later models.

Lubrication:

Every 12,000 miles unscrew the lubricator from the rear end of the generator, lift out the felt pad and spring and half fill the cap with high melting point grease. This lubricator will be found on early models only. On later cars there is a central hole in the rear end bearing. Squirt two or three drops of SAE 20 oil into the hole at regular intervals. The front ballbearing is packed with grease on assembly.

Checking generator output:

First make sure that there is no belt slip. Adjust according to the instructions in the Cooling Section.
1 Check the connections. Terminals 'D' and 'F' on the generator go to their respective terminals 'D' and 'F' on the control box (see **FIG 11:6**).
2 Switch off lights and accessories. Disconnect cable from generator terminals 'D' and 'F' and then join the two terminals with a short piece of wire.
3 Clip the negative lead of a 20-volt moving coil voltmeter to one generator terminal and the other to a good earth on the generator body.

4 Start the engine at idling speed and gradually increase speed. The voltmeter reading should rise rapidly without fluctuations. Do not allow the reading to reach 20 volts and do not race the engine in an attempt to increase the reading. A fast-idling speed should be sufficient.
5 If there is no reading check the brush gear.
6 If the reading is about $\frac{1}{2}$ to 1 volt the field winding may be faulty.
7 If it is about 4 to 5 volts the armature windings may be faulty.
8 If all is well, restore the original cable connections but leave the temporary wire in place and connect the voltmeter between the disconnected lead to the 'D' terminal on the control box and a good earth. Run the engine as before. The reading should be the same as that recorded on the generator. No reading indicates a broken cable connection. Repeat the process, connecting the meter between the disconnected 'F' lead at the control box and to earth.
9 If the readings are correct remove the temporary wire link. There may still be no charging current showing, however, and the control box must be tested. The procedure is covered in a later section.

11:4   Generator servicing

Dismantling generator:

1 Remove the generator by releasing the three nuts and bolts shown in **FIG 4:2** in the Chapter on Cooling. If the ignition coil is mounted on the generator, detach the coil leads too.
2 Remove the spindle nut and draw off the pulley, prising the Woodruff key 8 out of the keyway.
3 Where applicable, remove the nut and washers from the field terminal post 13. Then unscrew the two long through-bolts and lift off the commutator end bracket

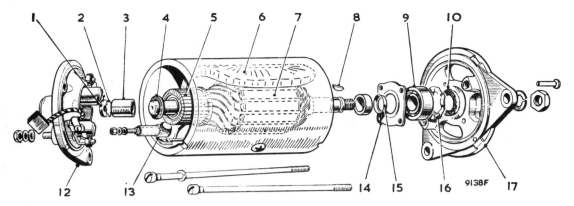

FIG 11 : 2   The generator on all cars except A30. The screwed terminals are replaced by Lucar connectors on later models

Key to Fig 11 : 2   1 Felt pad   2 Aluminium disc   3 Bronze bush   4 Fibre washer   5 Commutator   6 Field coils
7 Armature   8 Shaft key   9 Bearing   10 Felt washer   12 Commutator end bracket   13 Field terminal post
14 Bearing retaining plate   15 Cup washer   16 Corrugated washer   17 Driving end bracket

12. The armature can now be withdrawn from the other end, coming away with end bracket 17. There is no need to remove this end bracket unless the bearing 9 is worn. To replace the bearing, press out the armature shaft and unrivet the retaining plate 14.

Brushes:

1 Pull the brushes halfway out of the brush boxes and hold them there by letting the springs press on the brush sides. Replace the commutator end bracket on the armature. Release the brushes on to the commutator and pull them up and down by the flexible leads. The brushes should be quite free. If sluggish, remove, and ease the sides by rubbing on a smooth file.

2 Replace brushes which are worn down to $\frac{11}{32}$ inch on the C39 generator and $\frac{1}{4}$ inch on the C40/1 type. Bed new brushes by fitting them and sliding a strip of fine glass-paper round the commutator and under the brushes, then working to and fro. Always replace brushes in their own boxes and facing the way they did before removal.

Commutator:

1 Clean with a cloth moistened in petrol. If ineffective, polish by rotating the armature and using a fine glass-paper. Do not file, or use emery paper. Grains of emery may become embedded in the copper.

2 Given the use of a lathe the commutator can be skimmed to remove traces of wear, pitting or burning. Remove the minimum of copper, using a very keen tool and finally polish with fine glasspaper.

3 After skimming, the commutator insulation must be undercut as in **FIG 11 : 3**. Use a piece of hacksaw blade ground on the sides until it is the thickness of the mica. Undercut to a depth of $\frac{1}{32}$ inch.

4 Burnt commutator segments are a sign of broken armature wires. Shortcircuited windings cause darkening of the overheated coils and badly burnt commutator segments.

Field coils:

These are tested in the following way.

1 Connect a 12-volt battery between the field terminal 13 and the generator body, putting an ammeter in series. The reading should be about 2 amps. If the reading is much more it shows that field coil insulation has broken down. No reading indicates a break in the wiring of the coils.

Armature:

This can only be thoroughly tested with suitable equipment not normally available to the average owner. It can be tested by substitution, however. Do not attempt to straighten a bent shaft or to machine the armature core. Replacement of worn bearings is best left to an agent. The porous bronze bush 3 must not be reamed after fitting, so that a special pilot is needed when pressing it home.

Reassembling:

Proceed in the reverse sequence, lifting the brushes in their holders before fitting the commutator end cover and after replacing the armature. When the cover is within $\frac{1}{2}$ inch of the generator body, the brushes can be released on to the commutator by using a small screwdriver. Make sure that the springs are pressing on the brushes properly.

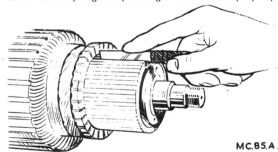

MC.85.A

FIG 11 : 3   Undercutting mica between commutator segments

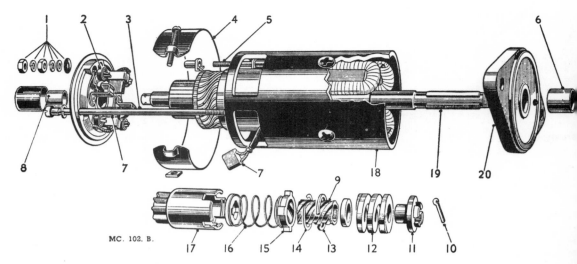

FIG 11:4   The starter motor exploded. The drive is shown in the lower section

Key to Fig 11:4

1 Terminal nuts and washers	2 Brush spring	3 Through-bolt	4 Cover band	5 Terminal pos
6 Bearing bush	7 Brushes	8 Bearing bush	9 Sleeve	10 Splitpin	11 Shaft nut	12 Main spring
13 Retaining ring	14 Corrugated washer	15 Control nut	16 Restraining spring	17 Pinion and barrel	18 Yok
19 Armature shaft	20 Driving end bracket			

11:5 The starter, testing and removing

This is shown exploded in **FIG 11:4**, the pinion assembly being drawn as if pulled off from the righthand end of the armature shaft 19.

Testing:

If the starter will not operate, first make sure that the battery is well-charged. If the lights go dim when the starter control is pulled, but there is no sound from the starter, it may be jammed. Turn the squared end of the starter armature shaft as shown in **FIG 11:5**. If it is tight at first and then comes free it shows that the pinion has been released from the engine starter ring. Another method is to engage bottom gear and rock the car gently backwards and forwards. This will often release a jammed pinion.

If the lights remain bright when the starter switch is pulled, check the switch and all the cable connections, particularly the battery terminals and those on the switch and starter. If the starter still refuses to turn it must be removed for examination.

Removing:

1 Remove the distributor as described in the Ignition Chapter.
2 Release the cable from the starter and unscrew the top bolt in the flange.
3 From below, release the dirt deflector under the starter and unscrew the bottom fixing bolt. Then pull the starter forward and clear of the engine.

Examination:

1 Remove cover band 4 and test the freedom of the brushes in their holders. Ease in the manner described

for the generator brushes, and replace those which are worn so short that they do not bear on the commutator
2 Clean the commutator with a petrol-moistened cloth while rotating the armature.
3 Hold the starter body in a vice and connect it to a 12-volt battery using heavy-gauge cables to carry the current required. One cable goes to the starter termina and the other to the starter body. The starter should now run at high speed. If it does not, it must be dismantled

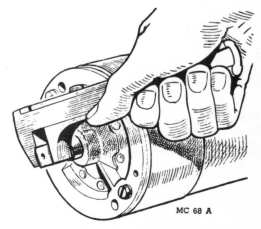

FIG 11:5   The squared end of the starter shaft can be turned to free a jammed drive

1 : 6 Starter servicing

Dismantling:

Hold back the brush springs with a wire hook and take out the brushes.

2 Remove the terminal nuts and washers 1.

3 Unscrew the through-bolts 3 and pull off the commutator end bracket.

4 Remove the driving end bracket complete with armature and drive.

Brushes:

To renew worn brushes, unsolder the flexible leads one at a time, solder a new one in place and slip each brush in turn into its correct holder so that there is no doubt about the right position. There is no need to bed-in starter brushes.

Pinion drive:

Wash the pinion and screwed sleeve in petrol and dry thoroughly. The pinion should be quite free when dry, and it must never be lubricated. If the starter spins but the pinion will not engage it is generally due to grit on the pinion and sleeve. If the parts are not oily there is less likelihood of grit sticking to them.

Dismantling drive:

Remove splitpin 10 and unscrew nut 11. On later cars, compress the spring and extract the circlip.

Remove the drive parts and unscrew pinion sleeve 9. If the sleeve is worn it must be replaced as a pair with the control nut 15. Renew broken springs and any badly worn parts. The barrel assembly 17 is further dismantled by removing the retaining ring 13.

The commutator:

This is reconditioned in the same way as that used for the generator commutator.

The mica insulation between the copper segments must not be undercut.

Field coils:

The test for an open circuit is made using a 12-volt battery with a bulb in one lead. Connect one lead to the terminal post 5 and the other to the tapping point where two of the brushes are connected to the field coils. If the bulb does not light there is a break in the field coil wiring.

If the bulb lights it is still possible that there is a breakdown to earth in the coils. Check this by removing the lead from the field coil tapping point and holding it on a clean part of the starter body. If the bulb still lights it means that the field coils are earthed.

Armature:

A likely cause of damage to the armature is the use of the starter control when the engine is running. This may lead to lifting of the conductors from the commutator due to excessive speed. It may also bend the armature shaft. Do not attempt to straighten a shaft nor to machine the armature core.

Bearings:

These are of porous bronze and renewing them is a job which should be left to the service agents, as they must not be reamed after fitting.

Reassemble the starter in the reverse order, lifting the brush springs with a wire hook to replace the brushes.

11 : 7 Control box

FIG 11 : 6 shows a typical control box with the cover removed. On later models the screws 1 and 2 have springs instead of locknuts; and terminal tags along the bottom instead of posts with screws. The regulator is on the left and the cut-out on the right.

The regulator controls the generator output in accordance with the load on the battery and its state of charge. The cut-out is an automatic switch for connecting or disconnecting the battery and the generator. Disconnection is necessary because the battery would otherwise discharge through a generator which was stationary or running slowly.

11 : 8 Regulator setting

Adjustment—electrical setting:

Normally it should not be necessary to alter the regulator setting but if the generator output is not enough, or does not fall when the battery is fully charged, the setting can be checked and altered.

It is important to check first that the low state of charge in a battery is not due to a defect in it, or to a slipping belt.

1 Withdraw the cables from the terminals marked 'A' and 'A1' on the control box and join them together. Connect the negative lead of a 20-volt moving coil voltmeter to the 'D' terminal on the generator. The other meter lead goes to a good earth.

2 Slowly speed-up the engine until the meter needle 'flicks' and steadies at a reading within the limits given in Technical Data for the appropriate temperature of the regulator. If the reading steadies outside these limits the regulator must be adjusted.

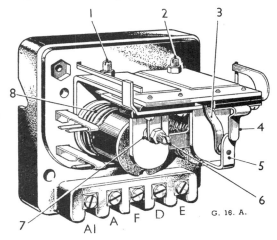

FIG 11 : 6 The regulator and cut-out control box. Later boxes have Lucar connectors instead of terminal posts

Key to Fig 11 : 6 1 Regulator adjusting screw 2 Cut-out adjusting screw 3 Fixed contact blade 4 Stop arm 5 Armature tongue and moving contact 6 Regulator fixed contact screw 7 Regulator moving contact 8 Regulator series windings

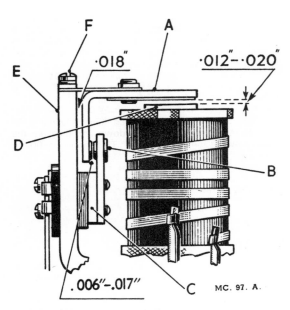

FIG 11:7 Mechanical setting of the A30 regulator

Key to Fig 11:7   **A** Armature   **B** Fixed contact
C Packing shims   **D** Bobbin core   **E** Regulator frame
F Armature fixing screws

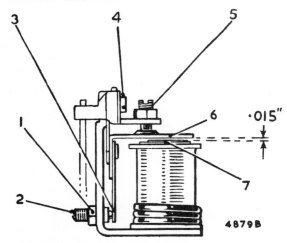

FIG 11:8 Mechanical setting of the regulator on all cars except A30

Key to Fig 11:8   1 Locknut   2 Voltage adjusting screw
3 Armature tension spring   4 Armature securing screws
5 Fixed contact adjustment screw   6 Armature   7 Core face and shim

3 Stop the engine and turn the adjusting screw 1 in **FIG 11:6** in a clockwise direction to raise the setting and anticlockwise to lower it. Do this a fraction of a turn at a time.

4 After each adjustment, test by running the engine at no more than half throttle. High speeds will produce a high voltage and false readings. These electrical

settings must be made as quickly as possible as the rapid temperature rise in the coils will affect the meter readings.

Mechanical setting—regulator:

A30: Refer to FIG 11:7:

1 Slacken the two armature fixing screws 'F' and insert a .018 inch feeler gauge between the back of the armature 'A' and the regulator frame 'E'.

2 Press the armature back against the frame and down on to the bobbin core 'D'. Keep the gauge in position and lock screws 'F'. Remove the feeler gauge.

3 Check the gap between the armature and the bobbin core. It should be within .012 to .020 inch. If outside these limits add or remove shims 'C' from behind the fixed contact.

4 Remove the gauge and press down the armature. The gap between the contacts should lie between .006 and .017 inch.

All other models: Refer to FIG 11:8:

If the mechanical setting has been altered or the armature removed, the regulator must be reset.

1 Slacken the fixed contact nut and unscrew the contact until it is well clear of the armature contact. Slacken the armature securing screws 4.

2 Slacken the voltage adjusting screw 2 until it is well clear of the armature tension spring 3.

3 Insert a .015 inch feeler gauge between the armature and the core face with shim 7. Be careful not to damage the edge of the shim. Press the armature firmly down against the gauge and tighten the screws 4.

4 Keeping the gauge in position, screw in the adjustable contact 5 until it just touches the armature contact. Tighten the locknut and remove the gauge.

5 Lastly, reset the voltage adjusting screw 2 by following the instructions given for adjusting the electrical setting.

Cleaning regulator contacts:

Use a fine carborundum stone or fine emery cloth. Afterwards, wipe away all traces of dust, using a non-fluffy cloth moistened with methylated spirit.

11:9 Cut-out setting

Cut-out electrical setting:

If the regulator is correctly set but the battery is still not being charged, the cut-out may need adjusting. Check the voltage at which the cut-out operates as follows.

1 Connect a voltmeter between the terminals 'D' and 'E' on the control box.

2 Start the engine and slowly increase the speed until the cut-out points are seen to close. This should happen between 12.7 and 13.3 volts.

3 If outside these limits, turn the adjusting screw 2 in **FIG 11:6**, first undoing the locknut if one is fitted. Turn the screw in a clockwise direction to raise the voltage setting, and anticlockwise to reduce it. Turn a fraction at a time and test after each adjustment. Like the regulator, electrical settings must be made very quickly or the rapid rise in coil temperature will affect the meter readings.

4 Adjustment of the 'drop off' voltage is done by care

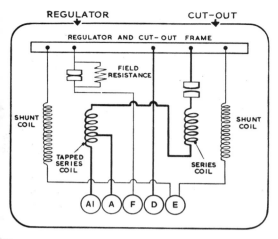

FIG 11:9   Circuit diagram of the control box

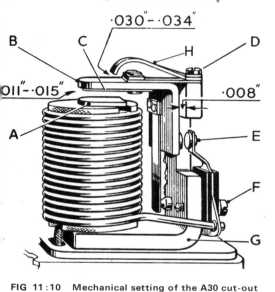

FIG 11:10   Mechanical setting of the A30 cut-out

Key to Fig 11:10   **A** Bobbin core   **B** Armature
C .005 inch brass shim   **D** Armature fixing screws
E Fixed contact   **F** Fixed contact screws   **G** Cut-out frame

fully bending the fixed contact blade. This point is covered in the next section.

If the cut-out does not operate there may be a break in the wiring of the regulator and cut-out unit. Testing will entail the removal of the control box. The circuit diagram is shown by **FIG 11:9**.

Cut-out mechanical setting:

A30: Refer to FIG 11:10 :

1 Slacken the two armature fixing screws 'D' and the fixed contact screws 'F'

2 Insert a .008 inch feeler gauge between the back of the armature 'B' and the cut-out frame 'G'. Put a .011 to .015 inch feeler between the underside of the armature shim 'C' and the core face 'A'. Press the armature down and back against the two feelers and tighten screws 'D'.

3 With the feeler gauges still in place, set the gap between the armature and the stop plate arm 'H' to .030 to .034 inch by carefully bending the arm.

4 Remove the gauges and tighten screws 'F'. Then insert a .025 inch feeler gauge between the core face and the armature. Press the armature down and measure the gap between the contacts at 'E'. This should be .002 to .006 inch. Adjust this gap by adding or removing shims beneath the fixed contact plate.

All other models: Refer to FIG 11:11 :

If the setting of the cut-out armature has been disturbed, the correct settings can be made as follows:

1 Slacken the locknut if fitted and unscrew the adjusting screw until it is well clear of the armature tension spring. Slacken the two armature securing screws.

2 Press the armature firmly down against the copper-sprayed core face and retighten the armature securing screws.

3 Using a pair of round-nosed pliers adjust the gap between the armature stop arm and the armature tongue by bending the arm. The gap should lie between .025 and .040 inch with the armature pressed squarely down on the core face.

4 In the same way the insulated fixed contact blade must be bent so that there is a 'follow-through' or deflection of the contact of .010 to .020 inch.

Finally, reset the cut-out adjusting screw according to the instructions for cut-out electrical setting.

Do not use emery cloth or carborundum stone for cleaning cut-out points, which are soft. If the contacts are dirty, rough or burnt, place a strip of fine glasspaper between them and draw it through, holding the contacts together. Do this two or three times then reverse the paper to clean the second contact. Use a non-fluffy cloth moistened in methylated spirit to clean away all dust.

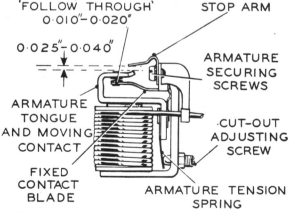

FIG 11:11   Mechanical setting of cut-out. All models except A30

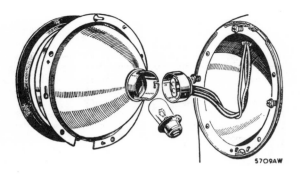

FIG 11:12 The headlamp unit showing the prefocus bulb and three adjusting screws

11:10 Fuses

The open-type fuse unit carries two 35-amp cartridge fuses held in spring clips. The fuse between terminal blocks A1 and A2 is to protect the general auxiliary circuits which are independent of the ignition switch, e.g. the horn. The other fuse between blocks A3 and A4 protects the ignition circuit and those auxiliaries which operate only when the ignition is switched on, e.g. fuel gauge, wiper motor and flashers.

11:11 Headlamps

With prefocus bulbs, refer to FIG 11:12 :

If the lamp is already correctly focused, no adjustment is required when a new bulb is fitted. To reach the bulb remove the bezel if fitted.

1 Remove the rim screw and lift the bottom of the rim outwards to release it.

2 Remove the dust-excluding rubber. Three spring loaded screws will now be seen. Press in the light unit against the springs and turn it anticlockwise until the screw heads can be disengaged. Do not disturb the screws as they adjust the beam setting. Remove the bayonet cap at the back of the reflector and remove the bulb. Locate the replacement bulb correctly.

3 When replacing the parts make sure that the dust excluding rubber has its thick inner edge resting in the recess in the light unit rim.

Beam setting :

The three screws which accept the keyhole slots of the light unit are the means of adjusting it for beam setting. Turn the top one for vertical setting and one or both of the others for horizontal setting.

Sealed beam headlamps :

After removing the rim, an inner rim will be seen. Take out its three securing screws and pull out the light unit. Pull off the three-pin socket from the back. The vertical

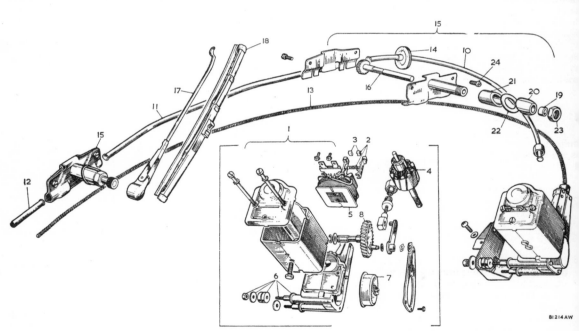

FIG 11:13 The wiper motor and drive exploded. Mounting brackets may differ

Key to Fig 11:13   1 Windshield wiper motor   2 Brush gear   3 Brush   4 Armature   5 Field coil   6 Fixing parts
7 Parking switch   8 Gear and shaft   10 Motor to wheelbox outer casing   11 Wheelbox to wheelbox outer casing
12 Wheelbox extension outer casing   13 Cross-head and rack assembly   14 Grommet   15 Wheelbox   16 Spindle and gear
17 Arm   18 Blade   19 Rubber tube   20 Front bush   21 Rear bush   22 Rubber washer   23 Nut
24 Cover screw

beam-setting screw will be found at the top, and there is a single screw on the righthand side for horizontal adjustment.

11:12 Windscreen wipers

The motor and drive assembly is shown in **FIG 11:13**. Note that the reciprocating rack 13 slides in the outer casing 11, engaging the gear on spindle 16 to produce the necessary arc of wiper movement. To remove the motor, disconnect the outer casing from the motor gearbox by unscrewing the union nut. Take off the wiper blades, remove the motor mounting nuts and washers and pull the motor away, bringing the inner rack 13 with it. To inspect the commutator and brush gear, remove the cover from the end opposite to the gearbox. Clean the commutator with a petrol-moistened cloth and examine the brush gear. The spring must have sufficient tension to keep the brushes in good contact, and the brush levers must be free. If the brush assembly is removed, mark it to ensure that it is replaced as before. Lubricate the bearings sparingly with SAE 20 oil. Grease is used in the gearbox, on the cable rack and in the wheelboxes.

Wiper parking:

The self-parking position can be adjusted by altering the limit switch 7. Slacken the four securing screws on the gearbox cover and note the projection near the rim of the limit switch. Position the projection in-line with the groove in the gearbox cover. Turn the limit switch 25 deg. in an anticlockwise direction and tighten the cover screws. If the wiping blades are required to park on the opposite side of the screen, turn the switch back 180 deg. in a clockwise direction. **Do not attempt to turn the switch through a full circle.**

11:13 Fuel gauge

If the gauge registers nothing or is incorrect, check that current is reaching the 'B' terminal on the gauge. If current is there, proceed as follows:
1 Disconnect the green with black cable from the 'T' terminal on the gauge. If it does not register 'FULL' with the ignition switched on, the gauge is faulty.
2 If the gauge seems correct, leave the cable still disconnected and connect a temporary cable from terminal 'T' to earth. If the gauge does not register 'EMPTY' with the ignition switched on, then the gauge is faulty.
3 If the gauge still seems to be sound, disconnect the green with black cable from the fuel tank unit, and then connect a temporary cable from the fuel gauge terminal 'T' to the tank unit terminal. If the gauge does not register according to the contents of the tank, or registers 'FULL' irrespective of it, then the tank unit is at fault. The ignition must be switched on during this test. If the contents of the tank are registered correctly when the temporary cable is connected, but 'EMPTY' when reverting to the normal wiring, then the cable between the gauge and the tank unit is earthed. **Do not connect the battery directly to the terminal of the tank unit.**

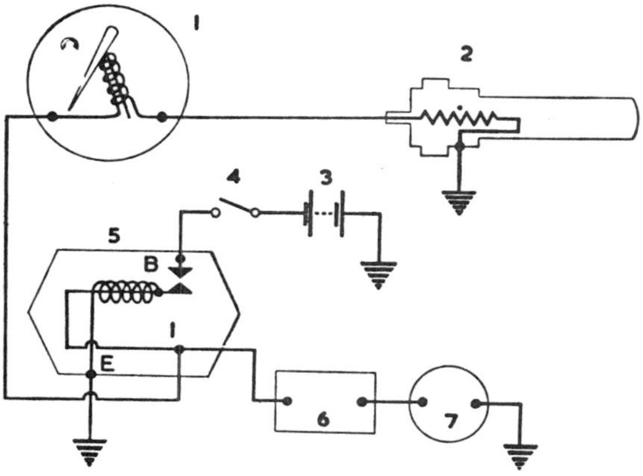

FIG 11:14 Circuit diagram of bi-metal instrumentation on later A40's

Key to Fig 11:14   1 Temperature gauge   2 Temperature gauge transmitter   3 Battery   4 Ignition switch   5 Voltage regulator   6 Fuel gauge   7 Fuel gauge transmitter

11:14 Bi-metal resistance instrumentation

Later A40 models are equipped with fuel and temperature gauges operating on a new principle. **FIG 11:14** is a circuit diagram showing that there are two transmitters 2 and 7. Each instrument 1 and 6 incorporates a bi-metal strip surrounded by a winding whose temperature varies according to the current supplied by the transmitter. The system is voltage-sensitive and the voltage regulator 5 is needed to ensure a constant supply at a predetermined voltage.

In case of trouble with the system do the following:
1 Check the wiring for continuity and leaks to earth, particularly in the wiring to the transmitters. Check that the voltage regulator and transmitters are earthed. **The instruments must not be checked by short-circuiting to earth.**
2 Check the voltage regulator for mean voltage between output terminal 'I' and earth. It should be 10 volts. Substitute with a new one if the regulator is faulty. It is essential, when replacing a regulator, that 'B' and 'E' are uppermost and do not exceed 20 deg. from the vertical.
3 Check each instrument for continuity between the terminals with the wiring disconnected. Renew a faulty instrument.
4 Check each transmitter for continuity between the terminal and case with the lead disconnected. Renew a faulty transmitter.

11:15 Flasher units

These cannot be dismantled for subsequent reassembly. A defective unit must be renewed, taking care to follow the original connections.

Checking faulty operation:
1 Check the bulbs for broken filaments.
2 Use the wiring diagram in Technical Data to check the connections.

3 Check the appropriate fuse.
4 Switch on the ignition and check with a voltmeter that there is battery voltage between the flasher unit terminal 'B' (or +) and earth.
5 Connect together flasher unit terminals 'B' (or +) and 'L'. Operate the direction indicator switch. If the flasher bulbs now light the unit is defective and must be renewed.

Before fitting a new flasher unit or installing a flashing light system, test the circuits. Join together the cables normally connected to the unit terminals. These are green, green with brown and light green. Operate the indicator switch and if a wrong connection has been made the ignition auxiliaries fuse will blow but there will be no damage to the flasher unit.

11:16 Fault diagnosis

(a) Battery discharged

1 Terminals loose or dirty
2 Lighting circuit shorted
3 Generator not charging
4 Regulator or cut-out units not working properly
5 Battery internally defective

(b) Insufficient charging current

1 Loose or corroded battery terminals
2 Generator belt slipping

(c) Battery will not hold charge

1 Low electrolyte level
2 Battery plates sulphated
3 Electrolyte leakage from cracked cell or top sealing compound
4 Plate separators ineffective

(d) Battery overcharged

1 Voltage regulator needs adjusting

(e) Generator output low or nil

1 Belt broken or slipping
2 Regulator unit out of adjustment
3 Worn bearings. Loose polepieces
4 Commutator worn, burned or shorted
5 Armature shaft bent or worn
6 Insulation proud between commutator segments
7 Brushes sticking, springs weak or broken
8 Field coil wires shorted, broken or burned

(f) Starter motor lacks power or will not operate

1 Battery discharged, loose cable connections
2 Starter pinion jammed in mesh with flywheel gear
3 Starter switch faulty
4 Brushes worn or sticking, leads detached or shorting
5 Commutator dirty or worn
6 Starter shaft bent
7 Engine abnormally stiff

(g) Starter motor runs but does not turn engine

1 Pinion sticking on screwed sleeve
2 Broken teeth on pinion or flywheel gears

(h) Noisy starter pinion when engine is running

1 Restraining spring weak or broken

(j) Starter motor inoperative

1 Battery discharged, loose cable connections
2 Armature or field coils faulty
3 Brushes worn or stuck

(k) Starter motor rough or noisy

1 Mounting bolts loose
2 Damaged pinion or flywheel gear teeth
3 Main pinion spring broken

(l) Lamps inoperative or erratic

1 Battery low, bulbs burned out
2 Faulty earthing of lamps or battery
3 Lighting switch faulty. Loose or broken wiring connections

(m) Wiper motor sluggish, taking high current

1 Faulty armature
2 Bearings out of alignment
3 Commutator dirty or shortcircuited
4 Wheelbox spindle binding, cable rack tight in housing

(n) Wiper motor operates but does not drive arms

1 Wheelbox gear and spindle worn
2 Cable rack faulty
3 Gearbox components worn

(o) Fuel gauge does not register

1 No battery supply to gauge
2 Gauge casing not earthed
3 Cable between gauge and tank unit earthed

(p) Fuel gauge registers 'FULL'

1 Cable between gauge and tank unit broken or disconnected

CHAPTER 12

THE BODYWORK

12:1 Body finishing

It is almost inevitable that the bodywork of the older car will suffer from some minor damage at least. This can be repaired by the operator who knows that a perfect finish can only be obtained by initial care in levelling up and rubbing down. Spray painting is the best method of matching new paintwork with old, and it is a good idea to leave large areas to the expert. This also applies to the repair of severe damage to sheet metalwork, where the specialized technique of panel beating is not usually within the powers of the amateur.

It is tempting to knock out small dents with a hammer, but too much beating may result in 'oil-canning' or popping in and out. Further hammering will only make matters worse. It is a better plan to fill such dents.

If a filler such as primer surfacer or a paste stopper is used, it is essential to remove any wax polish from the original finish by means of a solvent such as white spirit. When the filler is dry, rub it down with 400 grade 'Wet or Dry' paper until the surface is smooth and flush with the surrounding area. Apply the retouching paint by spray, keeping it wet in the centre and light and dry round the edges. After a few hours of drying time, use a cutting compound to remove the dry spray and finish with liquid polish. Colour-matching old and new paint is difficult, so spray a complete wing rather than a small patch. The following sections deal with the dismantling and adjustment of the mechanical parts of the bodywork.

12:2 Door servicing—A30 and A35

To remove the door trim refer to **FIG 12:1**. Lift the trim progressively free, using a screwdriver or the special tool depicted. Refit by holding the trim in place and then peel the rubber lip over the edge.

On later cars, take off the pull-strap and inner door handle first. The trim is then prised away using a screwdriver as shown in **FIG 12:4**. Pull the top away first and then lift the trim out of the bottom channel.

Locks:

Prise the private lock from outside, at the same time depressing the spring clips inside the door. When refitting, it is important to turn the square socket clockwise as far as it will go. With a rubber washer behind the lockplate, the lock can be pushed in until the clips spring into place.

Removing:

Remove the escutcheon plate and knob from the remote control lever. Extract the four screws from the remote control, the four screws from the bolt plate and withdraw the assembly. Old and new locks are shown in **FIG 12:2**.

Hinges:

If it is necessary to remove all the hinge screws, be careful that the hinges do not drop down inside the body. When replacing hinges do not fully tighten the screws until the door hangs and fits properly.

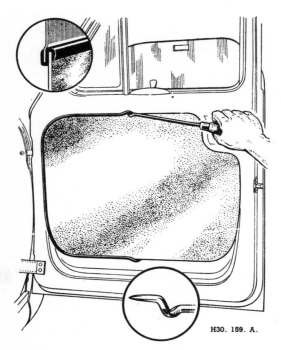

FIG 12:1 Fitting an A30 trim panel with the tool shown in the inset

Removing front windows:

1 Take away the door trim and the window arm shown in **FIG 12:3**. A small hole at the end of the arm carries a steel ball.
2 Remove the guide channels from the door frame by unscrewing the five fixing screws from the side and top. Free the channels from the fixing brackets at the lower end.
3 Work the glass out from below and the rear channel from above, then remove the other channel.

Replace by reversing the procedure but adjust the channels at their lower ends until the glass slides smoothly. With the remote control lever in the locking position the glass stop channel must engage with the stop bracket on the lever. On early cars the window should open one inch before engaging the stop bracket. Releasing the lock should allow the window to open fully under slight pressure. When fully open the arm should rest on the rubber stop. On later cars the remote control will lock the front glasses in the fully closed or partially opened position (see **FIG 12:2**).

Front and rear louvres—removing:

1 Withdraw the three securing screws inside the sealing rubber.
2 Close the louvre and support the inside of the glass with the hand. Strike the upper outside surface of the glass sharply with the other hand so that the top of the assembly will be forced free, and lift away.

Optional rear quarter lights—removing:

1 Open the window and release the catch from the door shell.
2 Open the hinge to its fullest extent and remove the four screws revealed. Lift away the window.

Rear door windows—removing:

1 Support on the inside and strike smartly with the flat of the hand on the outside at the top. When the top is released, the glass and weatherstrip can be lifted out from the inside.

Refit the glass by using the cord method described later for fitting windscreens.

12:3 Door servicing—A40

To lock the door and the window glass, the door must first be closed. Do not attempt to force the handle into the locked position while the door is open. To remove the

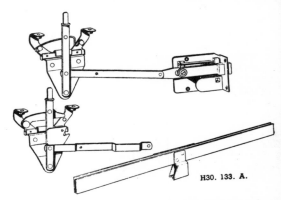

FIG 12:2 Door locks on A30 and A35. Early type (top) and later type (below), with glass channel

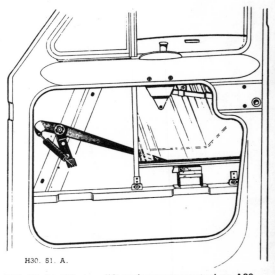

FIG 12:3 Window lift and remote control on A30

118

door trim set the interior handle to the 'normal' position with the window unlocked, and then remove the handle. Prise the trim panel away with a screwdriver to release the spring clips as in **FIG 12:4**. When replacing, locate the loose end of the plastic cover inside the lower aperture in the door.

Locks:

To remove the locks refer to **FIG 12:5**.

1 Remove screws 'C' and 'D', the door pull at 'E' and screw 'F'.
2 Release the remote control link by removing circlip and washer 'G'.
3 Take out the remote control screws 'H', press the loose end of the front window channel out of the way and remove the control.
4 Take out screws 'I' and 'J'. Pull the rear window channel away from the lock and turn it so that the lock can be manoeuvred round it and the outside push button passed through. Do not use force. The lock is then passed down until it is clear of the window channel and can be drawn out through the lower aperture.

To replace the locks refer to **FIG 12:6**.

1 Grease all moving parts, but never the private lock cylinder with anything but oil. Insert the lock and fixing screws. Move the latch downwards into the closed position 'L'.
2 The remote control is supplied with a peg 'M' to hold it in the locked position and must be fitted like this. Insert through the upper aperture connecting link first. Fit the three securing screws but do not tighten.

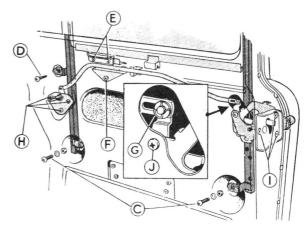

FIG 12:5 Lock and remote control mechanism on A40

3 Replace the link on the lock lever stud and fit the washer and circlip 'G' (see **FIG 12:5**). To align the lock assembly, slide the remote control towards the lock. The slotted end of the link and the stop on the lock lever will then be in position 'N'. Tighten the remote control screws and remove the temporary peg. Replace all the other parts.

The striker unit is fixed by screws 'K' in **FIG 12:6**. These screw into an adjustable tapping plate inside the door pillar. Do not disturb the setting unless adjustment is needed or a new assembly is to be fitted. To do this:

1 Attach the striker unit loosely, then move it to a position which seems suitable and tighten the screws.
2 Proceed to adjust the position until the door closes easily without rattling and does not lift or drop during closing.

The striker must be kept in a horizontal plane relative to the door axis during these adjustments. Finally, lubricate with oil.

Front ventilator removal:

1 Remove the inside door handle and the trim pad. Remove the window glass stop from the door, hold the regulator against the spring pressure and lower the glass as far as possible. Tie the regulator down.
2 Slide the clip along the top of the window moulding to expose the join and carefully prise the moulding away.
3 Remove the ventilator securing screws from the upper and lower front corners and those holding the window channel in position. Slide the channel downwards and remove the ventilator as the top of the frame is pulled gently rearwards and upwards. Reassemble in the reverse order.

Front ventilator adjustment:

The lower hinge pin of the ventilator carries a spring and two locknuts. To increase the friction unlock the nuts and screw upwards, locking them again when the ventilator remains in any required position. Conversely, slacken the nuts to reduce friction.

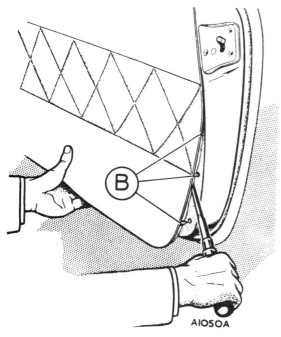

FIG 12:4 Removing an A40 trim panel. Spring clips lock in holes **B**

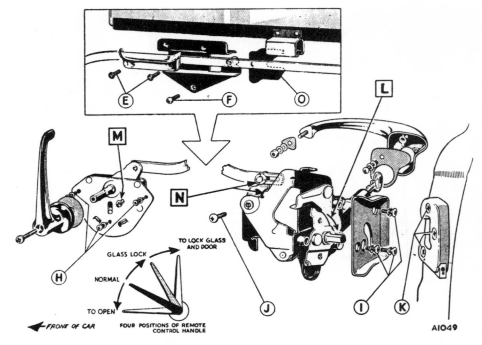

FIG 12:6 A40 lock and remote control exploded

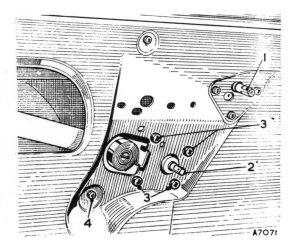

FIG 12:7 Window regulating mechanism on A40 Mk II

Window regulator—A40, Mk II:

The attachment screws are shown in **FIG 12:7**. To remove the mechanism:

1 Detach the interior door handle from shank 1. Press the regulator handle collar inwards against spring pressure to reveal the peg shown in **FIG 12:8** which can then be pushed out to release the handle.

2 Remove the door trim panel and plastic moisture deflector.

3 Remove screw 4, wind down the window about four inches and wedge it.

4 Remove the four screws 3 and lift the regulating arm out of its lifting channel.

5 Press the glass frame away from the door panel to allow the regulating mechanism and arm to be removed through the space at the bottom. Remove the three screws to detach the glass stop.

Replace in the reverse order. The plastic moisture deflector goes behind the door trim pad.

12:4 Fitting windscreens

It can be a puzzling problem to fit the rubber weatherstrip round a windscreen into the body aperture. This can be solved by using cords to peel the rubber lips over the steel flanges, as shown by **FIG 12:9**. The rubber stripping is first fitted to the glass and then cords are placed in the two grooves, or a single cord in the case of the backlight or rear window. An easy way to lay the cord is to insert the first six inches and feed the rest in using a short piece of small-bore tubing. The cord passes through the tube, the inner end of which is laid in the groove and drawn round. Start and finish at the same place, leaving generous lengths of the two cord ends to give good hand-holds. Press the glass into place and draw the cord out of the groove. This will peel the rubber lip over the body flange.

The last operation will be to make a watertight seal between the lips and the glass, or the lips and steel flange. Preferably using a nozzle, squeeze Seelastik well down into the groove so that there will be a surplus to be pressed out when the lip returns to normal.

12:5 Removing instrument panels

Early A30:

The panel is held in place by four recessed-head screws and four spire nuts behind the panel. The instruments and electrical connections are accessible on releasing the panel.

Later A30 and A35:

Remove the instrument panel by unscrewing the two knurled nuts, one on each side of the panel behind the facia. This releases the securing clips. The panel is drawn forward, all connections detached and the panel removed.

12:6 Removing facia—A30 and A35

Remove the fillets from the windscreen side pillars. Release the starter pull cable from the switch on the bulkhead and the choke cable at the carburetter, also releasing the choke outer cable from the bulkhead. Remove the trafficator control by unscrewing two set-screws and releasing three electrical cables. Release the demister pipes if a heater is fitted.

The facia is fixed to the scuttle by two hexagon bolts at each lower corner and four recessed-head screws underneath. Remove these and lift the facia off the four clips along the upper edge.

12:7 Heater

Adjustment of A30/A35 controls (later type):

Move the lower lever to the 'OFF' position. The air lever on the heater unit should now be right forward. With the fan motor running there should be practically no air entering the car. Now move the lever to 'HOT'. The lever on the unit should now be right back, with the water valve very slightly moved from the closed position.

If these settings are not obtainable, slacken the clamping screw on the cable trunnion and slide the inner cable through by a small amount and check after tightening the screw.

Move the lever to the 'COLD' position. The lever on the water valve should now be vertical and the water flow cut off. After two or three minutes with the engine and fan motor running, air entering the car should be cold. If it is not, the valve is not completely closed. Slacken the clamping screw securing the water valve operating rod beneath the cable attachment on the heater box. Move the valve lever and check that there is a slight increase in resistance as the lever passes the vertical position. If there is not, turn the centre screw on the lever a quarter of a turn clockwise and try again, adjusting a little more if necessary. With the lever vertical, retighten the clamping screw.

Move the demist lever to 'OFF'. The demist lever on the heater should now be right forward and no air should reach the screen with the fan motor running. In the 'DEFROST' position the lever on the heater should be right back.

Adjustment of A40 Mk II controls:

With the air control knob pulled right out, the lever on the air intake tube under the bonnet should be nearest to the cable clamp so that the rubber valve seals the tube.

Set the lefthand control on the blue arrow. In this position the lever on the water valve should be turned

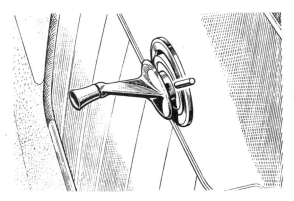

FIG 12:8 Locating peg on A40 Mk II window regulator handle

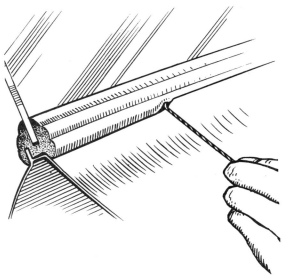

FIG 12:9 Using a cord to fit the windscreen weather-strip to the A30 scuttle

clockwise to the end of its slot. With the righthand control at the upward-pointing arrow, the heater outlet door should be closed.

Heater air lock:

Disconnecting the water hoses during an overhaul may lead to trouble with the heater due to an air lock in the system. If the engine has been running but the heater refuses to warm up when the fan is switched on, check the temperature of the water return hose. If it is cold, switch off the engine and disconnect the heater pipe from the lower radiator hose. Plug the hose temporarily. Extend the heater hose with a temporary pipe so that water can flow back into the radiator by way of the filler neck. Start the engine and check the flow into the radiator. When it is a smooth bubble-free stream, reconnect the hose to the lower radiator connection, tightening the clip as quickly as possible.

Note that heater units are not drained when the cooling system is emptied. For this reason it is essential to use anti-freeze in cold weather.

12:8 Seat belts

Fitting instructions—later A40 Mk I and II:

The upper bracket of the long belt is attached to the top of the centre door pillar. The lower bracket of the long belt is fitted to the floor panel adjacent to the lower door sill. The bracket for the short belt is attached to the side of the transmission tunnel farthest from the seat being equipped.

Pillar fixing:

At the top of the pillar feel for the hole beneath the trim and cut the trim in the form of a cross over the hole. Turn the edges of the trim under the trim panel. Pass a fixing screw through the belt bracket and feed on to the other side the anti-rattle washer and the shouldered distance piece. The concave side of the washer must contact the bracket and the large diameter of the distance piece must abut the pillar. Secure the bracket in place.

Floor sill fixing:

Locate the fixing point in the sill, low down and just forward of the central door pillar. Cut the carpet over the hole so that metal-to-metal contact can be made. Assemble the bolt, washer and distance piece as just described for the pillar fixing and secure the bracket.

Transmission tunnel fixing:

On the side opposite to the seat being equipped, lift the carpet and remove the two rubber plugs from the tunnel. Buckle the belt in position and mark the carpet where the bracket fits to the floor. Cut a slit in the carpet and pass the bracket through. From underneath, position the tapped plate and secure the bracket to it with the screws and lockwashers provided.

Fix the belt stowage clip $8\frac{1}{2}$ inches behind the centre pillar and just below the sill of the rear window on the same side. Drill two holes with a No. 31 drill and secure the clip with the self-tapping screws. Secure the warning label to the rear of the front seat, making the holes with a No. 38 drill and securing with two No. 6 screws.

APPENDIX

TECHNICAL DATA

WIRING DIAGRAMS

HINTS ON MAINTENANCE AND OVERHAUL

GLOSSARY OF TERMS

INDEX

NOTES

TECHNICAL DATA

Dimensions are in inches unless otherwise stated

ENGINE DETAILS

Bore and stroke (mm):
800 cc... ... ... 58 x 76.2
848 cc... ... ... 62.94 x 68.26
948 cc... ... ... 62.94 x 76.2
1098 cc ... ... 64.58 x 83.72
Compression ratio (low):
800 cc... ... ... 7.2:1
848 cc (A35) 8.1:1
948 cc (A35 and A40) 7.2:1
1098 cc (A35 and A40) 7.5:1
Compression ratio (high):
948 cc (A35 and A40) 8.3:1
1098 cc (A40)... ... ... 8.5:1
Firing order 1, 3, 4, 2
Main bearings, journal diameter:
All capacities ... ... 1.7505 to 1.7510
Main bearing liners, running clearance:
800 cc, 848 cc and 948 cc (A30 and A35) ... ... .0005 to .002
948 cc (A40) ... ... .0005 to .003
1098 cc (A35 and A40) ... ... .001 to .0027
Main bearings, lining material:
800 cc and 948 cc (A30, A35 and A40) ... ... Whitemetal
848 cc (A35) and 1098 cc (A35 and A40) ... ... Copper/lead
Crankshaft end float:
All capacities ... ... .002 to .003
Crankpin diameter:
800 cc... ... ... 1.4379 to 1.4384
All other capacities ... ... 1.6254 to 1.6259
Connecting rod centres:
All capacities 5.75
Big-end bearings, running clearance:
All capacities ... ... .001 to .0025
Big-end bearings, lining material:
800 cc (early A30) ... ... Whitemetal
800 cc (later A30) ... ... Copper/lead with lead/
    indium or lead/tin plating
848 cc (A35) ... ... Lead/bronze with lead/
    indium plating or copper/
    lead with lead/tin plating
948 cc (A35) ... ... Copper/lead with lead/
    indium or lead/tin plating
948 cc (A40) ... ... Copper/lead
1098 cc (A35 and A40) ... ... Copper/lead
Connecting rod end float on crankpin:
800 cc... ... ... .006 to .010
All other capacities ... ... .008 to .012
Clamped gudgeon pin:
Diameter (800 cc, 848 cc and 948 cc) ... ... .6244 to .6246
Clearance in piston (hand push) ... ... .0001 to .0003
Fully floating gudgeon pin:
Fit in piston (1098 cc) ... ... Hand push
Piston type ... ... Aluminium alloy

Standard piston, suitable bore size:	
800 cc...	2.2807 to 2.2810
948 cc...	2.4778 to 2.4781
1098 cc	2.5424 to 2.5447
Piston oversizes:	
800 cc, 848 cc and 948 cc	+.010, +.020, +.030 and +.040
1098 cc	+.010 and +.020
Piston clearance, bottom of skirt:	
800 cc and 948 cc (A35)	.0006 to .0014
848 cc (A35) and 948 cc (A40)	.0006 to .0012
1098 cc	.0005 to .0011
Piston clearance, top of skirt:	
848 cc (A35)	.0026 to .0032
1098 cc	.0021 to .0037
Piston rings, compression:	
Top	Plain
Second	Taper
Third	Taper (early A30, plain)
Fourth piston ring, all capacities except 1275 cc and later 1098 cc	Slotted scraper
Later 1098 cc	Duaflex 61
Width of compression rings:	
800 cc, 848 cc and 948 cc	.069 to .070
1098 cc (top ring)	.062 to .0625
1098 cc (second and third rings)	.0615 to .0625
Width of slotted scraper ring:	
All capacities except later 1098 cc	.124 to .125
Ring gap, fitted (all capacities)	.007 to .012
Duaflex 61 (rails and side spring)	.012 to .028
Ring clearance in groove:	
800 cc, 848 cc and 948 cc (top, second and third)	.0015 to .0035
1098 cc	.002 to .004
Camshaft journal diameters:	
Front	1.6655 to 1.666
Centre	1.62275 to 1.62325
Rear	1.3725 to 1.3735
Camshaft bearings:	
Front	Steel-backed whitemetal
Centre and rear (except 1098 cc)	Direct in crankcase
1098 cc (all three)	Steel-backed whitemetal
Camshaft clearance:	
Front bearing (also centre and rear when linered)	.001 to .002
Centre and rear bearings	.00125 to .00275
Camshaft end float	.003 to .007
Timing chain	Single roller
Timing chain, pitch	.375
Timing chain, length	52 pitches
Valve seat angle	45 deg.
Valve lift:	
800 cc, 848 cc and 948 cc (A30, A35, A40 Mk I and II) ...	.285
1098 cc	.312
Valve head diameter, inlet:	
800 cc (A30) and 848 cc (A35)	1.093 to 1.098
948 cc (A35, A40 Mk I and II)	1.093 to 1.098
1098 cc	1.151 to 1.156
Valve head diameter, exhaust:	
All capacities	1.000 to 1.005

Valve stem diameter, inlet:
    All capacities ...   .   .2793 to .2798
Valve stem diameter, exhaust:
    All capacities ...   .   .2788 to .2793
Valve stem clearance, inlet:
    All capacities ...   .   .0015 to .0025
Valve stem clearance, exhaust:
    800 cc...   ...   .   .001 to .002
    848 cc, 948 cc and 1098 cc   ...   .   .002 to .003
Valve rocker clearance (cold):
    All capacities 012
For checking timing only:
    800 cc and 948 cc 019
    848 cc and 1098 cc 021
Valve springs, free length:
    800 cc, 848 cc (early) and 948 cc (A30, A35 and A40 Mk I and II)   1.625
    848 cc (from Engine No. 10875) 1.75
    1098 cc (A35 and A40 Mk II)...   ...   .   1.75
Valve spring pressure (valve closed):
    800 cc, 848 cc (early) and 948 cc (A30, A35 and A40)   ...   35.5 to 39.5 lb
    848 cc (from Engine No. 10875)   ...   .   55.5 lb
    1098 cc (A35 and A40 Mk II)...   ...   .   52.5 lb
Valve timing (A30, 848 cc and 948 cc A35, A40):
    Inlet opens   ...   .   5 deg. before TDC
    Inlet closes   ...   .   45 deg. after BDC
    Exhaust opens...   ...   .   40 deg. before BDC
    Exhaust closes...   ...   .   10 deg. after TDC
    With rocker clearance of .019, **for checking only** (or .021 on 848 cc A35)
Valve timing (1098 cc):
    Inlet opens   ...   .   5 deg. before TDC
    Inlet closes   ...   .   45 deg. after BDC
    Exhaust opens...   ...   .   51 deg. before BDC
    Exhaust closes...   ...   .   21 deg. after TDC
    With rocker clearance of .021, **for checking only**
Oil sump capacity including filter (pints):
    All capacities ...   . $6\frac{1}{2}$
Oil pressure relief valve spring, free length:
    A30, A35 and A40 Mk I   ...   . $2\frac{7}{8}$
    A40 Mk II 2.86
Oil pressure (normal running), lb/sq in:
    A30   ...   .   50 to 55
    All others   60

TORQUE WRENCH SETTINGS

Tightening torque (lb ft):
    Cylinder head nuts   40
    Main bearing cap bolts   60
    Big-end cap bolts   35
    Gudgeon pin clamp screw   25
    Flywheel bolts...   ...   .   35 to 40
    Rocker pedestal nuts   25
    Sump to crankcase bolts   6
    Rocker cover nuts   4
    Oil pump securing bolts   12
    Deep-pressed cylinder side cover   5
    Timing cover ($\frac{1}{4}$ inch UNF bolts)   6
    Timing cover ($\frac{5}{16}$ inch UNF bolts)   14
    Oil filter (fullflow)   16

| Manifold to cylinder head | ... | ... | ... | ... | ... | 15 |
| Crankshaft pulley screw | ... | ... | ... | ... | ... | 70 |

IGNITION SYSTEM

Spark plug type, all capacities	...	...	...	...	... Champion N5
Spark plug gap ...	...	...	...	...	... .025
Contact breaker gap	...	...	...	...	... .014

Static setting, Premium fuel:
   A30 ... ... 11 deg. before TDC
   848 cc A35 (Premium fuel distributor) ... ... TDC
   948 cc (high compression) A35 and A40 ... ... 5 deg. before TDC
Static setting, 848 cc A35 (Regular fuel distributor) ... ... 7 deg. before TDC
Static setting (low compression):
   A30 (Commercial fuel) ... ... 6½ deg. before TDC
   948 cc (A35 and A40, Commercial fuel) ... ... 2 deg. before TDC
   1098 cc (A35 and A40) ... ... 3 deg. before TDC
Stroboscope setting at 600 engine rev/min:
   1098 cc (A40)... ... ... 6 deg. before TDC
   848 cc A35 (Premium fuel distributor) ... ... 2 to 2½ deg. before TDC
   848 cc A35 (Regular fuel distributor) ... ... 9 to 9½ deg. before TDC
Distributor type (Lucas):
   A30, 948 cc A35 and A40 Mk I DM2
   848 cc and 1098 cc 25 D4
Coil type (Lucas):
   Early A30 ... ... Q12
   All other models LA12

CARBURETTER DETAILS

Type (early A30) ... ... Zenith 26 JS
Choke 18
Main jet ... ... 95 or 113
Main air jet 160
Slow-running jet 40
Slow-running air bleed 80
Needle and seating ... ... 1.5 mm
Type (later A30, 948 cc A35 and A40 Mk I) ... ... Zenith 26 VME

	A30 (later)	A35	A40 Mk I
Choke	20	22	22
Main jet	70	80	80
Compensating jet...	57	57	57
Slow-running jet	50	50	50
Screw over capacity well...	2.5 mm	2 mm	2 mm
Needle and seating	1.5 mm	1.5 mm	1.5 mm
Progression	—	100	—

Type (early A40 Mk II) SU.HS2
Needle ... ... M
Spring ... ... Red
Type (848 cc A35) SU.HS2
Needle (Standard) ... ... EB
Spring ... ... Red
Type (1098 cc A35 and A40) SU.HS2
Needle (Standard) ... ... AN
Needle (Rich) H6
Needle (Weak) ... ... EB
Spring ... ... Red
Fuel pump (all models except A40 Mk II) ... ... AC 'Y' type (Mechanical)
A40 Mk II (early) ... ... SU type SP (Electric)
A40 Mk II (later)... ... ... SU type AUF (Electric)

GEARBOX

	Oil capacity							2⅓ pints	

Gear ratios (overall):

	First	Second	Third	Top	Reverse
A30 (up to chassis 1018) ...	19.94	12.63	8.19	5.143	25.25
A30 (after chassis 1018) ...	19.94	12.63	8.19	5.125	25.25
A30 (later)	19.94	12.63	8.19	4.875	25.25
A35 and 948 cc A40 ...	16.51	10.8	6.42	4.55	21.22
A35 (848 cc)	17.68	10.59	6.882	4.875	22.75
1098 cc A35 and A40 ...	15.276	9.169	5.95	4.22	19.665

BATTERY AND GENERATOR

Battery (positive earth):

	Type (Lucas)	Normal capacity (amp/hr)
A30	GLTW 7A	30
A35 (early)	GTW 7A	38
A35 (later) and A40 Mk I	BT 7A	43
1098 cc A35 and A40 (early)	N9 or NZ9	—
A40 Mk II (from Car No. 161047)	D9	40

Generator type (Lucas):

A30, A35 (early) and A40 Mk I (early)	C/39 PV2
A35 (later), A40 Mk I (later) and A40 Mk II	C/40—1

Cut-out (all types):

Cut-in voltage	12.7 to 13.3
Drop-off voltage (RB 106/1)	9 to 10
Drop-off voltage (RB 106/2)	8.5 to 11

Voltage regulator:

Control box RB 106/1 used with early C/39 PV2 generator
Open-circuit setting at 3000 rev/min ...

Voltage	Temperature correction
16.1 to 16.7	10°C (50°F)
15.8 to 16.4	20°C (68°F)
15.6 to 16.2	30°C (86°F)
15.3 to 15.9	40°C (104°F)

Control box RB 106/2 used with later C/39 and C/40 generators
Open-circuit setting at 3000 rev/min ...

Voltage	Temperature correction
16.1 to 16.7	10°C (50°F)
16.0 to 16.6	20°C (68°F)
15.9 to 16.5	30°C (85°F)
15.8 to 16.4	40°C (104°F)

COOLING SYSTEM

Radiator capacity:

All models (add one pint if heater fitted)	8½ pints

Thermostat opening temperature:

All 800 cc and 948 cc models	70°C to 75°C
848 cc and 1098 cc...	82°C to 83°C

FRONT SUSPENSION

Springs (free length):

A30 and A35	9.94
A40	10.04

STEERING

	A30 and A35	A40
Castor angle (deg.)	3	3½
Swivel pin inclination (deg.)	6½	6½ (Mk I)
Camber angle (deg.)	1	0
Toe-in (inches)	$\frac{1}{16}$ to $\frac{1}{8}$	$\frac{1}{8}$ to $\frac{3}{16}$

Measured with the car in a static unladen condition.

REAR AXLE

Oil capacity ... ... $1\frac{3}{4}$ pints

BRAKES

Brake fluid (all models) ... ... Lockheed Super Heavy Duty

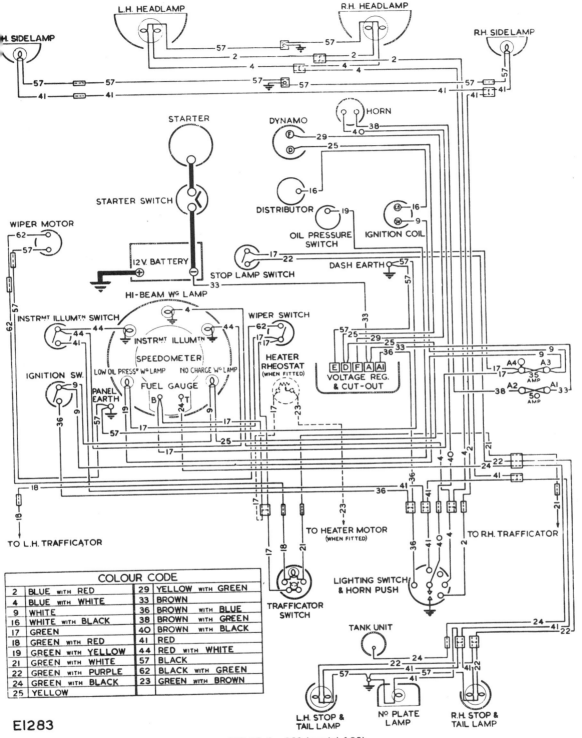

COLOUR CODE

2	BLUE with RED	29	YELLOW with GREEN
4	BLUE with WHITE	33	BROWN
9	WHITE	36	BROWN with BLUE
16	WHITE with BLACK	38	BROWN with GREEN
17	GREEN	40	BROWN with BLACK
18	GREEN with RED	41	RED
19	GREEN with YELLOW	44	RED with WHITE
21	GREEN with WHITE	57	BLACK
22	GREEN with PURPLE	62	BLACK with GREEN
24	GREEN with BLACK	23	GREEN with BROWN
25	YELLOW		

E1283

FIG 13:1   A30 (model AS3)

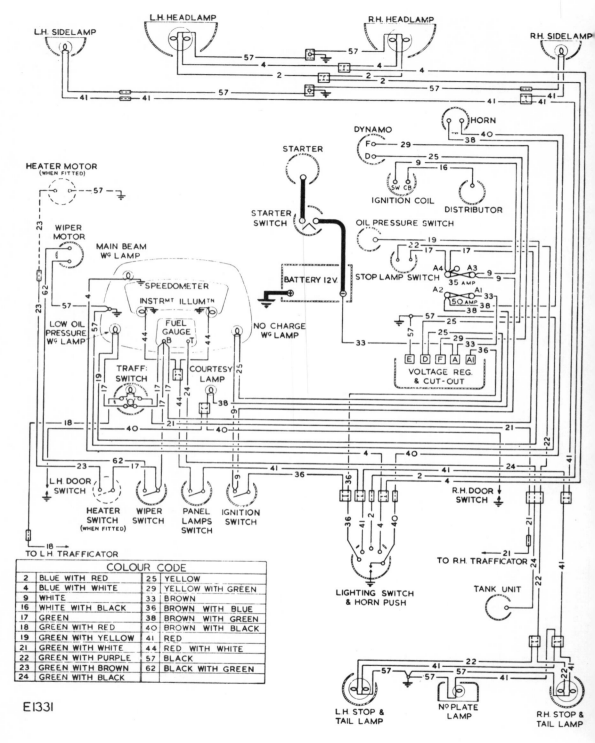

COLOUR CODE

2	BLUE WITH RED	25	YELLOW
4	BLUE WITH WHITE	29	YELLOW WITH GREEN
9	WHITE	33	BROWN
16	WHITE WITH BLACK	36	BROWN WITH BLUE
17	GREEN	38	BROWN WITH GREEN
18	GREEN WITH RED	40	BROWN WITH BLACK
19	GREEN WITH YELLOW	41	RED
21	GREEN WITH WHITE	44	RED WITH WHITE
22	GREEN WITH PURPLE	57	BLACK
23	GREEN WITH BROWN	62	BLACK WITH GREEN
24	GREEN WITH BLACK		

E1331

FIG 13:2   A30 (models A2S4, AS4, AP4 and AV4). A35 (models AP5 and AV5)

132

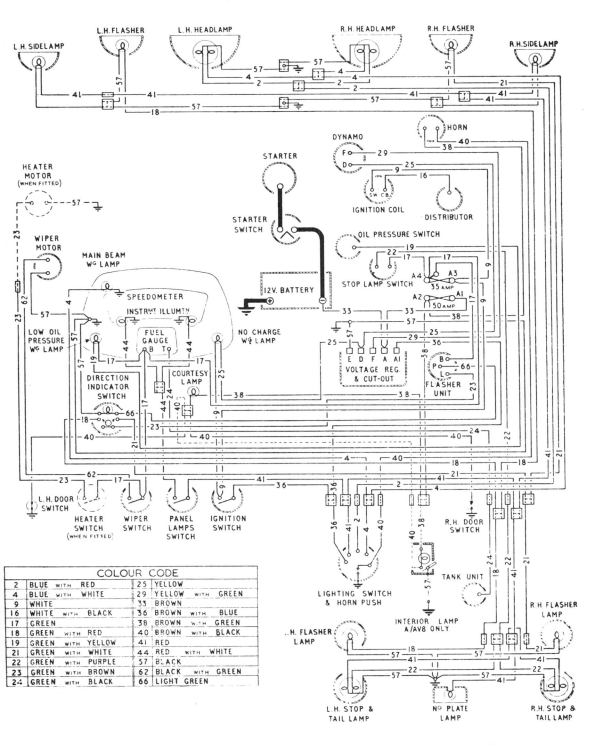

COLOUR CODE			
2	BLUE with RED	25	YELLOW
4	BLUE with WHITE	29	YELLOW with GREEN
9	WHITE	33	BROWN
16	WHITE with BLACK	36	BROWN with BLUE
17	GREEN	38	BROWN with GREEN
18	GREEN with RED	40	BROWN with BLACK
19	GREEN with YELLOW	41	RED
21	GREEN with WHITE	44	RED with WHITE
22	GREEN with PURPLE	57	BLACK
23	GREEN with BROWN	62	BLACK with GREEN
24	GREEN with BLACK	66	LIGHT GREEN

FIG 13:3   A35 (models A2S5, AS5, AK5, AV6, AP6 and A/AV8)

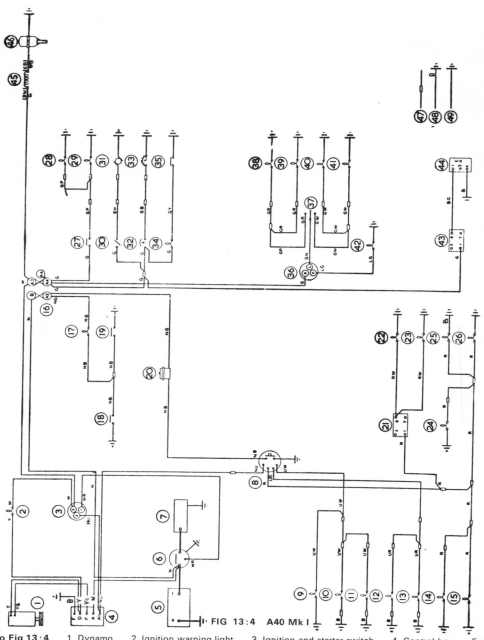

Key to Fig 13:4 1 Dynamo 2 Ignition warning light 3 Ignition and starter switch 4 Control box 5 12-volt battery
6 Starter solenoid switch 7 Starter motor 8 Lighting switch and horn push 9 Main beam warning light
10 RH headlight main beam 11 LH headlight main beam 12 LH headlight dip beam 13 RH headlight dip beam
14 LH sidelight 15 RH sidelight 16 Fuse unit 17 Courtesy light 18 Courtesy light switch
19 Courtesy light switch 20 Horn 21 Panel light switch 22 Panel light 23 Panel light 24 LH tail light
25 Number plate light 26 RH tail light 27 Stoplight switch 28 LH stoplight 29 RH stoplight 30 Heater switch
31 Heater motor 32 Fuel gauge 33 Fuel tank unit 34 Oil pressure warning light 35 Oil pressure warning light switch
36 Flasher unit 37 Flasher switch 38 LH rear flasher 39 LH front flasher 40 RH front flasher 41 RH rear flasher
42 Flasher warning light 43 Windshield wiper switch 44 Windshield wiper switch motor 45 Ignition coil 46 Distributor
47 Snap connectors 48 Earth connections made via cable 49 Via fixing bolts

Cable Colour Code: **B** Black **U** Blue **N** Brown **G** Green **P** Purple **R** Red **S** Slate **W** White
Y Yellow **L** Light **D** Dark **M** Medium

Note: When a cable has two colour code letters the first denotes the main colour and the second denotes the tracer colour.

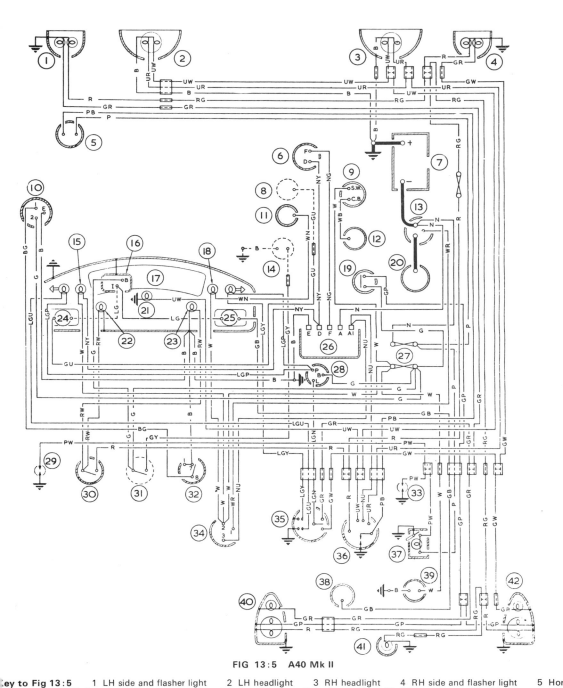

FIG 13:5   A40 Mk II

Cable Colour Code: **B** Black   **U** Blue   **N** Brown   **G** Green   **P** Purple   **R** Red   **S** Slate   **W** White
Yellow   **L** Light   **D** Dark   **M** Medium
Note: When a cable has two or three colour code letters the first or first two denote the main colour and the last the tracer colour.

Inches	Decimals	Milli-metres	Inches to Millimetres — Inches	Inches to Millimetres — mm	Millimetres to Inches — mm	Millimetres to Inches — Inches
1/64	.015625	.3969	001	.0254	.01	.00039
1/32	.03125	.7937	.002	.0508	.02	.00079
3/64	.046875	1.1906	.003	.0762	.03	.00118
1/16	.0625	1.5875	.004	.1016	.04	.00157
5/64	.078125	1.9844	.005	.1270	.05	.00197
3/32	.09375	2.3812	.006	.1524	.06	.00236
7/64	.109375	2.7781	.007	.1778	.07	.00276
1/8	.125	3.1750	.008	.2032	.08	.00315
9/64	.140625	3.5719	.009	.2286	.09	.00354
5/32	.15625	3.9687	.01	.254	.1	.00394
11/64	.171875	4.3656	.02	.508	.2	.00787
3/16	.1875	4.7625	.03	.762	.3	.01181
13/64	.203125	5·1594	.04	1.016	.4	.01575
7/32	.21875	5.5562	.05	1.270	.5	.01969
15/64	.234375	5.9531	.06	1.524	.6	.02362
1/4	.25	6.3500	.07	1.778	.7	.02756
17/64	.265625	6.7469	.08	2.032	.8	.03150
9/32	.28125	7.1437	.09	2.286	.9	.03543
19/64	.296875	7.5406	.1	2.54	1	.03937
5/16	.3125	7.9375	.2	5.08	2	..07874
21/64	.328125	8.3344	.3	7.62	3	.11811
11/32	.34375	8.7312	.4	10.16	4	.15748
23/64	.359375	9.1281	.5	12.70	5	.19685
3/8	.375	9.5250	.6	15.24	6	.23622
25/64	.390625	9.9219	.7	17.78	7	.27559
13/32	.40625	10.3187	.8	20.32	8	.31496
27/64	.421875	10.7156	.9	22.86	9	.35433
7/16	.4375	11.1125	1	25.4	10	.39370
29/64	.453125	11.5094	2	50.8	11	.43307
15/32	.46875	11.9062	3	76.2	12	.47244
31/64	.484375	12.3031	4	101.6	13	.51181
1/2	.5	12.7000	5	127.0	14	.55118
33/64	.515625	13.0969	6	152.4	15	.59055
17/32	.53125	13.4937	7	177.8	16	.62992
35/64	.546875	13.8906	8	203.2	17	.66929
9/16	.5625	14.2875	9	228.6	18	.70866
37/64	.578125	14.6844	10	254.0	19	.74803
19/32	.59375	15.0812	11	279.4	20	.78740
39/64	.609375	15.4781	12	304.8	21	.82677
5/8	.625	15.8750	13	330.2	22	.86614
41/64	.640625	16.2719	14	355.6	23	.90551
21/32	.65625	16.6687	15	381.0	24	.94488
43/64	.671875	17.0656	16	406.4	25	.98425
11/16	.6875	17.4625	17	431.8	26	1.02362
45/64	.703125	17.8594	18	457.2	27	1.06299
23/32	.71875	18.2562	19	482.6	28	1.10236
47/64	.734375	18.6531	20	508.0	29	1.14173
3/4	.75	19.0500	21	533.4	30	1.18110
49/64	.765625	19.4469	22	558.8	31	1.22047
25/32	.78125	19.8437	23	584.2	32	1.25984
51/64	.796875	20.2406	24	609.6	33	1.29921
13/16	.8125	20.6375	25	635.0	34	1.33858
53/64	.828125	21.0344	26	660.4	35	1.37795
27/32	.84375	21.4312	27	685.8	36	1.41732
55/64	.859375	21.8281	28	711.2	37	1.4567
7/8	.875	22.2250	29	736.6	38	1.4961
57/64	.890625	22.6219	30	762.0	39	1.5354
29/32	.90625	23.0187	31	787.4	40	1.5748
59/64	.921875	23.4156	32	812.8	41	1.6142
15/16	.9375	23.8125	33	838.2	42	1.6535
61/64	.953125	24.2094	34	863.6	43	1.6929
31/32	.96875	24.6062	35	889.0	44	1.7323
63/64	.984375	25.0031	36	914.4	45	1.7717

UNITS	Pints to Litres	Gallons to Litres	Litres to Pints	Litres to Gallons	Miles to Kilometres	Kilometres to Miles	Lbs. per sq. In. to Kg. per sq. Cm.	Kg. per sq. Cm. to Lbs. per sq. In.
1	.57	4.55	1.76	.22	1.61	.62	.07	14.22
2	1.14	9.09	3.52	.44	3.22	1.24	.14	28.50
3	1.70	13.64	5.28	.66	4.83	1.86	.21	42.67
4	2.27	18.18	7.04	.88	6.44	2.49	.28	56.8
5	2.84	22.73	8.80	1.10	8.05	3.11	.35	71.12
6	3.41	27.28	10.56	1.32	9.66	3.73	.42	85.34
7	3.98	31.82	12.32	1.54	11.27	4.35	.49	99.56
8	4.55	36.37	14.08	1.76	12.88	4.97	.56	113.79
9		40.91	15.84	1.98	14.48	5.59	.63	128.00
10		45.46	17.60	2.20	16.09	6.21	.70	142.23
20				4.40	32.19	12.43	1.41	284.47
30				6.60	48.28	18.64	2.11	426.70
40				8.80	64.37	24.85		
50					80.47	31.07		
60					96.56	37.28		
70					112.65	43.50		
80					128.75	49.71		
90					144.84	55.92		
100					160.93	62.14		

UNITS	Lb ft to kgm	Kgm to lb ft	UNITS	Lb ft to kgm	Kgm to lb ft
1	.138	7.233	7	.967	50.631
2	.276	14.466	8	1.106	57.864
3	.414	21.699	9	1.244	65.097
4	.553	28.932	10	1.382	72.330
5	.691	36.165	20	2.765	144.660
6	.829	43.398	30	4.147	216.990

HINTS ON MAINTENANCE AND OVERHAUL

There are few things more rewarding than the restoration of a vehicle's original peak of efficiency and smooth performance.

The following notes are intended to help the owner to reach that state of perfection. Providing that he possesses the basic manual skills he should have no difficulty in performing most of the operations detailed in this manual. It must be stressed, however, that where recommended in the manual, highly-skilled operations ought to be entrusted to experts, who have the necessary equipment, to carry out the work satisfactorily.

Quality of workmanship:

The hazardous driving conditions on the roads to-day demand that vehicles should be as nearly perfect, mechanically, as possible. It is therefore most important that amateur work be carried out with care, bearing in mind the often inadequate working conditions, and also the inferior tools which may have to be used. It is easy to counsel perfection in all things, and we recognize that it may be setting an impossibly high standard. We do, however, suggest that every care should be taken to ensure that a vehicle is as safe to take on the road as it is humanly possible to make it.

Safe working conditions:

Even though a vehicle may be stationary, it is still potentially dangerous if certain sensible precautions are not taken when working on it while it is supported on jacks or blocks. It is indeed preferable not to use jacks alone, but to supplement them with carefully placed blocks, so that there will be plenty of support if the car rolls off the jacks during a strenuous manoeuvre. Axle stands are an excellent way of providing a rigid base which is not readily disturbed. Piles of bricks are a dangerous substitute. Be careful not to get under heavy loads on lifting tackle, the load could fall. It is preferable not to work alone when lifting an engine, or when working underneath a vehicle which is supported well off the ground. To be trapped, particularly under the vehicle, may have unpleasant results if help is not quickly forthcoming. Make some provision, however humble, to deal with fires. Always disconnect a battery if there is a likelihood of electrical shorts. These may start a fire if there is leaking fuel about. This applies particularly to leads which can carry a heavy current, like those in the starter circuit. While on the subject of electricity, we must also stress the danger of using equipment which is run off the mains and which has no earth or has faulty wiring or connections. So many workshops have damp floors, and electrical shocks are of such a nature that it is sometimes impossible to let go of a live lead or piece of equipment due to the muscular spasms which take place.

Work demanding special care:

This involves the servicing of braking, steering and suspension systems. On the road, failure of the braking system may be disastrous. Make quite sure that there can be no possibility of failure through the bursting of rusty brake pipes or rotten hoses, nor to a sudden loss of pressure due to defective seals or valves.

Problems:

The chief problems which may face an operator are:
1 External dirt.
2 Difficulty in undoing tight fixings.
3 Dismantling unfamiliar mechanisms.
4 Deciding in what respect parts are defective.
5 Confusion about the correct order for reassembly.
6 Adjusting running clearance.
7 Road testing.
8 Final tuning.

Practical suggestions to solve the problems:

1 Preliminary cleaning of large parts—engines, transmissions, steering, suspensions, etc.,—should be carried out before removal from the car. Where road dirt and mud alone are present, wash clean with a high-pressure water jet, brushing to remove stubborn adhesions, and allow to drain and dry. Where oil or grease is also present, wash down with a proprietary compound (Gunk, Teepol etc.,) applying with a stiff brush—an old paint brush is suitable—into all crevices. Cover the distributor and ignition coils with a polythene bag and then apply a strong water jet to clear the loosened deposits. Allow to drain and dry. The assemblies will then be sufficiently clean to remove and transfer to the bench for the next stage.

On the bench, further cleaning can be carried out, first wiping the parts as free as possible from grease with old newspaper. Avoid using rag or cotton waste which can leave clogging fibres behind. Any remaining grease can be removed with a brush dipped in paraffin. If necessary, traces of paraffin can be removed by carbon tetrachloride. Avoid using paraffin or petrol in large quantities for cleaning in enclosed areas, such as garages, on account of the high fire risk.

When all exteriors have been cleaned, and not before, dismantling can be commenced. This ensures that dirt will not enter into interiors and orifices revealed by dismantling. In the next phases, where components have to be cleaned, use carbon tetrachloride in preference to petrol and keep the containers covered except when in use. After the components have been cleaned, plug small holes with tapered hard wood plugs cut to size and blank off larger orifices with greaseproof paper and masking tape. Do not use soft wood plugs or matchsticks as they may break.

2 It is not advisable to hammer on the end of a screw thread, but if it must be done, first screw on a nut to protect the thread, and use a lead hammer. This applies particularly to the removal of tapered cotters. Nuts and bolts seem to 'grow' together, especially in exhaust systems. If penetrating oil does not work, try the judicious application of heat, but be careful of starting a fire. Asbestos sheet or cloth is useful to isolate heat.

Tight bushes or pieces of tail-pipe rusted into a silencer can be removed by splitting them with an open-ended hacksaw. Tight screws can sometimes be started by a tap from a hammer on the end of a suitable screwdriver. Many tight fittings will yield to the judicious use of a hammer, but it must be a soft-faced hammer if damage is to be avoided, use a heavy block on the opposite side to absorb shock. Any parts of the steering system which have been damaged should be renewed, as attempts to repair them may lead to cracking and subsequent failure, and steering ball joints should be disconnected using a recommended tool to prevent damage.

3 It often happens that an owner is baffled when trying to dismantle an unfamiliar piece of equipment. So many modern devices are pressed together or assembled by spinning-over flanges, that they must be sawn apart. The intention is that the whole assembly must be renewed. However, parts which appear to be in one piece to the naked eye, may reveal close-fitting joint lines when inspected with a magnifying glass, and, this may provide the necessary clue to dismantling. Left-handed screw threads are used where rotational forces would tend to unscrew a right-handed screw thread.

Be very careful when dismantling mechanisms which may come apart suddenly. Work in an enclosed space where the parts will be contained, and drape a piece of cloth over the device if springs are likely to fly in all directions. Mark everything which might be reassembled in the wrong position, scratched symbols may be used on unstressed parts, or a sequence of tiny dots from a centre punch can be useful. Stressed parts should never be scratched or centre-popped as this may lead to cracking under working conditions. Store parts which look alike in the correct order for reassembly. Never rely upon memory to assist in the assembly of complicated mechanisms, especially when they will be dismantled for a long time, but make notes, and drawings to supplement the diagrams in the manual, and put labels on detached wires. Rust stains may indicate unlubricated wear. This can sometimes be seen round the outside edge of a bearing cup in a universal joint. Look for bright rubbing marks on parts which normally should not make heavy contact. These might prove that something is bent or running out of truth. For example, there might be bright marks on one side of a piston, at the top near the ring grooves, and others at the bottom of the skirt on the other side. This could well be the clue to a bent connecting rod. Suspected cracks can be proved by heating the component in a light oil to approximately 100°C, removing, drying off, and dusting with french chalk, if a crack is present the oil retained in the crack will stain the french chalk.

4 In determining wear, and the degree, against the permissible limits set in the manual, accurate measurement can only be achieved by the use of a micrometer. In many cases, the wear is given to the fourth place of decimals; that is in ten-thousandths of an inch. This can be read by the vernier scale on the barrel of a good micrometer. Bore diameters are more difficult to determine. If, however, the matching shaft is accurately measured, the degree of play in the bore can be felt as a guide to its suitability. In other cases, the shank of a twist drill of known diameter is a handy check.

Many methods have been devised for determining the clearance between bearing surfaces. To-day the best and simplest is by the use of Plastigage, obtainable from most garages. A thin plastic thread is laid between the two surfaces and the bearing is tightened, flattening the thread. On removal, the width of the thread is compared with a scale supplied with the thread and the clearance is read off directly. Sometimes joint faces leak persistently, even after gasket renewal. The fault will then be traceable to distortion, dirt or burrs. Studs which are screwed into soft metal frequently raise burrs at the point of entry. A quick cure for this is to chamfer the edge of the hole in the part which fits over the stud.

5 **Always check a replacement part with the original one before it is fitted.**

If parts are not marked, and the order for reassembly is not known, a little detective work will help. Look for marks which are due to wear to see if they can be mated. Joint faces may not be identical due to manufacturing errors, and parts which overlap may be stained, giving a clue to the correct position. Most fixings leave identifying marks especially if they were painted over on assembly. It is then easier to decide whether a nut, for instance, has a plain, a spring, or a shakeproof washer under it. All running surfaces become 'bedded' together after long spells of work and tiny imperfections on one part will be found to have left corresponding marks on the other. This is particularly true of shafts and bearings and even a score on a cylinder wall will show on the piston.

6 Checking end float or rocker clearances by feeler gauge may not always give accurate results because of wear. For instance, the rocker tip which bears on a valve stem may be deeply pitted, in which case the feeler will simply be bridging a depression. Thrust washers may also wear depressions in opposing faces to make accurate measurement difficult. End float is then easier to check by using a dial gauge. It is common practice to adjust end play in bearing assemblies, like front hubs with taper rollers, by doing up the axle nut until the hub becomes stiff to turn and then backing it off a little. Do not use this method with ballbearing hubs as the assembly is often preloaded by tightening the axle nut to its fullest extent. If the splitpin hole will not line up file the base of the nut a little.

Steering assemblies often wear in the straight-ahead position. If any part is adjusted, make sure that it remains free when moved from lock to lock. Do not be surprised if an assembly like a steering gearbox, which is known to be carefully adjusted outside the car becomes stiff when it is bolted in place. This will be due to distortion of the case by the pull of the mounting bolts, particularly if the mounting points are not all touching together. This problem may be met in other equipment and is cured by careful attention to the alignment of mounting points.

When a spanner is stamped with a size and A/F it means that the dimension is the width between the jaws and has no connection with ANF, which is the designation for the American National Fine thread. Coarse threads like Whitworth are rarely used on cars to-day except for studs which screw into soft aluminium or cast iron. For this reason it might be found that the top end of a cylinder head stud has a fine thread and the lower end a coarse thread to screw into the cylinder block. If the car has mainly UNF threads then it is likely that any coarse threads will be UNC, which are not the same as Whitworth. Small sizes have the same number of threads in Whitworth and UNC, but in the $\frac{1}{2}$ inch size for example, there are twelve threads to the inch in the former and thirteen in the latter.

7 After a major overhaul, particularly if a great deal of work has been done on the braking, steering and suspension systems, it is advisable to approach the problem of testing with care. If the braking system has been overhauled, apply heavy pressure to the brake pedal and get a second operator to check every possible source of leakage. The brakes may work extremely well, but a leak could cause complete failure after a few miles.

Do not fit the hub caps until every wheel nut has been checked for tightness, and make sure the tyre pressures are correct. Check the levels of coolant, lubricants and hydraulic fluids. Being satisfied that all is well, take the car on the road and test the brakes at once. Check the steering and the action of the handbrake. Do all this at moderate speeds on quiet roads, and make sure there is no other vehicle behind you when you try a rapid stop.

Finally, remember that many parts settle down after a time, so check for tightness of all fixings after the car has been on the road for a hundred miles or so.

8 It is useless to tune an engine which has not reached its normal running temperature. In the same way, the tune of an engine which is stiff after a rebore will be different when the engine is again running free. Remember too, that rocker clearances on pushrod operated valve gear will change when the cylinder head nuts are tightened after an initial period of running with a new head gasket.

Trouble may not always be due to what seems the obvious cause. Ignition, carburation and mechanical condition are interdependent and spitting back through the carburetter, which might be attributed to a weak mixture, can be caused by a sticking inlet valve.

For one final hint on tuning, never adjust more than one thing at a time or it will be impossible to tell which adjustment produced the desired result.

NOTES

GLOSSARY OF TERMS

Allen key   Cranked wrench of hexagonal section for use with socket head screws.

Alternator   Electrical generator producing alternating current. Rectified to direct current for battery charging.

Ambient temperature   Surrounding atmospheric temperature.

Annulus   Used in engineering to indicate the outer ring gear of an epicyclic gear train.

Armature   The shaft carrying the windings, which rotates in the magnetic field of a generator or starter motor. That part of a solenoid or relay which is activated by the magnetic field.

Axial   In line with, or pertaining to, an axis.

Backlash   Play in meshing gears.

Balance lever   A bar where force applied at the centre is equally divided between connections at the ends.

Banjo axle   Axle casing with large diameter housing for the crownwheel and differential.

Bendix pinion   A self-engaging and self-disengaging drive on a starter motor shaft.

Bevel pinion   A conical shaped gearwheel, designed to mesh with a similar gear with an axis usually at 90 deg. to its own.

bhp   Brake horse power, measured on a dynamometer.

bmep   Brake mean effective pressure. Average pressure on a piston during the working stroke.

Brake cylinder   Cylinder with hydraulically operated piston(s) acting on brake shoes or pad(s).

Brake regulator   Control valve fitted in hydraulic braking system which limits brake pressure to rear brakes during heavy braking to prevent rear wheel locking.

Camber   Angle at which a wheel is tilted from the vertical.

Capacitor   Modern term for an electrical condenser. Part of distributor assembly, connected across contact breaker points, acts as an interference suppressor.

Castellated   Top face of a nut, slotted across the flats, to take a locking splitpin.

Castor   Angle at which the kingpin or swivel pin is tilted when viewed from the side.

cc   Cubic centimetres. Engine capacity is arrived at by multiplying the area of the bore in sq cm by the stroke in cm by the number of cylinders.

Clevis   U-shaped forked connector used with a clevis pin, usually at handbrake connections.

Collet   A type of collar, usually split and located in a groove in a shaft, and held in place by a retainer. The arrangement used to retain the spring(s) on a valve stem in most cases.

Commutator   Rotating segmented current distributor between armature windings and brushes in generator or motor.

Compression   The ratio, or quantitative relation, of the total volume (piston at bottom of stroke) to the unswept volume (piston at top of stroke) in an engine cylinder.

Condenser   See capacitor.

Core plug   Plug for blanking off a manufacturing hole in a casting.

Crownwheel   Large bevel gear in rear axle, driven by a bevel pinion attached to the propeller shaft. Sometimes called a 'ring gear'.

'C'-spanner   Like a 'C' with a handle. For use on screwed collars without flats, but with slots or holes.

Damper   Modern term for shock-absorber, used in vehicle suspension systems to damp out spring oscillations.

Depression   The lowering of atmospheric pressure as in the inlet manifold and carburetter.

Dowel   Close tolerance pin, peg, tube, or bolt, which accurately locates mating parts.

Drag link   Rod connecting steering box drop arm (pitman arm) to nearest front wheel steering arm in certain types of steering systems.

Dry liner   Thinwall tube pressed into cylinder bore

Dry sump   Lubrication system where all oil is scavenged from the sump, and returned to a separate tank.

Dynamo   See Generator.

Electrode   Terminal, part of an electrical component, such as the points or 'Electrodes' of a sparking plug.

Electrolyte   In lead-acid car batteries a solution of sulphuric acid and distilled water.

End float   The axial movement between associated parts, end play.

EP   Extreme pressure. In lubricants, special grades for heavily loaded bearing surfaces, such as gear teeth in a gearbox, or crownwheel and pinion in a rear axle.

Fade	Of brakes. Reduced efficiency due to overheating.
Field coils	Windings on the polepieces of motors and generators.
Fillets	Narrow finishing strips usually applied to interior bodywork.
First motion shaft	Input shaft from clutch to gearbox.
Fullflow filter	Filters in which all the oil is pumped to the engine. If the element becomes clogged, a bypass valve operates to pass unfiltered oil to the engine.
FWD	Front wheel drive.
Gear pump	Two meshing gears in a close fitting casing. Oil is carried from the inlet round the outside of both gears in the spaces between the gear teeth and casing to the outlet, the meshing gear teeth prevent oil passing back to the inlet, and the oil is forced through the outlet port.
Generator	Modern term for 'Dynamo'. When rotated produces electrical current.
Grommet	A ring of protective or sealing material. Can be used to protect pipes or leads passing through bulkheads.
Grubscrew	Fully threaded headless screw with screwdriver slot. Used for locking, or alignment purposes.
Gudgeon pin	Shaft which connects a piston to its connecting rod. Sometimes called 'wrist pin', or 'piston pin'.
Halfshaft	One of a pair transmitting drive from the differential.
Helical	In spiral form. The teeth of helical gears are cut at a spiral angle to the side faces of the gearwheel.
Hot spot	Hot area that assists vapourisation of fuel on its way to cylinders. Often provided by close contact between inlet and exhaust manifolds.
HT	High Tension. Applied to electrical current produced by the ignition coil for the sparking plugs.
Hydrometer	A device for checking specific gravity of liquids. Used to check specific gravity of electrolyte.
Hypoid bevel gears	A form of bevel gear used in the rear axle drive gears. The bevel pinion meshes below the centre line of the crownwheel, giving a lower propeller shaft line.
Idler	A device for passing on movement. A free running gear between driving and driven gears. A lever transmitting track rod movement to a side rod in steering gear.
Impeller	A centrifugal pumping element. Used in water pumps to stimulate flow.
Journals	Those parts of a shaft that are in contact with the bearings.
Kingpin	The main vertical pin which carries the front wheel spindle, and permits steering movement. May be called 'steering pin' or 'swivel pin'.
Layshaft	The shaft which carries the laygear in the gearbox. The laygear is driven by the first motion shaft and drives the third motion shaft according to the gear selected. Sometimes called the 'countershaft' or 'second motion shaft.'
lb ft	A measure of twist or torque. A pull of 10 lb at a radius of 1 ft is a torque of 10 lb ft.
lb/sq in	Pounds per square inch.
Little-end	The small, or piston end of a connecting rod. Sometimes called the 'small-end'.
LT	Low Tension. The current output from the battery.
Mandrel	Accurately manufactured bar or rod used for test or centring purposes.
Manifold	A pipe, duct, or chamber, with several branches.
Needle rollers	Bearing rollers with a length many times their diameter.
Oil bath	Reservoir which lubricates parts by immersion. In air filters, a separate oil supply for wetting a wire mesh element to hold the dust.
Oil wetted	In air filters, a wire mesh element lightly oiled to trap and hold airborne dust.
Overlap	Period during which inlet and exhaust valves are open together.
Panhard rod	Bar connected between fixed point on chassis and another on axle to control sideways movement.
Pawl	Pivoted catch which engages in the teeth of a ratchet to permit movement in one direction only.
Peg spanner	Tool with pegs, or pins, to engage in holes or slots in the part to be turned.
Pendant pedals	Pedals with levers that are pivoted at the top end.
Phillips screwdriver	A cross-point screwdriver for use with the cross-slotted heads of Phillips screws.
Pinion	A small gear, usually in relation to another gear.
Piston-type damper	Shock absorber in which damping is controlled by a piston working in a closed oil-filled cylinder.
Preloading	Preset static pressure on ball or roller bearings not due to working loads.
Radial	Radiating from a centre, like the spokes of a wheel.

Radius rod	Pivoted arm confining movement of a part to an arc of fixed radius.	**TDC**	Top Dead Centre. The highest point reached by a piston in a cylinder, with the crank and connecting rod in line.
Ratchet	Toothed wheel or rack which can move in one direction only, movement in the other being prevented by a pawl.	**Thermostat**	Automatic device for regulating temperature. Used in vehicle coolant systems to open a valve which restricts circulation at low temperature.
Ring gear	A gear tooth ring attached to outer periphery of flywheel. Starter pinion engages with it during starting.	**Third motion shaft**	Output shaft of gearbox.
Runout	Amount by which rotating part is out of true.	**Threequarter floating axle**	Outer end of rear axle halfshaft flanged and bolted to wheel hub, which runs on bearing mounted on outside of axle casing. Vehicle weight is not carried by the axle shaft.
Semi-floating axle	Outer end of rear axle halfshaft is carried on bearing inside axle casing. Wheel hub is secured to end of shaft.		
Servo	A hydraulic or pneumatic system for assisting, or, augmenting a physical effort. See 'Vacuum Servo'.	**Thrust bearing or washer**	Used to reduce friction in rotating parts subject to axial loads.
		Torque	Turning or twisting effort. See 'lb ft'.
Setscrew	One which is threaded for the full length of the shank.	**Track rod**	The bar(s) across the vehicle which connect the steering arms and maintain the front wheels in their correct alignment.
Shackle	A coupling link, used in the form of two parallel pins connected by side plates to secure the end of the master suspension spring and absorb the effects of deflection.	**UJ**	Universal joint. A coupling between shafts which permits angular movement.
		UNF	Unified National Fine screw thread.
Shell bearing	Thinwalled steel shell lined with anti-friction metal. Usually semi-circular and used in pairs for main and big-end bearings.	**Vacuum servo**	Device used in brake system, using difference between atmospheric pressure and inlet manifold depression to operate a piston which acts to augment brake pressure as required. See 'Servo'.
Shock absorber	See 'Damper'.		
Silentbloc	Rubber bush bonded to inner and outer metal sleeves.	**Venturi**	A restriction or 'choke' in a tube, as in a carburetter, used to increase velocity to obtain a reduction in pressure.
Socket-head screw	Screw with hexagonal socket for an Allen key.	**Vernier**	A sliding scale for obtaining fractional readings of the graduations of an adjacent scale.
Solenoid	A coil of wire creating a magnetic field when electric current passes through it. Used with a soft iron core to operate contacts or a mechanical device.	**Welch plug**	A domed thin metal disc which is partially flattened to lock in a recess. Used to plug core holes in castings.
Spur gear	A gear with teeth cut axially across the periphery.	**Wet liner**	Removable cylinder barrel, sealed against coolant leakage, where the coolant is in direct contact with the outer surface.
Stub axle	Short axle fixed at one end only.		
Tachometer	An instrument for accurate measurement of rotating speed. Usually indicates in revolutions per minute.	**Wet sump**	A reservoir attached to the crankcase to hold the lubricating oil.

NOTES

INDEX

NOTES

Alfa Romeo Giulia 1600,
1750 1962 on
Aston Martin 1921-58
Auto Union Audi 70, 80,
Super 90, 1966 on
Audi 100 1969 on
Austin, Morris etc.
1100 Mk. 1 1962-67
Austin, Morris etc. 1100
Mk. 2, 3, 1300 Mk. 1, 2, 3
America 1968 on
Austin A30, A35, A40
Farina
Austin A55 Mk. 2, A60
1958-69
Austin A99, A110 1959-68
Austin J4 1960 on
Austin Maxi 1969 on
Austin, Morris 1800
1964 on
Austin, Morris 2200 1972 on
Austin Kimberley, Tasman
1970 on
Austin, Morris 1300, 1500
Nomad 1969 on
BMC 3 (Austin A50, A55
Mk. 1, Morris Oxford
2, 3 1954-59)
Austin Healey 100/6,
3000 1956-68
Austin Healey, MG
Sprite, Midget 1958 on
Bedford CA Mk2 1964-69
Bedford Beagle HA Vans
1964 on
BMW 1600 1966 on
BMW 1800 1964 on
BMW 2000, 2002 1966 on
Chevrolet Corvair 1960-69
Chevrolet Corvette V8
1957-65
Chevrolet Corvette V8
1965 on
Chevrolette Vega 2300
1970 on
Chrysler Valiant V8
1965 on
Chrysler Valiant Straight
Six 1966-70
Citroen DS 19, ID 19
1955-66
Citroen ID 19, DS 19, 20,
21 1966 on
Colt 1970 on
Daf 31, 32, 33, 44, 55
1961 on
Datsun 1200 1970 on
Datsun 1300, 1400, 1600
1968 on
Datsun 240C 1971 on
Datsun 240Z Sport 1970 on
De Dion Bouton
1899-1907
Fiat 124 1966 on
Fiat 124 Sport 1966 on
Fiat 125 1967 on
Fiat 128 1969 on
Fiat 500 1957 on
Fiat 600, 600D 1955-69
Fiat 850 1964 on
Fiat 1100 1957-69
Fiat 1300, 1500 1961-67

Ford Anglia Prefect 100E
1953-62
Ford Anglia 105E, Prefect
107E 1959-67
Ford Capri 1300, 1600 OHV
1968 on
Ford Capri 1300, 1600,
2000 OHC 1972 on
Ford Capri 2000, 3000
1969 on
Ford Classic, Capri
1961-64
Ford Consul, Zephyr,
Zodiac, 1, 2 1950-62
Ford Corsair Straight
Four 1963-65
Ford Corsair V4 1965-68
Ford Corsair V4 2000
1969-70
Ford Cortina 1962-66
Ford Cortina 1967-68
Ford Cortina 1969-70
Ford Cortina Mk. 3
1970 on
Ford Escort 1967 on
Ford Falcon 6 1964-70
Ford Falcon XK, XL
1960-63
Ford Falcon 6 XR/XA
1966 on
Ford Falcon V8 (U.S.A.)
1965-71
Ford Falcon V8 (Aust.)
1966 on
Ford Pinto 1970 on
Ford Maverick 1969 on
Ford Maverick V8 1970 on
Ford Mustang 6 1965 on
Ford Mustang V8 1965-71
Ford Thames 10, 12,
15 cwt 1957-65
Ford Transit 1965 on
Ford Zephyr Zodiac Mk. 3
1962-66
Ford Zephyr Zodiac V4,
V6, Mk. 4 1966-72
Ford Consul, Granada
1972 on
Hillman Avenger 1970 on
Hillman Hunter 1966 on
Hillman Imp 1963-68
Hillman Imp 1969 on
Hillman Minx 1 to 5
1956-65
Hillman Minx 1965-67
Hillman Minx 1966-70
Hillman Super Minx
1961-65
Holden V8 1968 on
Holden Straight Six
1948-66
**Holden Straight Six
1966 on**
Holden Torana 4 Series
HB 1967-69
Jaguar XK120, 140, 150,
Mk. 7, 8, 9 1948-61
Jaguar 2.4, 3.4, 3.8 Mk.
1, 2 1955-69
Jaguar 'E' Type 1961 on
Jaguar 'S' Type 420
1963-68

Jaguar XJ6 1968 on
Jowett Javelin Jupiter
1947-53
Landrover 1, 2 1948-61
Landrover 2, 2a, 3 1959 on
Mazda 616 1970 on
Mazda 808, 818 1972 on
Mazda 1200, 1300 1969 on
Mazda 1500, 1800 1967 on
Mercedes-Benz 190b,
190c, 200 1959-68
Mercedes-Benz 220
1959-65
Mercedes-Benz 220/8
1968 on
Mercedes-Benz 230
1963-68
Mercedes-Benz 250
1965-67
Mercedes-Benz 250
1968 on
Mercedes-Benz 280
1968 on
MG TA to TF 1936-55
MGA MGB 1955-68
MGB 1969 on
Mini 1959 on
Mini Cooper 1961 on
Morgan 1936-69
Morris Marina 1971 on
Morris (Aust) Marina
1972 on
Morris Minor 2, 1000
1952-71
Morris Oxford 5, 6 1959-71
NSU 1000 1963 on
NSU Prinz 1 to 4 1957 on
Opel Ascona, Manta
1970 on
Opel GT 1900 1968 on
Opel Kadett, Olympia 993cc
1078cc 1962 on
Opel Kadett, Olympia 1492,
1698, 1897cc 1967 on
Opel Rekord C 1966 on
Peugeot 204 1965 on
Peugeot 304 1970 on
Peugeot 404 1960 on
Peugeot 504 1968 on
Porsche 356A, B, C 1957-65
Porsche 911 1964-69
Porsche 912 1965-69
Porsche 914 S 1969 on
Reliant Regal 1952 on
Renault R4, R4L, 4 1961 on
Renault 6 1968 on
Renault 8, 10, 1100 1962 on
Renault 12, 1969 on
Renault R16 1965 on
Renault Dauphine
Floride 1957-67
Renault Caravelle 1962-68
Rover 60 to 110 1953-64
Rover 2000 1963 on
Rover 3 Litre 1958-67
Rover 3500, 3500S 1968 on
Saab 95, 96, Sport
1960-68
Saab 99 1969 on
Saab V4 1966 on
Simca 1000 1961 on
Simca 1100 1967 on

Simca 1300, 1301, 1500,
1501 1963 on
Skoda One (440, 445, 450)
1955-70
Sunbeam Rapier Alpine
1955-65
Toyota Corolla 1100 1967 on
Toyota Corona 1500 Mk. 1
1965-70
Toyota Corona 1900 Mk. 2
1969 on
Triumph TR2, TR3, TR3A
1952-62
Triumph TR4, TR4A
1961-67
Triumph TR5, TR250,
TR6 1967 on
Triumph 1300, 1500
1965 on
Triumph 2000 Mk. 1, 2.5 PI
Mk. 1 1963-69
Triumph 2000 Mk. 2, 2.5 PI
Mk. 2 1969 on
Triumph Dolomite 1972 on
Triumph Herald 1959-68
Triumph Herald 1969-71
Triumph Spitfire, Vitesse
1962-68
Triumph Spitfire Mk. 3, 4
1969 on
Triumph GT6, Vitesse
2 Litre 1969 on
Triumph Toledo 1970 on
Vauxhall Velox, Cresta
1957-72
Vauxhall Victor 1, 2, FB
1957-64
Vauxhall Victor 101
1964-67
Vauxhall Victor FD 1600,
2000 1967 on
Vauxhall Victor 3300,
Ventora 1968 on
Vauxhall Victor FE
Ventora 1972 on
Vauxhall Viva HA 1963-66
Vauxhall Viva HB 1966-70
Vauxhall Viva, HC Firenza
1971 on
Volkswagen Beetle 1954-67
Volkswagen Beetle 1968 on
Volkswagen 1500 1961-66
Volkswagen 1600 Fastback
1965 on
Volkswagen Transporter
1954-67
Volkswagen Transporter
1968 on
Volkswagen 411 1968 on
Volvo 120 1961-70
Volvo 140 1966 on
Volvo 160 series 1968 on
Volvo 1800 1960 on

NOTES

NOTES

NOTES